To Michael

Hope you kick up
some tips.

Love.

Lorraine . x x

What You'll Never Learn on the Internet

BY THE SAME AUTHOR:

What They Don't Teach You at Harvard Business School

What You'll Never Learn on the Internet

MARK H. McCORMACK

HarperCollinsBusiness
An Imprint of HarperCollins*Publishers*

HarperCollinsBusiness
an imprint of HarperCollins*Publishers*
77–85 Fulham Palace Road,
Hammersmith, London W6 8JB

www.**fire**and**water**.com/business

Published by HarperCollins*Publishers* 2000
1 3 5 7 9 8 6 4 2

A catalogue record for this book is
available from the British Library

ISBN 0 00 257171 4
ISBN 0 00 710634 3 (TPB)

Set in Utopia and Stone Sans by
Rowland Phototypesetting Ltd, Bury St Edmunds, Suffolk

Printed and bound in Great Britain by
Clays Ltd, St Ives plc

To my four children: Breck, Todd and Leslie, who are helping to guide me through, and make sense out of, the beginning stages of this exciting Internet revolution; and dearest little Maggie, my two-year-old daughter, who will live her life in a new era of technology, which heretofore has never even been contemplated.

I would like to acknowledge the tireless and inspired help that my trusty associate, Mark Reiter, has given me in pulling together the material for this book.

Contents

Introduction

A person would have to be deaf and blind and locked away in a cave today not to notice the emergence of the Internet as a powerful and legitimate field of business, an 'industry' as real and dynamic as auto manufacturing or oil refining or film-making. That's certainly the overwhelming impression you'd get if you relied on coverage of the Internet in the business media. It's not just the bootstrapping stories about entrepreneurs plunging into Internet-based businesses, raising venture capital, and becoming instant millionaires (if not billionaires) when they take the company public that feed this impression. It's also the tidal wave of stories about how traditional companies are responding to the 'challenge' of the Internet. The Internet will completely change how we sell and buy, how we gather and distribute information, how we communicate, even how we behave – and if you don't get on board with that concept, you'll be left in the dust. You'll be the 21st century equivalent of horsewhip manufacturers who insisted that the first automobiles would never displace the horse and carriage as the preferred means of transportation. In the media today, the overwhelming message seems to be 'The Internet changes everything!'

It's probably true. But let's say I'm a reluctant convert to the Internet gospel.

Don't get me wrong. I'm not a complete Luddite who thinks the Internet is a fad. It's here to stay. There's too much money – trillions of dollars – invested in the Internet infrastructure for it to do anything but grow. And, if past is prologue, it will grow more rapidly than any business we have ever seen. My problem is that I don't understand what it will grow into. I can barely comprehend its impact today, so I certainly don't have a clue what it will be a few years from now. And, frankly, I don't think anyone else does either. We're all wishing, hoping, or praying that we'll be there when the money starts rolling in.

You could argue that my lack of evangelical fervour for the Internet is based on sheer ignorance. I don't use a computer. I've never sent an e-mail. I don't have an on-line account. I've never bought anything over the Internet. I'm computer-illiterate. No wonder I'm sceptical.

But that would miss the point. I have several assistants who are computer-literate. They send and receive hundreds of e-mail messages each day for me. Computers and the Internet may not intrigue me personally. But I recognize that I could not lure talented people to work for me if I didn't provide them with at least the same office equipment the rest of the world is using. As a result, I've spent tens of millions of dollars in recent years to make sure that each of the 2500 people in our company's 80 offices in 31 countries has a computer and is connected via the Internet to everyone else in the company. While you may be agonizing about spending $500 to upgrade to Windows 98, I have been writing enormous cheques to Microsoft and Hewlett-Packard and Oracle and SAP to make sure our company keeps up the pace with everyone else. So, don't blame my scepticism on a reluctance to accept new technology and change. Heck, I even have my own web site – www:successecrets.com. I may not be computer literate but I still know how to compete.

My scepticism stems from other things.

For one thing, to me computers and the Internet are now a fact of life, not a phenomenon. They are like the telephone or automobile. I appreciate the value of a telephone. But I don't need to know how it works or what the whiz kids at the phone company are doing to improve the device to maintain that appreciation. I simply accept that I need the telephone to conduct business. Likewise, with a car. I don't need to know how the car was built or where that car company's stock price closed that day to appreciate that I need a car to get around.

The Internet is no different. It's an immutable fact of life. We can't turn back the clock and pretend that business will not be changed by it. I accept that.

What I'm not ready to accept, however, is the notion that 'The Internet changes everything' – because there are some things that you can't learn on the Internet and they happen to be the most important things you need to learn.

If I owned a bookstore and found myself suddenly competing with (and losing customers to) the online bookstore Amazon.com perhaps I wouldn't hold that view. Likewise, if I were any kind of retail merchant selling a commodity product that could be purchased over the phone as easily as in person, I would be paying serious attention to the Internet.

But I have the luxury of being in the sports business, which as far as I can tell, is one 'industry' that's completely immune to the Internet. There's nothing happening on the Internet that poses a challenge to our company's slice of the sports marketplace. People have always enjoyed watching talented athletes compete in a stadium or on a field – and I don't see anything on the Internet that threatens to erase that simple emotional urge among human beings. (The Internet may be taking 'eyeballs' away from traditional media such as magazines, books, newspapers, and television, but sports continues to grow and proliferate in all those media. There's more sports programming – i.e., more hours of sports – on television around the world than ever before. Newspaper sports pages are thicker, not thinner, than they were ten years ago.) Quite frankly, if the sports business is a steady growth business, then the Internet, with its web sites that attract fans who want updated scores and more facts and statistics than traditional broadcasts provide, only adds to that growth.

As for the nuts and bolts of our business – which is representing athletes, creating events for them, and making sure those events are seen by as wide an audience as possible – the Internet is not a threat. We are in the personal services business – and the Internet can't provide our kind of personal service. The Internet can't help us discover a tennis prodigy. It can't recognize talent or talk to a young athlete's parents about nurturing that talent properly. It can't help us negotiate a contract or construct a tournament schedule or hire a coach. We have to rely on our experience and judgment to do that.

That experience and judgment is the most valuable 'product' we sell in our business. And you can't learn these or, for that matter, any other worthwhile interpersonal skill from the Internet. That's the big reason I feel so indifferent to both the challenge and the opportunity posed by the Internet. Our business is largely a one-on-one people business. It consists of salespeople talking to customers and managers talking to clients, each dealing with the other as an individual rather than a commodity or statistic. And that sort of connection will never be threatened by the Internet.

It's easy to forget that, however. The other day one of our executives was boasting to me about how he and a new customer handled a client endorsement contract from start to finish via e-mail. He pitched the idea via e-mail. He negotiated the deal points back and forth with the customer via e-mail. They even did all the contract drafting and revision via e-mail.

We didn't have to talk on the phone once, said the executive.

I wasn't sure what this executive was bragging about – was it the ease of doing business via e-mail or was it the way he avoided the nuisance of endless phone calls to make the transaction work? – but I wanted to burst his bubble slightly about the wonders of e-mail. I didn't want him thinking that e-mail was somehow a substitute for actually seeing customers face to face. So I asked how he knew the customer.

'He invited me to lunch a year ago because a friend had recommended me as someone who could help him with a problem. He wanted to pick my brain,' said the executive.

'How do you know you can trust him?' I continued.

'We're friends now. I've kept in touch with him and invited him to a golf tournament a few months ago when we both happened to be in the same city. In fact, we cooked up this endorsement idea walking the course following Tiger Woods and Mark O'Meara. The gallery was so big we couldn't see any golf, so we discussed business.'

I rest my case.

The endorsement deal may have been concluded on the Internet. But in my mind, the business that was done via e-mail – the negotiating over deal points and drafting of the contract – was nothing more than rudimentary housekeeping, the endgame of a long process. The sale itself began a year earlier when these two individuals decided to meet and became friends. But what sealed the sale in my mind is our man displaying the common sense and gumption to invite the customer to the golf tournament because they were in the same town that weekend.

That experience and judgment – that increasingly rare brand of people skill – is something you'll never learn on the Internet.

This book is all about people skills and using those skills in a time of momentous change.

It's been 15 years since I wrote my first business book, *What They Don't Teach You at Harvard Business School.* Back then there were no such things as plain-paper fax machines or mobile phones. Our company didn't own one personal computer. Executives and their assistants still answered their own telephones; there was no voice mail. Microsoft was still a small privately held company. Nike sold running shoes and almost nothing else. Of course, there was no e-mail and no Internet or World Wide Web.

I could go on listing dozens of now-everyday phenomena that didn't exist in 1984. There's nothing particularly interesting in the fact that some things that are ubiquitous now didn't exist 15 years ago. I could do the same comparing 1949 to 1963, citing the arrival of jet planes, colour television, and the Beatles. But I cite these specifically because (a) everyone reading this is surely aware of mobile phones and Nike and the Internet and (b) those three items (out of thousands I could have chosen) are emblematic of what is surely the biggest change in how business is conducted since 1984 – that is, the *speed of change* in business.

Back then, it would have been unthinkable that you could contact anyone anywhere anytime with a mobile phone and that you would reach them because they had a mobile phone too. If the other party were out of the office, you would have to wait.

Back then it was unfathomable that a Japanese auto manufacturer could introduce an expensive model such as the Lexus and turn it into a raging success in three years. Building a powerful luxury brand was supposed to take a decade or more.

Likewise, it was hard to conceive that someone would have the audacity to challenge the three major American television networks with a fourth network called Fox and, even more inconceivable, that the challenge would work with hit programs such as 'The Simpsons' and 'The X Files.'

When I wrote my book, progress in business was steady but slow. Those were the halcyon days when business schools still taught their MBA candidates how to write exquisite five-year business plans – because companies still thought in five-year time frames. (Back then, major Japanese corporations prided themselves on envisioning their businesses 10 and 20 years ahead. I doubt if they would be as confident or reckless today.) Today, if someone showed me a five-year plan, I'd toss out the pages detailing Years Three, Four and Five as pure fantasy. If I were a business school professor, I'd tell my students, 'Anyone who thinks he or she can evaluate business conditions five years from now, flunks.'

The overwhelming impression to me is that you can reach someone, get information, make a decision, build a brand, finance a start up, and create a personal fortune a lot faster today than you could 15 years ago. Of course, the converse is also true: you can be overwhelmed by your competitors and wiped out of business much more quickly as well.

Some people, particularly those in the high technology sector where the speed of change is blinding, know this intuitively – and behave accordingly. They build their businesses to respond to change, not to follow a business plan.

But there are also a lot of people in more traditional sectors of the economy who haven't adapted as well. They're still thinking in terms of the calendar and their one- or two-year plans while circumstances are changing around them on a daily basis – and *not according to plan*. Their business clock is out of synch with the times.

I hope this book, which focuses on the need for both agile thinking and humane behaviour, will help both kinds of people. I hope it provides a brush-up course in people skills to the speed junkies out there whose impatience and brusqueness often comes at other folks' expense. I also hope it gives clarity and a sense of urgency to the folks out there who are befuddled by the rapid changes around them.

IT TAKES TALENT TO SEE THE NEED TO CHANGE

One of the most interesting aspects of the rapid growth of the Internet is how quickly some people have come to embrace it as an engine of entrepreneurial promise and wealth. I have never seen so many people thinking and exploring ways to get in on this phenomenon. It's the end-of-the-century gold rush. People with minimal interest in information technology and even more minimal computer skills are dreaming up web sites and forming teams of talented friends to write business plans for viable e-businesses, all in the hopes of finding a venture capitalist who will fund their start-up that will ultimately lead to the fabulous wealth that comes with taking the business public. They've seen it happen for other people. Now they want it to happen to them.

There's nothing wrong with that. The people I've been observing are talented and successful in their traditional lines of business. But they see something going on (how could they miss it?) and, to their credit, they're not ignoring it or denying its significance or writing it off as a passing fancy. They're diving into it. They don't want it to pass them by.

These folks are displaying another skill that you can't learn on the Internet: recognizing the need to change sooner rather than later. It's a talent that certainly pre-dates the Internet – by centuries. In every era, there have always been people who recognized social or commercial or technological forces that would change everything. And there have always been people who couldn't see what was plainly in front of their eyes.

I'm not sure how you develop this talent. But I do know that the first step is accepting that it is a valuable skill in its own right.

I remember having lunch with a very successful magazine publisher in September 1997, about two weeks after the death of Princess Diana. The facts of Diana's life, the circumstances surrounding her horrible death, and the unprecedented outpouring of grief among the British and American people were the only thing the news media were interested in covering at the time. All Diana all the time was *the* news story that month.

Personally, I wasn't surprised by the phenomenal attention accorded Diana's death, but I could see that it confounded my publisher friend and even pushed him into a career crisis of sorts. As he explained it, 'As a publisher, it's my job to know what people are thinking and feeling. I'm supposed to have my finger on the readers' pulse. But this Diana circus took me by complete surprise.'

And that worried him. It made him feel that maybe he was out of touch, that he had fallen a step or two behind in spotting important trends and shifts in taste in his business. After all, even the lowliest editor on his staff knew that when Diana was alive, putting her on the magazine's cover was the easiest way to boost news-stand sales. So why was he surprised by the massive interest in her death? If he had been on top of his game, he would have seen it coming miles away.

So I was a little taken aback about six months later when this publisher called me to say he was leaving the magazine to explore new opportunities. He wasn't being forced out. He wasn't jumping to a new job. He was just leaving. 'What's going on?' I asked.

Apparently, the Diana episode (though not by itself) had precipitated a career crisis in this very successful executive. The fact that he had missed this shift in public taste surrounding her death made him question his ability to recognize important swings in the public temperament and in market forces. And in turn, it made him re-examine some of the changes in his own career. Was he alert to all the changes swirling around him? Or was he missing a critical signal or two?

In this man's case, he concluded that the ground was shifting under his feet. There had been a change in leadership at his magazine's parent company: the founder of the company had died suddenly and his children had assumed control.

Remarkably, he hadn't given much thought to the new leadership. Why should he? His job was safe. His magazine was tops in its field, and the founder's children knew he was responsible for this success.

The Diana episode, however, shook him out of his comfort zone. After all, only a fool ignores the fact that a new set of bosses signals new (and possibly big) changes in any organization. And yet, when you work inside an organization, you not only grow comfortable with the day-to-day routines of your job, you become sheltered from the significance of internal or external changes, even major ones. You can even be blithely unaware that a new group of bosses almost always means a new way of doing things.

Fortunately, my publisher friend regained his alertness to changing forces at work and his ability to adapt accordingly. In this case, he concluded that it was time to move on. He had peaked in his job, hit all his financial targets and done everything he was asked to do, but he could see there was no room for advancement for him in the organization. He was not a member of the controlling family and never would be. At best, he would be a valuable and respected outsider. So he decided to leave.

He wasn't troubled that he was leaving with no job in place. What would have troubled him more, he said, was if he had missed the signals and stayed in the position too long, when it might be too late to leave on his own terms.

He likened this recognition to hiking with friends in the woods and getting lost. There is always someone in the group who realizes early in the hike that the group is lost. Then there are others who only acknowledge it deep into the trip when the evidence is overwhelming. And then there are a few people who simply refuse to admit they are lost, despite the evidence; they always believe the right path is just around the next tree or hill.

As the publisher put it, 'I didn't want to be the kind of guy who's always in that last group, refusing to see or admit the truth.'

How about you? Could you say the same thing about your career and seeing the need to change? Do you have your finger on the pulse of your business? Have you thought about the nature of your business and where it's headed in the next few years? Is it an industry with a future, and one you want to continue in? Is your company in a strong position and likely to succeed? Do you have the skills to succeed as the industry changes? Do you have the support and confidence of the people leading your organization in this new landscape?

If you've been blithely going along, never thinking about these factors, you might be more lost in the woods than you imagine.

FIND THE HUMAN MOMENT IN EVERY TRANSACTION

There is no doubt that the ease of communication the Internet provides has changed the way people conduct business. But is it possible that our slavish connection to the world via a computer screen is eroding our people skills?

This occurred to me the other day when one of our executives reported on her meeting at a major Internet company. I had asked her to call on the company because they had just sponsored their first sports event. I wanted to know if our company could fit into their plans.

Her report was not encouraging – and it all centred on people skills. 'The sponsorship director, a fairly young woman, met me in the lobby. I thought that was nice,' she said. 'But then she led me down about a quarter-mile of hallways without saying a word. That was awkward. When we sat down in her office, the first thing she said was that she would have to end the meeting in 20 minutes because something else had come up. That didn't bother me. Twenty minutes was enough for a first meeting. But I wasn't sure I would get the full twenty. I certainly didn't have her full attention. She had a computer on her desk that beeped to signal incoming e-mail. It beeped several times during the meeting, and each time she turned to the computer to check the message while I was talking. That was rude (though I suspect she couldn't help herself).

'Even worse, she didn't know anything about our company, even though I had sent materials the week before. I outlined the kinds of events we had produced for other sponsors. She had no follow-up questions. I asked her the most basic questions about their budgets, their timetables, the consumer they were trying to reach, and what sports interested them the most. She ignored each of these questions, saying she was not at liberty to divulge that information. I wasn't asking her to share nuclear secrets with China. I just wanted to know if her CEO liked golf!

'It was the strangest, most hostile sales call – and it was going nowhere. I politely told her I had taken enough of her time. The *coup de grâce*, though, came as I showed myself to the door. I turned around to say goodbye, but she was already glued to her computer screen.'

I was disappointed for our executive. No one should have to bear such oafish behavior. But a part of me wasn't surprised. I've always worried that as people rely more on technology, particularly e-mail and voice-mail, for communicating, they rely less and less on their face-to-face personal skills. And slowly but steadily, those everyday skills – the common decencies like politeness and sensitivity to other people's feelings – erode away.

At some point, people may be so reliant on technology, they won't even feel the need for human contact. After all, if you can get your message across via e-mail, who needs face-to-face contact?

I'm seeing this in its infant stages at our company. I had to resolve a dispute between two executives the other day. They each came to my office armed with an e-mail history of their communication. Seventeen e-mails went back and forth, each stating their author's position. It was interesting to see how each successive message was written. As the dispute continued, the messages became shorter and testier, with the net effect of escalating the disagreement rather than resolving it. They were torturing each other with e-mail.

I tossed the e-mails in the wastebasket and said, 'You both work in the same building. Why didn't one of you visit the other's office and talk this over?'

They looked at me as if the thought had never entered their mind.

I guess that's another thing you can't learn on the Internet: the value of human contact.

It's a factor that will only increase in importance as we become more dependent on technology for communicating. The people who remember that something meaningful and constructive happens when two people are in the same room having a face-to-face conversations and conversely, that something destructive happens when people hide behind technology to communicate will be happiest and most successful in the new environment.

People, say things in e-mail that they would never say to someone's face.

I've been fascinated by the US government's anti-trust case against Microsoft. The trial has been going on for months in a Federal court in Washington, DC and gets daily coverage in the business press.

I'm not interested in the legal issues. I don't have a strong opinion about whether Microsoft has abused its monopolistic power in the software industry (as the government contends) or whether it is simply a very aggressive competitor in an ultra-dynamic industry (as Microsoft argues).

What fascinates me is the evidence the government prosecutors are using. It's all e-mail.

It seems as if the government attorneys have combed through every memo and e-mail ever written by Microsoft executives and they have made their findings the centre of their prosecution. The government strategy is simple: Whatever Microsoft's executives say on the witness stand, don't believe them. They have no credibility – and we have their e-mails to prove it.

Thus, during weeks of endless testimony, whenever a Microsoft witness made a statement favorable to the defense, there was a government attorney brandishing an e-mail that clearly contradicted the testimony. *US vs. Microsoft* is the most significant corporate trial of the decade, and it may be the first ever to hinge in large part on e-mail.

It's incredibly unfair. The problem with e-mail is that it only reveals a fraction of the message: the terse, blunt, just-the-facts side. What's missing is the nuance, the tone of voice, the irony or humour underlying the same message that comes when you say it aloud to someone else. An e-mail, like a memo or letter, lacks nuance. Depending on the tone of voice, a conversation using the same words can sound conciliatory, sceptical, even innocent.

Unfortunately for Microsoft, everyone at the company, from the chairman on down, communicates via e-mail. They should have had more face-to-face meetings.

Technology is wonderful and seductive. But it's also insidious, especially if it chips away at our appreciation of the value of constant human contact – because without these moments of face-to-face exchanges we lose a vital regulator in our lives. Human contact controls our behaviour. Remove it and people's baser instincts appear. For this reason an executive can walk into my office and complain about a colleague. But if I invite that colleague into our meeting, the complaining executive will totally change his tune. He may not back down completely, but his tone and choice of words will become more civil. He won't repeat to the colleague's face what he was willing to say behind his back.

Remember this as you march into the future with your laptops, Palm Pilots, and digital communicators. No matter how tempting it is to hide behind technology, there's more to be gained by looking into another person's face than by staring at a screen.

1 Giving Yourself a Reality Check

THE PERSON WHO WILL CHANGE YOUR LIFE IS NOT IN IT NOW

I used to think that the best person to solve a problem in our organization was the person who first recognized the problem and presented it to me. Someone smart enough to detect, say, a flaw in our accounts receivables system was probably smart enough to correct it.

But one of my advisors challenged my thinking on this not long ago. We were discussing some troubling developments in one of our divisions. True to form, I announced how I wanted the situation resolved and then delegated the solution to the division head who had brought it to our attention.

'That's locked-room logic, Mark,' said the advisor. 'The best solution to a problem isn't always going to come from the people you've locked in a room to discuss it. If you take that attitude to its logical extreme, you'd be talking to the same people every day of your life – and getting the same routine answers to every set of new problems. You have to open the door and let some fresh faces in. The people who will have the biggest impact on your business are probably not in it right now.'

That last line caught me by surprise. It made me wonder whether I was a prisoner of 'locked-room logic' or whether I believed in opening the door to let new voices and new ideas in.

On reflection, I'm convinced that I am closer to the latter than the former. I've always fashioned my problem-solving skills to be slightly contrary and unpredictable. For example, years ago when our Cleveland accounting system needed a drastic overhaul, I transferred a senior executive from our London office, a trained attorney as well as a salesman, to oversee the project. He had a lawyer's rigorous mind, understood contracts, and knew what kind of data the sales force needed. He was also an outsider who would be indifferent to the entrenched relationships in the Cleveland office. And he wasn't an accountant. In other words, he was as fresh a face as I could find.

I guess I had forgotten some of that 'open-door logic' over the years. But my friend's point that the people who can change your world the most are not in it right now has snapped me back.

If you think about it, you'll see it can be applied productively in almost any business context.

It's certainly true in sales. Consider my theory that our sales executives should meet five new people each year. I take this objective so seriously that I literally expect our senior executives to report who these five people are and how these contacts can develop into business relationships for our company.

Of course, this assignment is not as easy as it sounds. Some people claim they don't have time to meet five new people. They have more business than they can handle. Then there's the inherently incestuous nature of many organizations. It's hard for people to break out of their friendly, familiar cliques. Worst of all, perhaps, is the fact that as people grow in seniority they find it easier to go back to the familiar names in their Rolodex than to break new ground with new people. (Actually, I encourage this 'knock on old doors' strategy. But it shouldn't deter people from knocking on new doors too.)

Yet the logic here is irrefutable. To test the theory, I went through my list of customers from as far back as 20 years ago. It was dramatically different than my list from ten years ago, and my ten-year-old list was unrecognizable against last year's list, while last year's list differed significantly from this year's list. Of course, some of the same names appear on each list (I knock on old doors too), but the most compelling and lucrative names are the new ones. They are the engines of growth in our sales. If my personal history is any indication, I'm sure the most lucrative names on my list in the next two or three years are customers I haven't called on yet or even imagined.

I'm also sure the same is true for everyone who sells for a living. The customers who will have the most impact on your sales performance are not your customers now. They're not even on your prospect list. They probably don't know you exist. What are you doing to change that?

This sort of logic also applies to career development. When people are concerned about their careers – for example they want a big raise or promotion or they want to switch jobs – they almost always turn to people they know. If they want a raise or promotion, they talk to their boss. If they're fishing for a new job at another company, they ask their friends to keep an eye on open positions at other organizations.

There's nothing wrong with that. If you're doing a great job, there's no one better than your boss to evaluate you and set your compensation. Your boss is the one who knows how valuable you are, who can't afford to lose you, and who will do anything within reason to keep you happy.

But if you have greater career ambitions – if you want your boss's job or something even bigger – you will have to look elsewhere. You might turn to your superiors in other parts of the company who don't have preconceptions about you and are open to helping you make a giant leap in your career. More likely, though, you will have to turn to decision-makers at other firms. These are the people who won't be pigeon-holing you into a specific job level or category. These are the people who hold the highest opinion of you, because their opinion is not tainted by memories of you at the start of your career. These are also the people who are eager to export your talent, contacts, and experience into their organization.

By definition, these people are not in your world right now. If they were, you'd know them and they would be calling you. The key to making a giant career leap is appreciating that you don't yet know the people who can help you achieve your goals. Once you realize that, you'll know how and where to find them.

BEWARE THE SMALL DEFINING MOMENTS

There's a little scene in the movie *Out of Africa* that has always stuck with me. The Meryl Streep character based on the writer Isak Dinesen comments to a friend that the Robert Redford character, Denys Finch Hatton, has a lovely book collection.

'Does he lend them?' she asks the friend.

The friend responds with an anecdote about how Denys once loaned a book to a fellow named Hopworth, who failed to return it.

The fellow telling the anecdote asked Denys about it: 'You wouldn't lose a friend for the sake of a silly book?'

Denys replied: 'No, but he has, hasn't he?'

The scene sticks in my mind because it points up one of the more interesting myths about how friendships and relationships are formed or broken in life.

It's easy to think that our character and reputation are formed by how we perform in the big moments in our career. We get this message all the time from sports. If an athlete performs well at a pivotal moment in a game or match, that crucial performance can have a lasting impression on the athlete's image and reputation. It can define his or her career forever after, regardless of what he or she does elsewhere.

But actually, in everyday life, the opposite is true. Unlike in sports, where athletes get a chance to be heroes or goats on an almost daily basis, ordinary life doesn't present that many opportunities for glory and heroism. Our criteria for judging people are more modest. As a result, it's the small, almost petty moments that define our character and reputation, that tell people whether we can be trusted or not, that attract potential friends and allies or repel them.

How we behave at these small but pivotal moments reveals as much about us as most people need to know and determines if our path through life will be rocky or smooth. Here are five everyday defining moments that are a lot bigger than they seem.

1. When you're considerate

I remember a few years ago observing a chill develop between two executives at our company who had been the closest of friends. When I asked one of the executives what happened, he said, 'I've never gotten over the fact that he sent a card when my mother died. He didn't call me or come to the funeral. He just sent a card.'

When I asked the other executive if he knew what went wrong in their relationship, he replied, 'Oh yes, I know. It's because I didn't call him when his mother died. It was too awkward for me. I didn't know what to say or how to deal with his grief, so I sent a card. That's what did it.'

What's interesting here is that both men knew the moment was a test of character. The man who lost his mother was looking for empathy and consideration. The other friend failed to supply it. Such small moments not only test a relationship, they can break it.

2. When you show backbone

People are incredibly alert to displays of courage and, conversely, spinelessness in the workplace. We've all seen it. The meek, mild-mannered employee who stands up to the bullying boss in a meeting soars in our estimation instantly. We automatically see the scene as a crucial display of true character. We think, 'I didn't think he had it in him.' But now we know better.

More important, the brave employee soars in the boss's estimation too. Bosses, even the bullies in the crowd, save their greatest respect for the people who are willing to disrespect them when they think they're wrong.

It's such a cliche, I don't know why more people don't appreciate it. If you want to give your reputation a quick lift, show backbone.

3. When you keep a confidence

How people deal with secrets is as sure a test of character as any I know. It's a virtue that people take for granted. No one goes around describing you by saying, 'Boy, that Jim, he can keep a secret.' You are probably defined by other more obvious virtues. But it's a virtue that, in a snap, can turn into a character flaw if you aren't careful during those small vital moments when you should be keeping a secret rather than sharing it.

If you want to fracture a relationship, break a confidence. If you want to lower people's opinions of you, be a gossip.

4. When you anticipate the other side's point of view

If pressed, I'd say my most valuable managerial skill is anticipating how other people will react to our company's actions. I can't count how many times I've quashed our people's strong ideas because I knew that taking them further would upset relationships in other parts of the company. It's not the sort of thing an executive gets credit for; after all, people rarely notice when you *avoid* an error. But they certainly do when you *commit* one. Anticipating the other side's reaction can be one of those small defining moments in a relationship.

For example, perhaps you've seen the Tiger Woods commercial for Nike where he bounces a golf ball off his wedge twenty times through his legs and around his back and then flips the ball up in the air and whacks it 200 yards down the course. It is one of the most talked-about sports commercials of the decade. When it first aired around the 1999 US Open, the media immediately started asking questions about this remarkable display of athletic skill. Was it trick photography? (No.) Clever editing? (No.) Computer enhanced? (No.) Did Tiger do it one take? (No, it took four tries to get it perfect.) And it was all unscripted. Tiger was doing his bouncing ball routine while he was idly waiting for the cameras on a totally different commercial. The director noticed Tiger's antics and asked if he could repeat it with the cameras rolling. Tiger said yes and wrapped up the spot in twenty minutes.

It quickly became a dream spot for Nike, entertaining to people who aren't interested in golf and riveting to those who are. It has generated great word of mouth for Nike and inspired kids all over to emulate Tiger Woods.

You'd think this would be a simple feel-good story about a successful marketing campaign, with everyone involved walking away happy.

But no. A fine company in Greenwich, Connecticut named Acushnet was not happy with the commercial. Acushnet makes Titleist golf balls, the same golf balls that Tiger Woods endorses and, in fact, used in the Nike commercial.

But when it comes to the category of golf apparel and footwear, Tiger endorses Nike's line. It probably didn't help that Nike recently introduced its own line of golf balls to compete with Acushnet's Titleist brand. Acushnet felt the commercials carried an implied message that Tiger had switched to Nike golf balls.

They interpreted the spots as an ambush by Nike and blamed us, as Tiger's representatives, for not anticipating their reaction. (By the way, I'm not revealing anything confidential here; that would be breaking rule no. three above. All of this was amply reported in the press.)

I mention this not to take sides with Nike or Acushnet (I admire both companies) but to marvel at how, even in the most innocent-seeming situations, where it seems there can be only one way to interpret the situation, there's always someone who sees it differently.

As the saying goes, 'No matter how thin you pour the batter, there's always two sides to a pancake.'

5. When you see an accident waiting to happen

People always have their reasons for not interfering when they suspect something bad is about to happen. Some people don't care. Others are overly impressed by group thinking and don't have the mental toughness to buck popular opinion. They're also afraid of being wrong. Then there are the people who look away because they simply want to see a colleague fail.

None of these reasons strikes me as being particularly admirable. In fact, I can't think of any pure, noble motive for holding your tongue when you see a colleague turning onto a potentially disastrous path.

I was watching from the sidelines some years ago as a friend of mine, a CEO at another company, allowed his people to commit themselves to putting on a sports event that had never been tried before. The concept was so glamorous and compelling that everyone at his company wanted to be involved with it. So the company opened up a special office dedicated to the event. They hired new people, commissioned marketing studies, and spent a lot of money seeking sponsors and courting civic leaders and community groups to support the event. This development process continued for 18 months with the blind, unwavering support of every senior manager at the company – until one day a sharp-eyed accountant, analyzing the project's costs and projected revenues, concluded that the event would never make money. None of the senior managers wanted to hear this, of course. They were so in love with the project they couldn't tolerate any dissent. They dismissed the account-ant's analysis as the predictable consequence of unimaginative bean counting.

But the accountant firmly believed the numbers didn't add up and ultimately took his case to the CEO, who agreed with him and killed the project immediately.

I have to believe that most people at the company respected the accountant for speaking up. I know the CEO took notice, because three years later he promoted the young man to be his chief financial officer.

The next time you waver between speaking up or shutting up about an accident waiting to happen, don't think of it as a choice between meddling and being a team player. What's really at stake is your reputation as a thinker and adviser. These are the moments when your reputation for intelligence and wisdom (an even rarer quality) is formed. The wisest counsellors aren't afraid to speak up or offer advice that runs counter to the conventional thinking. Somehow they know that when everyone assumes something to be true, it usually isn't.

6. When you remain loyal

In my mind, loyalty is the greatest virtue. It's the emotional glue that keeps organizations from crumbling, that keeps employees on board dur-ing tough times, that keeps customers on your side when competitors try to lure them away. But again, it's a virtue that reveals itself in small ways more often than it does in grand dramatic gestures. The fact is, there are very few moments in the workplace that call for grand dramatic gestures, for egregious displays of loyalty or disloyalty, where you are forced to cross some line with everyone watching which way you go.

Loyalty isn't extracted by huge public displays. More often than not, it shows up in small private moments – for example, when someone attacks your boss and you defend him or her. Your character and reputation are shaped by such small tests. If nothing else, I guarantee that the person attacking your boss will be impressed by your defence. I know I would be.

KNOW YOUR MENTAL YARDSTICK
FOR PERSONAL SUCCESS

I think everyone in business has a mental yardstick for their on-the-job performance, a secret form of measurement that motivates them and tells them how they're doing. For many people, the obvious yardstick is money.

Yet for others it may be status or control or being liked by everyone or having the freedom to come and go as they please.

My mental yardstick is time. I'm a fanatic about maximizing not only my days and hours but my minutes and seconds. Everything I do is filtered through the clock. Everyday business decisions such as where I travel and whom I meet are guided by how much time they require of me and how much reward will result from the investment of that time. If the time investment outweighs the reward, I'll usually say no to an opportunity to which other less time-conscious executives might say yes.

The larger point I'm trying to make is not what my mental yardstick says about me, but what it should be saying to people who deal with me.

A person who knows that time is my yardstick can get a lot more out of me than someone who doesn't appreciate it. They can use my yardstick to persuade, impress, and control me.

If the head of our office in New Zealand (where I haven't been in years) thinks it's worthwhile for me to visit there, he's more likely to get me to make the trip if he crowds my schedule with high-level meetings from 6 a.m. to 6 p.m. than if my schedule is only half full. He's telling me in advance that I won't be wasting my time.

Our company is too big for me to have met every employee or know each one by name. But I will make the time to meet any employee who writes me a note that says, 'I need to talk to you for 15 minutes at your convenience.' whereas I would be reluctant to meet with someone who neglected to mention how much time they needed. A time-specific request impresses me. An open-ended one scares me.

As a manager, I'm always trying to figure out an employee's mental yardstick, seeking clues in his speech, appearance, and work habits to answer the question: How does this individual measure personal happiness and success?

If I can figure out the unit of measurement, I can usually figure out how to manage them. I haven't run into many employees whose mental yardstick is time, but here are four common yardsticks to look for:

1. Money

Money may be the universal unit of measurement for keeping score in business, but some employees try to conceal their feelings about it. However, an employee's true feelings about money are inevitably revealed at salary review time. That's when a normally agreeable or docile individual can turn into a rapacious dynamo who has itemized the dollar value of every contribution he has made at work during the previous year. There's nothing wrong with this. I actually prefer dealing with these types, because they're so direct. Their effort on the job is in direct proportion to their monetary reward. It's not clouded by 'warm and fuzzy' factors like recognition or praise or self-esteem. It's commerce in its simplest form: quid pro quo.

2. Status

Status is a trickier yardstick to manage – because (a) it's not a private matter like money and (b) one employee's obsession with status can have a snowball effect on everyone else in the organization. You can't give one employee a bigger job title or office (two of the more obvious status indicators in the workplace) and not expect his peers to seek a comparable title or office. If status is one employee's yardstick, it soon becomes the yardstick for his peers. As a manager I pay extra attention to the status seekers on the staff because the entire organization can get out of control.

3. Being liked by everyone

Some people simply want to be liked by everyone. They are helpful, accommodating, and reluctant to make waves. They gauge their success by how well they get along. Again, there's nothing wrong with this. It's nice to work with pleasant people. But as a manager, you might not want these types in positions where hard decisions need to be made. The company might be better off filling those slots with people who don't care if everyone likes them.

4. Autonomy

Some people measure happiness and success by how much they can control their own destiny. They will sacrifice money and status for the sense that they have autonomy at work, that no one is looking over their shoulder, questioning their whereabouts and judging their every move. As a manager, I've found this is the easiest yardstick to accommodate. As long as the employee performs as expected, I leave him or her alone.

DON'T BE DELUDED ABOUT YOUR PRIORITIES

The terrible truth about priorities is that they exert far more control over us than we do over them. This is ironic because of all the forces at play in the workplace, you would think that we have more control over our priorities than almost anything else. After all, priorities, by definition, are the goals, dreams, and concepts that *we* deem important. Other people may have the power or authority to tell us what *they* think our priorities should be, but we still have the freedom and will to decide whether or not we accept their priorities as our own. If there's a conflict, we can walk away.

And yet, after years of observing people at work, I'm convinced that there are few greater sources of delusion in business than how people establish priorities and how well they stick to them.

For one thing, very few people actually know what their priorities are.

I recently saw an article about an expert in time management who was lecturing to a group of business students. As this man stood in front of the group of bright, accomplished students, he said, 'It's time for a quick quiz.' He pulled out a wide-mouthed gallon jar and set it on a table in front on him. Then he produced a dozen fist-sized rocks and dropped them one at a time into the jar.

When the jar was filled to the top and no more rocks would fit inside, he asked, 'Is this jar full?'

Everyone in the class said, 'Yes.'

'Really?' the man asked. He reached under the table and pulled out a bucket of gravel. He poured some gravel into the jar and shook it, causing pieces of gravel to work themselves down into the spaces between the rocks.

Then he asked the group again, 'Is the jar full?' By this time the class was onto him. 'Probably not,' one of them suggested.

'Good.' he replied. And he reached under the table and brought out a bucket of sand. He started dumping the sand in and it went into all the spaces between the rocks and the gravel. Once more he asked the question, 'Is the jar full?'

'No,' the class shouted in unison. Once again, he said, 'Good.' Then he picked up a pitcher of water and poured it in until the jar was filled to the brim. Then he looked up at the class and asked, 'What's the point of this demonstration?'

One student raised his hand and said, 'The point is no matter how full your schedule is, if you try really hard, you can always fit some more things into it.'

'No,' the speaker replied. 'that's not the point at all. The lesson is this: if you don't put the big rocks in first, you'll never get them in at all!'

I submit, via this artful illustration, that few people ever establish in their minds what the 'big rocks' are in their lives. The options are numerous, from the obvious appeal of fame and fortune to the simpler pleasures of spending more time with your family to the noble cause of improving your community to the mundane matters of finishing a project that's important to you. But how many of us have clearly spelled out in our minds which of these numerous options is number one in our life?

The delusion doesn't stop here. Even when we have our priorities straight in our minds, not all of us are adept at keeping them in order in our hearts – that is, in actual practice.

For example, if you ask most married male executives in their mid-30s to early 50s what their priorities are, they'd answer family first, then career, community, and if they are religious, church. The order on the last three items may vary, but I don't know many men with wives and children who are willing to admit that their career is their number one priority.

And yet . . . how many men actually practise what they preach? Given the choice between having a dinner in town to close on a huge sale or going home early to see their daughter's soccer match, how many people are willing to sacrifice the clear material reward of the former for the warm and fuzzy payoff of the latter?

That's a thorny dilemma for many men, even in today's enlightened climate of salary families where dads are expected to share the child-rearing responsibilities and there's general approval for anyone who has the nerve to sacrifice his career for his family. ('That fellow has his priorities in order,' we tell ourselves, with admiration for the individual in question.) The man tells himself that he's putting in the extra hours at work precisely *for* his family. The better his career, the better he can provide for them. But for many men, it's not quite the truth. Their jobs and maintaining a steady upward arc in their careers are as important, if not more so, than anything else in their lives, including their families.

I'm not making a value judgment here, saying that family should take precedence over career (or vice versa). I'm merely pointing out that there is a disparity between the priorities we claim to have and the priorities we actually adhere to. It would be healthier for everyone if we were a little more honest about where our priorities really are.

There's another slightly more subtle delusion about priorities. It's the notion that we are somehow betraying ourselves if we change our priorities in midstream.

Establishing our priorities is how we develop our code of behaviour in life. If something is important to us, that fact determines the choices we make and colours how we behave in almost any critical situation. But circumstances change, either because of us or despite us, and it often takes wisdom for people to notice the change and courage to alter their priorities accordingly.

I've been around long enough to see some of my contemporaries accumulate fairly substantial fortunes – more than enough so that they and their heirs and their heirs' heirs would be well taken care of. It's interesting how differently people deal with their success.

For some, the fact that they have as much money as they'll ever need has no altering effect on their priorities. They like what they're doing, regardless of the material reward, and they intend to continue doing it until the passion disappears. Nothing wrong with that. They know their priorities – and live by them. (That's one reason they're so successful.)

But there's an equivalent group who reach a certain level of success – and then stop what they're doing. They change their focus from accumulating worldly success to giving something back. It's the reason you see so many wealthy individuals 'retire' in their prime and turn to public service and philanthropic work.

What strikes me about such career shifts is the willingness to change priorities. Most of us don't even know what our priorities are, and even fewer of us have the courage to follow them faithfully when we do know them. So when we see someone who not only knows his or her priorities but can actually alter them in midstream, it's an even more impressive display of wisdom and character.

A GOAL IS MORE ACHIEVABLE IF YOU BREAK IT DOWN INTO ITS MOST MANAGEABLE PARTS

For most of his NBA career Michael Jordan kept his scoring average at 32 points per game (he retired in 1999 with an NBA record 31.5 point career average). It didn't matter who his teammates were, what offence they were running, what injuries he was nursing, or who was guarding him, Michael Jordan would get his 32 points.

When reporters asked him how he maintained that consistency for more than a decade, Jordan said, 'I simplified it a few years ago: 32 points per game is really just eight points a quarter. I figure I can get that in some kind of way during the course of a game.'

I like that. It's clear and elegant explanation of how to set a high standard for yourself and then achieve it: You start with the end result (32 points), break it down into its most easily do-able components (8 points per quarter), and then focus on each component. If you're successful with each component, you'll achieve the goal.

It's a wonder more people don't adopt this strategy. I wonder how many starters in the NBA, with half of Jordan's talent and the same amount of playing time, could average 16 points per game if they broke down their scoring goals to 4 points a quarter. I wonder how many of these highly disciplined professionals even think in terms of quarters rather than the full game?

If professional basketball is anything like the professional workplace, the number is probably not very high. My impression is that most people in the workplace are not particularly goal-oriented or, if they do have goals, they are not particularly smart about how to achieve them. They may want a better job, better pay, and a better life for themselves and their family. But those are dreams more than goals. If they were real goals, they would be specific and they would be broken down into easily doable components.

Take, for example, a young sales executive at a new company. He's hired to produce X dollars in annual revenues. If he produces X, he keeps his job. If he does a little better than X, he gets a bonus. If he does much better than X, he gets a bonus and a promotion. That's the standard reward procedure in any meritocracy.

If I were that salesperson on the hook to produce X, I'd simplify the sales process into its most do-able component – namely, the sales call. Anyone can make a sales call. (Making the sale is another matter.) I'd find out the company's average sales transaction. Then I'd calculate how many sales at that average I would have to close to make my quota. Dividing that number of successful transactions by 12 would tell me how many sales I was expected to make per month. That's a good number to know. With that in mind, I'd find out how many sales calls the company's sales force makes for each sale. That would tell me the minimum number of sales calls I would need to make per month to have a good chance of producing X. Then I would make sure to call on more prospects than the bare minimum.

That's breaking down a sales goal. Some unforeseen circumstance may prevent me from hitting my target, but it wouldn't be that I wasn't calling on enough prospects.

It's not a mentally taxing procedure. But without it, how can you tell if you're trying hard enough or seeing enough people? Yet I suspect a lot of salespeople ignore this aspect of goal setting, preferring instead to flail about, making calls whenever they pick up leads, hoping for that one big score that will make their year.

Goal setting isn't the only area where this break-it-down mental exercise is useful. It shows up in the most mundane activities – like getting somewhere on time.

How often has this happened to you? You and a friend agree to meet for dinner at a downtown restaurant in 60 minutes. But first your friend has to run some errands. You arrive at the restaurant. The friend arrives 40 minutes late. The friend uses traffic and long customer lines as an excuse. But when you review his activities, you realize there was no way he could have made it to the restaurant in 60 minutes.

If your friend had broken down each segment of his itinerary into increments of time – 20 minutes to get across town. 15 minutes to exchange a gift, 10 minutes to get to the next shop, 5 minutes to make a purchase, 10 minutes to drop off a package, 20 minutes to the restaurant – and allowed 15 to 20 minutes as a margin of error, he would have arranged to meet you in 90 minutes instead of keeping you waiting.

But some ornery impulse prevents many people from tackling this sort of simple arithmetic. They'd rather put their faith in good luck and their own ingenuity than go through a few dull, uninspired calculations.

Actually, I think this type of thinking is the height of originality. It demonstrates a unique way of seeing the world that will set you apart – and usually above – the crowd.

LETTING THINGS GO IS A GOOD GOAL, TOO

For most of us, setting goals is an exercise in addition.

If you decide to learn to speak Italian, you are adding a new language to your repertoire. If you want a fatter pay cheque, you add hours to your schedule and more responsibilities to your job description. (Even a goal like losing weight, which should be the ultimate case of subtraction, is a process of addition – in this case. more exercise and discipline.)

In each case, setting a goal requires a commitment of additional time, effort, and willpower to achieve it. Of course, that's one reason so many people fall short of their goals: they simply don't have the additional time or energy for the effort.

But setting goals can also be an exercise in subtraction. In our constant striving for more skills, more power, more contacts, more recognition, etc. – we often overlook the obvious merits of eliminating some of the more troubling components in our lives and careers. Subtraction is a worthwhile goal, too.

Some years back we were considering hiring a sales executive. He had all the tools: brains, self-confidence, a solid list of contacts. It wasn't just cosmetics. He could sell. But I was troubled by his résumé, which did not disguise the fact that he had switched jobs five times in eight years, all lateral moves. Clearly, his career had stalled. But I wasn't sure I wanted to find out why by letting him into our company. So we hired someone else.

I ran into him seven years later when he had become a senior executive at a major retailer that I wanted to do business with. He reminded me that I had interviewed him for a job and rejected him. (He had not lost any of his self-confidence!) I mumbled something about how he seemed to be in a rut at the time but that he had recovered nicely. I asked, 'What happened?'?

He said, 'My wife got fed up listening to me complain about how every-one else at work was stupid. After my fifth or sixth new job, she pointed out that maybe my co-workers weren't the problem, that maybe there was something unattractive in my personality and maybe I should work on it. Together, we listed all my positive and negative attributes. She was more brutal than I was. But we both agreed that I argued too much – which made me appear more unfriendly than I really was. So I eliminated this negative from my life. I stopped debating every point at every meeting. I didn't stop thinking I was the smartest guy in the room. I simply stopped telling the world about it. I guess it's made a difference.'

Everyone in business wants to be smarter or more charming or more articulate or more commanding. Perhaps more of us should reset our sights and try to be less. Less difficult. Less remote. Less paranoid. Less argumentative. Less obnoxious. It's a worthwhile goal – and so easy to do.

It's also good to remove a few things from your plate.

I don't know any ambitious people who do not feel they have too many projects on their plate. The most effective and successful people step back periodically, isolate a project or two, and remove it from their plate.

Shedding responsibilities and authority isn't the customary path to suc-cess at most companies. But if you're spending precious time on a project that

- you hate,
- is going nowhere fast,
- isn't teaching you anything, or
- you would never try to take credit for,

let it go.

PEOPLE WHO COUNT ON LUCK RARELY GET LUCKY

An entrepreneur I know was describing his elaborate campaign to win a major account. Landing the account wouldn't make or break his business, but it would be a nice feather in his cap and give his company a big revenue jolt. I was particularly impressed by the man's complete confidence that his pitch would be successful. In fact, he was so confident that he confessed that he had already signed a lease for a new office in Chicago to service the account.

'Isn't that a little premature and risky?' I asked. 'What will you do if you lose the bid?'

'I don't intend to lose,' he said. 'We did our homework on this campaign. We covered every contingency and prepared as well as we know how. If you do that, you don't need to wait till the end to find out who won. If you set yourself up to win, you can pretty much predict the winners and losers when the contest begins. It's going to take a miracle to beat us on this one, and I haven't seen anything that our competition has done to deserve a miracle.'

I'm not so sure you can always tell the winners and losers at the start. After all, that's why they play out the game: to see who wins. But there's more than a kernel of truth in this fellow's philosophy about setting yourself up to win.

It's certainly true about the athletes I've observed over the years. The athletes who win consistently are the ones who consistently set themselves up to win rather than fail. It's almost as if they have a checklists: they're well conditioned. They're well rested. They're peaking at the right moment. They've thought about their game plan. They're not nursing any nagging injuries.

If they don't meet these minimum requirements for excellence, they don't play – or at least they're not disappointed when they lose. More important, when they set themselves up to win, they're more likely to benefit from a little miracle.

In a golf tournament, it might be the way the course sets up to favour your particular style of play, or it might be one or two bounces that went for you rather than against you. Some people call this luck. I think it's all part of setting yourself up to win.

I'm always puzzled by how vividly people remember a lucky bounce or a controversial call in a pivotal moment of a sports event. For some reason, they believe this single moment determined the outcome of the match or game. What people forget, of course, are all the other things the athlete has done to get himself to that pivotal moment in a championship match or a final pairing on Sunday. They forget that the real reason the athlete got lucky was that he was uniquely positioned to get lucky.

To me, this is the paradox of miracles. The more you rely on luck to win, the less likely you are to get it. Conversely, luck tends to happen to people who need it the least. They're not counting on a miracle to win. They're counting on their hard work and talent. The lucky bounce or the call that went their way – the miracle – is simply the slightly extraordinary event that stands out in everyone's mind. And these winners have earned it. As Gary Player told me long ago, 'The harder I work, the luckier I get.'

I see the same dynamic all the time in business. Some people set themselves up to win. Some set up to fail. Guess which ones get lucky?

For example, I'm fascinated by a particular corner on Lexington Avenue in Manhattan near our Upper East Side office. During the past 15 years, I've seen a half dozen restaurateurs open up a fancy restaurant at this corner location. And the same thing happens every time: within two years, the restaurant goes out of business. It doesn't matter what kind of cuisine the kitchen offers or how generous the food critics are, the location is simply not congenial to a restaurant. And yet within months of one tenant's departure, there's another presumably smart restaurateur who thinks he's the one who can succeed at this accursed location.

Over the years, as the sad procession of openings and closings at this corner continue, I've always wondered. Haven't any of these business people researched the failure rate for restaurants here? Don't they see a pattern?

To me, that's not setting yourself up to win. Ignoring the harsh history at this location – and believing that you'll be the unique individual who can make it work – is setting yourself up to fail. It would take a miracle to make a restaurant successful here. But in choosing this particular spot, you don't deserve the miracle.

BE AS CREATIVE WITH PEOPLE AS YOU ARE WITH YOUR IDEAS

Creativity comes in all forms in business. You can be creative with words, computers, office design, purchasing procedures, cash management, the law, even the tax code. By creativity, I mean making the connection between two disparate concepts and coming up with a third concept that no one else sees as readily as you do. If people appreciate your creativity, you will be well compensated throughout your life.

But there is one form of creativity that often goes unappreciated. That is creativity with people, by which I mean linking individuals who are seemingly unconnected and finding a mutually beneficial reason for them to get together. It goes unnoticed because, in many ways, it's taken for granted. Business, after all, is all about bringing disparate people together – buyers and sellers, employers and employees, entrepreneurs and investors – and forging a commercial connection between them.

Creativity with people is a talent that you notice only when it is absent. It's a lot like being a guest at a wonderful party. If the host has a gift for entertaining large groups of people, many of whom are strangers to one another, you don't notice all the creative touches that go into making the party a success: how the bar is stocked with every drink imaginable, how the hors d'oeuvres appear at the precise moment when everyone is hungry, how the host gently steers you to a corner of the room, saying, 'There's someone I want you to meet.'

As the guest you may not give all this a moment's thought. But I guarantee you that the host has thought about it. Making something look effortless requires tremendous effort.

I also guarantee that you *would* notice if the party was a dud – if the bar only offered beer, if the food was cold, if you didn't meet anyone interesting – and you'd probably blame it on the host. As I say, you appreciate this sort of creativity only when it's missing.

Not long ago I asked a successful journalist I know how she got started in her career.

'I got a lucky break,' she told me, 'but it almost didn't happen. Straight out of college, I landed a copy editing job at a ridiculously boring magazine. I was stuck there for four years with no clue how to get out. Fortunately, one of my best friends heard about a job opening at a slick national magazine. She mentioned it to my husband, asking him if he knew anyone in the magazine trade who would be interested in applying. Now here's the interesting thing. This woman was a close friend, and yet it never entered her mind that I might be interested. Of course, my husband made the connection right away. I applied, got hired, and every good thing that has happened to me began with that job.

'But it was revealing that my friend didn't think of me for the job. She was a sweet and generous friend. She didn't ignore me because she was jealous or didn't want me to get ahead. She simply lacked the imagination to connect people. Her brain didn't work that way.'

I suspect there are a lot of people in business whose 'brains don't work that way.' But creativity with people is an invaluable talent and unlike other forms of creativity, it can be learned. It is virtually impossible to teach someone to be a creative designer or software programmer if he or she doesn't have some innate visual or mathematical gift. But all of us, to one degree or another, have a feel for people. All of us can become a little more creative in how we 'manage' the relationships of the people in our lives.

The problem here is not that people have no imagination. Rather, they're not applying it in the context of other people. Just like a lawyer who sees the world in the context of legal issues or an accountant who sees everything through the prism of dollars and cents, people who are creative with people see the world in terms of social connections and relationships.

How can you train your imagination to work that way? You can start by observing the 'social lions' at your company. They're the executives who are constantly calling *ad hoc* meetings of random employees to tackle a problem. They're the ones who offer you tickets to an important ballgame or invite you and your friends for a drink after work. They're the colleagues who invite the staff to their home for a summer barbecue. They think in the context of other people. Study them. Note how they are constantly connecting the human dots in and out of the workplace. Emulate them.

It also helps to have a generous spirit.

To connect people creatively, you need a selfless desire to see them get together and benefit from the connection. That requires a spirit of generosity that many people cannot muster within themselves. They would rather do nothing than do something to help a stranger or friend. I have no idea why people are built this way. But it's not attractive and it stifles any talent for bringing people together.

Without a generous spirit, you're not connecting people creatively, you're scheming (like Shakespeare's Iago).

Of course, part of being generous is not being overt about what's in it for you.

Let's face it, when we bring other people together, we expect a payoff for ourselves. Part of the payoff is the emotional gratification of seeing our creative manoeuvring work out for a friend or a business associate. But in the back of our minds we're also thinking that our efforts won't go unrewarded. We're holding an IOU from our friends that might come in handy in the future.

The point is, you can't be overt about this. You can't regard all your associates and friends as potential finder's fees. It makes people suspect your motives.

I once met with the marketing chief of a major mail-order company who was explaining how his company did one-fifth of their annual business around Valentine's Day.

'We own Valentine's Day,' he boasted.

'That's interesting,' I said. 'We have a client, the CEO of 1–800 Flowers, who thinks he owns Valentine's Day. The two of you should get together.'

I could see the marketing chief's eyes dancing with delight at my suggestion. He was very keen to find out who this 'flower CEO' was.

In the back of my mind, however, I was thinking, 'What's in it for me? If I connect these two companies and they make a ton of money from the relationship, how do I profit from it?' I didn't articulate my thoughts, of course. But I know a lot of people who would immediately start negotiating a finder's fee the moment they saw the marketing chief's eyes dancing.

That's not my style or motivation. Until these two companies get together and make money. I'm suspending my self-interest. I'd rather have these two executives focused on doing business together than worrying about me and my fee. In my experience, people remember who brought them together and they usually pay you back in ways that are more creative than you imagined.

GET A CROSSOVER SKILL

An entrepreneur and I were comparing notes about what we feared most in a competitor.

'That's an easy one,' said the entrepreneur. 'It's an accountant who can sell. I'd hate my nearest rival to be someone who had a salesperson's ability to get money out of customers and an accountant's financial discipline to squeeze the maximum profit out of the sale. Most people have one skill. Lots of salespeople can get the order. But not many of them pay attention to the finer financial points of the deal: how the money is paid out, when it's paid, who pays for shipping, and soon. And yet these points usually spell the difference between a double-digit profit margin or a single-digit margin or no margin at all. People with more than one skill scare me. That's why I try to get them to work for me rather than against me.'

I take his meaning.

For a long period of time when the ranks of upper and middle management were populated by generalists – reasonably intelligent people with no special expertise who were quick enough to understand a problem and clever enough to find someone to solve it. The lean-and-mean 1980s were not a good time for generalists. That decade came mighty close to wiping out the population. With alarming speed, organizations went into the market for 'specialists.' And job candidates began marketing themselves accordingly as narrow-focused talents who happen to be the best at what they do.

The tide has turned. With the workplace now crowded with individuals who excel at one thing, it's not surprising that the people rising above the pack now possess (or can develop) crossover skills – so they excel at two things.

The comeback of Andre Agassi in 1999, from a world ranking of number 143 to number one is a useful example of acquiring a crossover skill. Agassi always had the tennis skills to be a champion – the foot speed, the reflexes, the eye-hand coordination, the overpowering ground strokes – and indeed they brought him glory at various points in the 1990s. But at the end of the decade, as he was approaching the age of 29 (ancient in tennis terms), he realized he didn't have the conditioning to match up week after week against the various young studs across the net from him. On any given day, Andre was a sitting target for elite and not-so-elite players. He changed that with a strength and conditioning programme that totally reconfigured his body – and the results in 1999, his first French Open title and a second US Open triumph, speak for themselves. It might be hard to think of being in shape as a second skill for a world-class athlete. But in Agassi's case, it was the missing ingredient that put him back on top.

It works in business too. Having a talent that complements and enlarges an existing skill is a great career booster at any level of an organization.

The best CEOs I know are not just dynamic leaders. They also excel in specific areas, whether it's product design or cash management or managing inventory. That skill is how they got to the top. They didn't start out as 'leaders.' No one does. Invariably, they began as niche players who were good at product design or cash management or inventory control. That skill got them noticed. When their superiors looked closer, they saw another talent. Perhaps it was a hint of leadership ability, or organizational ability, or a talent for getting along with customers. That was the crossover skill that propelled them ahead of the pack.

It's not much different today – except it's more ruthless and competitive. In a world where everyone is a talented specialist, if you want to bust out from the pack, you need a crossover skill that's in short supply. After all, there's no point in perfecting a crossover skill that dozens of people in your company are already good at. You have to find a gap in your organization that no one is paying attention to and use your talent to fill it.

I remember some years ago, a friend of mine at an advertising agency made a radical shift in the accounts he was pursuing. He had been fairly effective handling the usual high-profile consumer and packaged-goods companies that are the lifeblood of any agency. But it was a very competitive scene. Everybody wanted the same accounts he was pursuing. Then one day he realized he had an edge that he wasn't exploiting. It was his master's degree in chemistry (don't ask how he got into advertising).

Realizing that no one at his agency and very few people at the competition had similar training, he focused his attention on chemical and pharmaceutical companies. His main skill was winning accounts, but his crossover skill in chemistry gave him an affinity with these advertisers that no one else could match. He eventually started his own medical advertising agency, with handsome results. I doubt if things would have turned out this way if he didn't have the degree in chemistry. That was the crossover skill that let him cross over to a new niche.

I also recommend consulting someone you respect or admire – i.e. a 'coach' – to help reveal your hidden talent.

Many people don't know what they are good at. That's ignorance. An equal number think they're good at something, but they're really not. That's delusion.

Whether you're ignorant or deluded, everyone needs an objective outside party to help them identify their true talent.

For example, the great Australian soprano, Joan Sutherland, built her phenomenal career around her ability to hit high notes in relatively light Italian and French operas. But it wasn't always so. She started out singing heavy German operas that gave her no chance to display her vocal pyrotechnics. Things changed when a rehearsal pianist in Europe told her she was singing the wrong repertory. He taught her more suitable roles and coached her into extending her vocal range. She eventually married the pianist, conductor Richard Bonynge, and together they built one of this century's great musical careers. But it would never have happened if she hadn't found the perfect coach, who heard something no one else was hearing.

Of course, once you identify a talent gap and find a coach, you'll discover that it's still an incredibly competitive environment. That's when you have to be creative about the skills that matter. Start with these three:

Talent no. 1. To sell

Perhaps I have a bias toward selling because I run a privately-held sales organization. We don't have capital markets and money from stock offerings to fall back on in tough times. We either sell our services or we're out of business.

Thus, I still place the highest premium on sales ability. I still believe that nothing happens until someone sells something, and I reward people accordingly. If working for yourself is the best way to get paid exactly what you're worth, then selling runs a close second.

The only change is my recently acquired scepticism about 'the all-purpose salesperson.' I used to believe that there were some people who had natural sales talent. Their personality and ability to read other people meant they could sell anything to anyone. It helped if they were passionately interested in what they were selling, but it wasn't my top priority. Because we were a sports company, I figured someone who had proven sales talent and a general knowledge of sports (the kind you can get from reading the daily newspaper) was a better hire than an unproven candidate who knew everything about a specific sport.

Times have changed. Our customers in the sports arena have become so sophisticated and demanding that sending an 'all-purpose salesperson' to call on them would be a suicide mission. The customers would eat him or her alive. Our salespeople now need sales talent *and* the kind of marketing expertise you can't read about in the sports pages. I suspect this applies to any salesperson in any field today.

Talent no. 2. To create or have a unique expertise

Not long ago, I met with four senior officers of a computer software company. I was trying to interest them in a sports sponsorship programme, but what stuck in my mind was the makeup of the group. There were two men and two women. None of the group had a traditional sales or marketing background. They were all engineers or programmers – and proud of it. Only two of them had finished college. None of them was over 40 years old.

(If I had had that meeting 20 years ago, the group would probably have been all male and over 40. They would all have college degrees and perhaps law degrees or MBAs as well. They would all have come up through the sales or marketing ranks.)

It occurred to me that this group represented a major shift in how companies value and promote talent. Each of these four people started with a technical expertise that had always kept them at the core of their company's business. In their hearts, they were programmers and technophiles. They're the ones who created what the company sold. Learning to be executives who could run a big business (at least one big enough to be interested in sports marketing) was a talent that they picked up along the way.

I see the same thing happening in other organizations. Creative employees with advanced technical skills have always been valued but have often been shut off from the mainstream executive track. They were considered more valuable working away in their isolated niches.

The big change, I guess, is that companies now not only recognize that their in-house experts deserve a shot at advancement, they rely on them. If you can't promote the experts and creative people at the core of your business, who can you promote?

In an era that glamorizes specialization, having a unique expertise or being a source of new ideas can propel you quickly through an organization, certainly faster than age or educational pedigree.

Talent no. 3. To own a relationship

For years, when I called on advertising agencies, I heard about agency executives who had major clients 'in their hip pockets.' I was warned that approaching these clients with my sports ideas was pointless. The account executive owned the relationship. No matter how mediocre the advertising created by the agency, the client would never leave the agency for me. Although I thought this was a strange way to do business, it taught me the tremendous value of owning relationships. A client who was loyal even when you didn't do your job well was a great client indeed.

If you measure an employee's value by how much it would hurt to lose him or her, then the people who own relationships at our company – whether it is a special bond with an athlete client, an athlete's parents, or a corporate decision-maker – may well be our most valuable assets. When all else fails, you know these relationships will come through for you.

The only difference today (and it's a big one) is how these relationships are formed. In the not-too-distant past, executives had someone in their hip pockets because of some personal tie. They were neighbours or played golf together or went to the same school. Today's relationships demand more substance. Excelling at talents 1 and 2 is not a bad place to start.

YOUR JOB IS JUST ANOTHER PROJECT

The incredible mobility of young executives in the workplace proves that there is a large cohort of people out there who no longer view their jobs as a long-term once-in-a-lifetime commitment. They regard their job as a project, a short-term play, with a finite beginning and end. In between, they can make a contribution, meet new people, gain some knowledge, earn a little more money than they did before, and hopefully become associated with a success that looks good on their résumé. If it all works out, they can leverage this experience into the next job-project. Their careers are a continuum of increasingly more important 'projects.'

There's nothing wrong with this attitude. You certainly can't criticize it as selfish or disloyal. In reality, it's the logical reaction to an uncertain workplace where downsized corporations have demonstrated no particular loyalty to their employees.

It's also a shrewd response to a business environment where entire industries seem to reinvent themselves every three or four years. In a climate of blinding change, people can no longer think of their careers in terms of decades. They have to think in much shorter increments. A project mentality suits the current climate.

What's interesting about this attitude, though, is that it's also valid for all those talented people out there who like where they're working and don't want to jump ship to a new company or a new city. Yet for various reasons, they find themselves stalled in their careers. Their boss may be holding them back. Their workload may be too heavy to let them branch out. Their part of the organization may simply be mature and no longer growing as fast as other parts of the company.

Unfortunately, this sort of career impasse is precisely the situation that befuddles most people. They don't know where to begin looking to make a change, they don't know who to talk to, and most of all, they want to be sure they're making the right choice. If any of this resembles your situation, you're ripe for a new project. Here's how to get started.

1. Who's the leader?

A project appeals to many people because it sounds more exciting than their current assignment, they like the people they'll be working with, and they believe the job suits their abilities. These are valid criteria, but they're not as important as figuring out the qualities of the project leader.

The ideal project leader is someone who a) will teach you but won't be looking over your shoulder every step of the way, b) is respected in the organization so your project will get serious attention and high visibility, and c) has a track record of sharing the credit with his or her associates. It's incredible to me how often people commit themselves to projects that are led by people who don't possess these simple but singular qualities.

If the whole point of a project is to lift you out of a career rut, you have to put yourself in the hands of a leader who has hoisted others out of their ruts in the past. Anything less in your leader puts you back to square one.

2. What can you contribute?

To make a strong impression in any project, you don't need to do every-thing well. You only need to do one thing better than anyone else on your team. That's your contribution, and you better know what it is before you sign up. That particular skill makes you indispensable – and everyone will remember you when they're handing out kudos at project's end. Without it, you're dead weight.

3. How much can you learn?

A lot of people assess projects by how much they can learn from them. They look at each project as a mini-graduate course, a chance to add to their skill set. This is fine – up to a point. But if you're so focused on learning, you're probably not contributing and you're certainly not leading. At some point, you have to do something productively with all the learning you've acquired.

In our company, for example, we could take someone out of our accounting department and put him on a project developing a new sports event. In six months on this project, I guarantee that this accountant would learn more about how to create and sell a sports marketing concept than he could at any university, business school, or other company. But once the project is over, what of it? If the accountant never uses this acquired expertise, the project has been an interesting diversion. On the other hand, if the accountant returns to his old job with a better understanding of the costs and profit potential of a sports event, everyone wins.

4. Who are the other people?

Poker players like to say there's a patsy in every game. If you look around the table and don't know who the patsy is, you're it.

It's not much different when assessing the personnel on a project. You always want to be on a project where your colleagues are at least as smart and capable as you think you are – and possibly a little smarter and more capable. That's the best way to learn and elevate your game. It's also the most positive form of guilt by association. If you're associated with smart, capable people, a little bit of that aura inevitably rubs off on you.

A lot of people miss this point when they join a project. They don't look around to honestly assess the abilities of their teammates. The truth is, you should never be far and away the strongest person on the project. If you look around and, by your estimation, all you see are lightweights, you're probably a lightweight too.

KNOW WHEN TO MAKE AN EXCEPTION TO THE 'RULES'

You will have noticed by now that I'm fond of using bullet points and rules to guide people's behaviour in business situations. This begs the question: Do I actually obey these rules?

The short answer is yes – with a few exceptions.

The best thing about establishing rules for yourself in business is sticking to them. The second best thing is knowing when to break them.

I live by a personal code of conduct in business, under which fall certain principles about honesty, thoughtfulness, and doing what you say you will do. I try my best not to compromise on my code – because I know that doing so will cost me more than the occasional deal. It can compromise my name, reputation, career, and company.

But 'rules' are different. In my mind, the myriad rules that surround all of us are merely mental shorthand to remind us to stay focused on what matters.

I once read a carpentry book whose chief rule (and actual title) was 'Measure Twice, Cut Once.' A cute, pithy rule that should stick with you if you work with wood. But reading beyond the title, I discovered a caveat to the rule. Inside the book, the advice was actually 'Measure twice, cut once, but don't measure at all if you can avoid it.' That's because experienced carpenters know that tape measures vary. The longer they're used, the more they stretch. After a while, the readings are not accurate. If you're working with other carpenters on a house, and they're using their own aged and imperfect tape measures, you can end up with a multiplicity of distorted measurements that can create havoc.

Thus, an experienced carpenter knows not to measure unless he has no choice. He would never measure an exterior wall for a piece of siding, then go off and measure a length of siding, cut it, and bring it back to the wall for installation. Rather, he would bring the length of the siding to the wall, hold it up against the wall, and measure it on the spot using nothing but his eye. He knows that it's the actual length that matters, not the numerical reading on his tape measure. The situation demands nothing less than that sort of common sense.

It's the same in business. The true measure of an effective executive or salesperson or service provider is having enough common sense to make an exception to the so-called rules when the situation demands it.

We've all had run-ins with bureaucracy in all its varied guises. Perhaps we forgot to answer a question on a government form. Perhaps we lost one of the four tickets to our reserved box at the ballpark. Now, the 'rules' demand that we fill out the form completely and that no one is admitted to the stadium without a ticket. Yet, the occasions we remember happily and gratefully are precisely those when the rules were not enforced, when some friendly 'bureaucrat' used his or her discretion to bend the rules in our favour. He or she stamped 'Approved' on our flawed form or let us take our seat without a fuss. We admire such people for demonstrating such common sense.

And yet many of us forget these moments of blinding common sense in business when we are the ones facing the choice of following the rules or making an exception.

For example, when I'm negotiating on behalf of a client (whether it's a talented athlete or performing artist), I have a personal rule that says, 'Talent should never touch the money.' That's my mental mantra that reminds me that clients should stay out of business deals. Talented clients should spend their time perfecting their sport or art, and they should let me sweat the details of a negotiation.

Ninety-nine per cent of the time, I stick to this rule. (I even apply this to myself. When I'm invited to speak for a fee to a business group, I let other people in our company negotiate the financial terms. I don't 'touch the money' because I don't want any ill will that may have arisen during the negotiation to intrude on the good will I want to generate during my speech.)

But there are exceptions when the client should be at the negotiating table. Sometimes the client is smarter than I am. If I am negotiating a merchandising agreement for a new gadget, I want to have the gadget's inventor by my side. I may be the expert on merchandising, but the client knows how the gadget works.

Sometimes the client's stature can help close the deal. Although the presence of a superstar client in a meeting can be a major distraction – especially if they talk too much and volunteer information that is none of the other side's business – it can also force the other side's hand. We could be going back and forth for months on a contract, but if I bring the superstar to the next meeting, his or her presence somehow has an energizing effect on the proceedings. Everyone is more alert, more responsive, and more accommodating. After all, it's one thing for the other side to tell me personally, 'Your superstar isn't worth the price.' It's another for them to say it to the superstar.

On such occasions, I gladly bend my rule about talent never touching the money. Sticking to the rule is clearly getting me nowhere. What have I got to lose by breaking it?

I think this is the sort of gamesmanship that makes business fun.

It's like triple-booking airline reservations to combat the institutional white lie of airline overbooking. This sort of gamesmanship is sometimes the traveller's only weapon to guarantee a seat on a plane.

The overwhelming majority of transactions and relationships in business and in life are fair and uncomplicated. But on occasion you may have to confront people who bend the rules at your expense. When you find yourself in that ethical grey area, a little bit of whitewashing doesn't hurt – and may be absolutely necessary.

Remember: a rule is dangerous if you don't know when to make an exception to it.

DON'T LOWER THE BAR FOR YOURSELF

An insurance company ran an advertisement a few years ago showing a powerful grizzly bear in the middle of a roaring stream, with his neck extended to the limit, jaws wide open, teeth flaring. The bear is about to clamp on to an unsuspecting airborne salmon jumping up stream. The headline reads: 'You probably feel like the *bear*. We'd like to suggest you're the *salmon*.'

The eye-grabbing ad was designed to sell disability insurance. But it struck me as a powerful statement about how people in the workplace delude themselves about their achievements and their careers. We all think we're performing like bears. But much of the time we're more like salmon.

As a manager who's overseen hundreds of performance reviews in my time, I'm always amazed at the blind spots people reveal when they evaluate themselves. What amazes me is the predictability of the exercise. When it comes to themselves, people tend to:

- overestimate their contribution to a project
- take credit (partial or complete) for successes that truly belong to someone else
- have an elevated opinion of their professional skills or their standing within the company
- conveniently ignore their costly failures or time-consuming dead-ends
- exaggerate a project's impact on our company's net profits because they don't appreciate the hidden (yet very real) costs of operating a business

In short, people are too easy on themselves. They lower the bar. They don't apply the same harsh standards to themselves that they would to a subordinate or a rival. It's easy to see why people behave this way. If you're negotiating with your boss for a promotion or a raise, you should be accentuating the positive. It's the boss's job to play hardball or, at least, invoke reality.

However, it would occasionally be nice if the employees did some of the work themselves, if they played a little hardball with their own achievements, if they separated the real from the bogus and showed they were aware of their delusions. For example:

1. What do I actually do?

The disparity between what you and your boss think you should be doing is probably the source of greatest disappointment at performance reviews.

For some people this is an easy one. The Honda associate installing windshields on a Marysville, Ohio assembly line knows exactly what he does. He installs windshields. It's a small, albeit vital, contribution. He may do it very well. He may set an example for others on the line to perform as well as he does. But he doesn't dress up his job into anything more than it is.

The question is more complicated in any sort of entrepreneurial environment where everyone is dashing around, trying to make things happen. Surrounded by numerous open-ended opportunities, people can easily be pulled in several directions at once. People in our company often approach me to say there are other areas where they feel their particular talents would be useful. An accountant who handles a golf client's taxes might want to get more involved in the golfer's business affairs, to the point where the accountant thinks he should be managing golf clients. An attorney who's spent months writing a complex licensing contract, talking to the other side daily and in the process becoming an expert on the subject, might get the notion that he should be going around the world drumming up licensing deals. Quite often, I see their point. They are at least showing initiative in trying to progress their careers. But it's also my job to remind them they're getting paid to handle taxes and contracts first.

There's a difference between *what you do* and *what you can do*. You have to stay focused on the former before you can even think about the latter.

2. What have I actually done?

People are usually clear about what they've actually done during the year. If they've brought in $2 million in tangible revenue, it's easy to quantify that. Just look at the cheques. Where they tend to fudge, though, is when other people deserve some of the credit, too.

Personally, I don't care if they hit their home runs single-handedly or with someone else's help. An executive smart enough to recruit other people to get things done is just as impressive as the one working solo. But I worry when people claim their achievements are theirs alone and the facts support another conclusion. It makes me wonder what agenda they're pursuing, what else are they exaggerating or not fully disclosing.

It would be refreshing to hear someone say, 'Joe, Sally, and I made that $2 million sale happen – and 40% of it was me.' It would be even more refreshing if that person's contribution was actually closer to 60%, indicating that they were generous to others rather than themselves in this vague territory, that they didn't automatically award any benefit of doubt to themselves. It would be more refreshing still if that person got the $2 million customer to confirm that 40% figure. But people rarely do. They think (and want me to think) they did it all.

Some personal hardball in this area is infinitely better than trying to throw me a curve.

3. How does the rest of the world think you're doing?

I have always been fascinated by the dichotomy between how severely we gauge excellence in sports and how loosely we appraise it in the business world.

In sports you have very clear objective standards for what constitutes excellence. When you play at Wimbledon, you have either won or lost. It's there in the score for everyone to see. It's definitive.

The standards in business are a lot fuzzier. They're more subjective and considerably more forgiving.

A ballplayer can string together four incredible years, but if he has one or two off years people may think he's lost a step or is past his prime. It won't be long before people are saying, 'He used to be great.' Sport is brutal that way.

On the other hand, an executive who is supposedly very good at what he does can go for years before people notice that he may have lost a step or two. If he enters the room with a solid-gold reputation, he will invariably walk out with that reputation intact. Unless he does something completely idiotic, it will take years of mediocre performances for people to catch on to the gap between reputation and reality.

As a result. I think business people are not as tough on themselves as athletes. They know what they can get away with. They kid themselves about how much they have to prepare for an important meeting or a conference call. They can wing it and slide by. Sometimes they're actually surprised when someone suggests that they're not as clued up as they should be.

If that sort of carelessness crops up when the world is watching you, it can be the ultimate career killer. You may not be judging yourself harshly, but you ought to have enough sense to spot those occasions when other people are. In that sense, success is a simple equation of identifying the occasions when you need to be at your best, and then preparing sufficiently so that you rise to the occasion.

4. What is the 'but . . .' about you?

Nobody's perfect. Everyone has some qualifier attached to them.

'Joanne is a talented producer, *but* . . . you can't depend on her to make a deadline.'

'Fred is a great negotiator, *but* . . . he always ticks off the customers.'

'Tom is terrific on his own deals, *but* . . . he doesn't help out anyone else.'

What's interesting about this delusion is that even when people recognize this 'but . . .' in themselves, they have an amazing capacity to deny it – or at least not correct it. It's as if they feel they can award themselves a flaw or two because of all their other good points. Worse, they think this is a permanent entitlement. That's softball, not hardball.

I'm impressed by any employee who recognizes a character flaw. But I'm not impressed for very long. If the same employee is owning up to the same flaws a year or two later, that's depressing.

2 Speed, the Defining Factor

IT IS BETTER TO BE A RACEHORSE THAN A PLOUGH-HORSE

I'm always on the lookout for outstanding talent in sports. The criteria vary from sport to sport, but the basics are the same: you want someone who wins more often than he loses, of course. You're also looking for less quantifiable qualities such as competitiveness, mental toughness, intelligence, personality and personability, an appreciation of the long term, even an understanding of how our business operates.

In much the same way, as a manager of a company, I'm also scouting for standout talent in our organization. Over the years, I've developed some criteria to distinguish the racehorses from the plough-horses in our company. Admittedly, the criteria are highly idiosyncratic and are a function of the business we are in, but I doubt if the following attributes will ever work against you.

1. Speed

I think speed is the most obvious indicator that you have a racehorse working for you. When people say someone is 'bright,' they're usually impressed by how fast that person grasps a situation and figures out a way to deal with it. In that sense, intelligence is a function of speed. That's what people mean when they call someone a 'quick study.' It's an intuitive judgment, but you can spot it early on in true racehorses. You see it in the quickness of their wit, their ability to get up in a presentation and surprise everyone by their eloquence, or their ability to articulate a complicated transaction.

Racehorses also tend to be speedy in how they sink their teeth into an assignment. If someone in our company says, 'Gee, we ought to sign Joe

Jones as a client,' the plough-horse will sit around for months wondering how to do it. He'll call friends who can introduce him to Joe Jones. He'll research Joe Jones's background, family, and career. He'll go through the proper channels (whatever they are!). The racehorse will simply get on a plane and approach Joe Jones.

Plough-horses tend to overthink things. Racehorses are sometimes guilty of underthinking. Sometimes they go too fast and overshoot their target. But the superstars at a company are mostly racehorses. They're the people on the go, moving places in a positive direction, stirring things up, making things happen.

2. Knowing the boss

Racehorses tend to have a sixth sense of how to use the boss to their advantage.

In our company, for example, I encourage people to use me to advance their business interests. There are many occasions when my presence at a meeting can elevate the significance of the subject under discussion. (You know the logic: 'if the chairman's here, it must be important.') Sometimes I can actually make a substantive contribution.

Here's the interesting thing. Over the years I've noticed that racehorses are very sensitive to when I should be involved and when I shouldn't. They can smell that in the air. They're not afraid to enter my garden, so to speak, because they're confident they can learn where the paths are and not trample on my flowers.

The plough-horse is afraid of getting near anything I'm involved in. There are people in our company who, if they know I'm quarterbacking a project, will stay as far away from it as possible. I suspect they're afraid that whatever they do, they will expose their performance to my scrutiny. I'll observe how they work, how they deal with people, how they conduct themselves in meetings, how they write agreements – and they're not comfortable with that exposure.

I don't think the plough-horse's paranoia is unique to our company.

Take a copywriter at Microsoft's advertising agency working on the launch of the company's new networking software. Would he relish or resist being in the same room with Microsoft chairman Bill Gates to talk about his creative concepts?

The racehorse would relish it. He would be delighted at the chance to meet Bill Gates, the industry visionary and competitor *par excellence.*

The plough-horse would be scared to death. He would rather have the comfort of dealing with his copy supervisor who in turn would deal with the account manager who in turn would have to deal with Gates. That's the sign of most plough-horses. They prefer to plough around in their own field.

3. Endurance

Another racehorse indicator that I value is endurance, which usually manifests itself in how well people follow up. There are people in our company whom I regard as racehorses simply because of their persistence, their diligence, their ability to outlast the other guy.

4. Chaos in the hierarchy

Because of the speed they work at and the velocity of their ascent through the organization, racehorses can create chaos in your hierarchy.

We once hired a young man in our London office who turned out to be a genuine thoroughbred compared to his plough-horse boss. The disparity in their abilities was obvious to everyone and soon created an awkward situation. The racehorse had a remarkable affinity for closing deals. He had six major projects going on while his boss, whose job ostensibly was to manage the racehorse, had nothing to do.

Ultimately, with the racehorse running around creating more and more work, the boss was reduced to following up on his subordinate's sales. The boss had the senior title and salary, but in fact their status at our company was turned upside down. Of course, making it official by promoting the racehorse above his old boss would have created enormous morale and organizational problems. Instead, we transferred the racehorse to another office, gave him the title he deserved, and let him continue his racehorse ways.

(Warning to managers: you can always tell a racehorse by the respect mixed with envy he or she breeds in his colleagues. Your job is to prevent that envy from turning into jealousy and resentment.)

5. Plough-horse activities

The irony about racehorses versus plough-horses is that a big part of being a racehorse is having the willingness to do what everyone else regards as plough-horse work.

I've said for years that I think it's easier to do a hundred $1000 deals than one $100,000 deal. It might take more time, but plodding along, making the small $1000 deals, and nurturing them into bigger and better deals is sort of a 'racehorsey' thing to do – although many people don't see it that way.

For example, I've always thought that if a salesperson in our company was really smart, he would start at the top of the Empire State Building, which houses dozens of small apparel and sporting goods companies, and work his way down floor by floor with our corporate brochure, cold-calling each company, asking, 'Which of our athletes would you like to work with?' I have to believe that, given our client list, some manufacturer or marketer would say, 'Yes, I'd pay $35,000 for the right to put Derek Jeter's face on t-shirts.'

But nobody does that. It sounds too dull. It's not perceived as 'race-horsey.'

Instead, they spend their time trying to reinvent the wheel, calling on a big-spending car manufacturer or soft-drink company to sell some zillion-dollar sponsorship idea, which may have a 'racehorsey' image but more often than not will blow up in their face.

Aim to be a racehorse and know how to be one.

END YOUR DAY ON TIME

You can tell a lot about an individual's time-management skills by how he or she ends a business day. I've always thought it's ironic that reasonably well-organized people have a solid grip on every minute of their day – they know when they'll arrive at work; what they're discussing at their 10:15 meeting; when, where, and with whom they've having lunch: why they have a 2:45 conference down on their calendar, and what to expect at their 4:30 interview with a client. But unless they have a plane to catch or a dinner engagement that evening, they often have no idea what time they intend to snap their briefcase shut, turn off the computer, and call it a day.

Everything about their workday has a defined beginning, middle, and end – except the time when they intend to stop working. (If you don't believe me, when was the last time you wrote 'Go home!' in your daily diary?)

That goes a long way to explaining why so many people tell me that they're working too many hours and feel that their personal and professional lives are out of balance.

Of course, there's an easy solution to this problem: schedule a reasonable time to stop working each day and stick to it. But that can create more problems than it solves, especially if it forces you to end each day with a lot of crucial items left untackled or unfinished. Eventually, that sort of negligence catches up with you.

A much better solution: schedule a stop-work time, stick to it, *and* make one or two behavioural changes that add efficiency to the rest of your day. Here are a half dozen that anybody could live with:

1. Steal an early hour

If you want to go home at a reasonable hour, come to work earlier. I don't know why more people don't try this. They're missing the huge perk of working before the rest of the world shows up. It's the purest work environment. There are no distractions, no noise, no ringing phones, no colleagues walking through your door with their first cup of coffee wanting to chat about last night's playoff game.

If everybody in your office wanders in around 9 o'clock and you show up at 7:30 a.m., those 90 minutes can be as productive as three or four hours in the middle of the day. With that kind of efficiency payoff, imagine how early you can leave at day's end.

2. Close your door

You're not being hostile or anti-social. You're merely constructing a barrier that makes your colleagues think twice before interrupting you. For many gregarious people, that often makes all the difference between efficiency and chaos.

3. Eliminate unnecessary travel

I know people who claim they don't have time for a ten-minute discussion with a colleague and yet they wouldn't hesitate to jump on a plane for a half-hour meeting with a prospect or customer.

The reality is that there are very few situations that cannot be handled by a phone conversation or delayed until a more convenient travel date.

I'm not minimizing the value of being there in person. I realize that there are still many situations that demand an urgent face-to-face conversation. All I'm suggesting is that you pause before you book that hurried flight and think about all the time you're spending on something that may be just as easily handled from your desk. If that hesitation eliminates only two or three trips a year, you've gained 25 to 30 hours of time for other things.

4. Find a surrogate

One of the biggest reasons people put in long hours is that they don't have a capable replacement, someone to share their work load or pick up the slack when they're busy elsewhere. They think they're indispensable. They have to do everything themselves or it won't get done correctly.

For example, if they're about to go on vacation for two weeks, they feel compelled to work into the night and on weekends to get everything done before their departure. (Has this happened to you?)

To me, that's comically inefficient. No one is so unique or irreplaceable that some of his or her work cannot be done by someone else. The problem for most people is that they are unaware that they need a surrogate or unwilling to make the effort to find one. By surrogate, I'm not talking about an assistant or subordinate to whom you delegate boring or onerous tasks. Rather, I mean finding a peer who can back you up when you're swamped or fill your shoes when you're away (and for whom you can return the favour when the situations are reversed).

This is more advanced than the usual delegating procedure (although delegating, in my mind, is still the greatest time-management tool of all!) It is more like creating an internal partnership where your partner gives you the gift of time.

5. Appreciate that you are always getting better at what you're already good at

People waste a lot of time each day because they don't appreciate that, as their business skills and acumen evolve, they get better at what they do – and can do it in less time than they used to.

I can get through to busy people more quickly, conduct meetings in half the time I required in my relative youth, dictate more letters in a morning, and handle more phone calls per day. Given all the high-tech communication tools at my disposal now, I can even close deals more quickly. All this increased efficiency is a function of greater experience.

What's strange, however, is the number of people who don't appreciate or take advantage of the fact that age and experience have made them better. They still take the same time to do something today as they did five or ten years ago.

If you're good at something and do it long enough, you get better at it – and you should do it in less time. This applies to every time-consuming event, whether it's a meeting or a negotiation or dictating a letter. If you're still allotting the same time for these activities that you did a few years ago, you're cheating yourself – and it will catch up with you at the end of the day.

6. Work when you are at work

I know an editor/writer at a monthly magazine in New York whose sole responsibility is to edit a section of the magazine and write a thousand-word column each month. Yet whenever I call him at home on a weekend, he's holed up in his office working on the column. This has been going on for years. I asked him if he enjoyed giving up his weekends to write the column.

'No, I hate it,' he said.

'So why don't write it during the week?' I asked.

'Because I'm too busy having meetings, going out to lunch, talking on the phone, and pushing paper to get any work done,' he said.

I suspect that's true for a lot of people in office jobs. Going to work offers so many distractions, they don't have time to actually work when they are allegedly working.

7. Don't invest your time on puny payoffs

Have you ever been in a meeting presenting an idea that you think has great potential for the company? And then the boss makes you conduct a reality check? The boss wants to know how much time you'll be working on the project, how many different people you'll have to persuade to sign off on the concept, and most important, what the financial reward might be in two or three years. As you answer the questions, it slowly dawns on you that your brilliant idea is very labour intensive and once all the costs are factored in the payoff is puny.

That's what bosses are supposed to do. They exist, in part, to make employees appreciate that every investment of time, energy, and resources in business is a risk–reward decision – and that there ought to be a considerable reward if you risk a lot of your time on an idea.

It's no different with personal time management. The most efficient people – i.e., the ones who leave work when they want to – are the ones who don't accept every idea or account or client that crosses their path. They're selective. They can say no to an 'opportunity' where the risk–reward ratio is out of balance. It's not that they're afraid of hard work. Rather, they appreciate that hard work with no chance of a commensurate financial payoff is wasted work.

Being able to assess and reject dead-end opportunities may be the greatest business discipline you can master. It's certainly the best way to end your day on time.

PICK UP THE PACE WITH THE LITTLE TASKS

We agree that we live in an accelerated age. Conditions change at an alarming pace that none of us has ever seen before. So it should be easy to accept that all of us need to do some everyday tasks more speedily. After all, if the world around us is speeding up, we need a speedier response simply to keep up. Here are 12 small but eminently achievable goals that can bring anyone up to speed.

1. Shorten your response time

I'm amazed by how much lag time people give themselves between a request and their response. In an accelerated world, there's no allowance for delay, for extra time to let the request sink in or to get your other priorities out of the way. The only correct response is the immediate one. This isn't because the world is clocking your response time. It's is precisely because things change so quickly. If you're slow, your response may be moot by the time you get around to it. In which case, you'll not only appear unresponsive but you may have also rendered yourself moot too.

2. Return all telephone calls within 24 hours

In any business, but especially a personal services business, this is a noble goal – not so much because if demonstrates your efficiency to the rest of the world but rather because it sends the message to the people who call you that they are important to you, that you care. The unexpected benefit of speeding up your returned calls, of course, is that they make you more efficient in other areas – because you don't have all those message slips hanging over your head.

3. Shorten your phone calls

This is the corollary to returning calls more quickly. If you can limit each telephone conversation to, say, five minutes or less, you'll not only have more time for more calls but you'll find it has an accelerating effect on everything else you do, including the people who work with you. They'll step up their pace to match yours.

There are some executives who take pride in the fact that they answer their own phones and they're always accessible. That's laudable – within reason. But if you accept every phone interruption during your day you must also accept that your schedule will always be at the mercy of every one who has your number.

Long ago, even before I really controlled my schedule, I made up my mind that I would rather make than take calls. True, I would drop everything if Palmer, Player, or Nicklaus called; that was, after all, my job. But I also figured out that there was a specific time of day when I could reach each of them at home. So I started calling them before they called me. I have to believe that helped me establish a daily schedule that otherwise could have easily gone out of control.

4. Learn to say no (and enjoy it)

Some people are constitutionally incapable of saying no when colleagues ask for help. They're so agreeable, so eager to please. This isn't all bad, of course. Every organization wants people willing to pitch in.

But at some point, being agreeable becomes counterproductive. In my experience, people who can't say no are often the least organized people in a company. They don't know their limits. It's as if someone put a sign on their back saying, 'Go ahead. Interrupt my day.' It's not surprising that their colleagues oblige by piling on the work. Who would you turn to? Someone who always says yes, or someone who might say no?

5. Apologize quickly

People take too long to apologize when they're wrong. For starters, they don't believe they were wrong. Then as it dawns on them that they are to blame for hurting someone, they are slow to make amends. They procrastinate (because apologizing is awkward for many people). They wait for the 'appropriate' moment (because they want it to be as painless for them as possible). During all this time, of course, someone's feelings remain hurt. That's rarely a productive period for all involved. The longer you delay, the greater the resentment that builds up.

So, if you're wrong, admit it. If you hurt someone, apologize. The faster you do it, the faster everyone can move on.

6. Speed up lunch

I appreciate the value of a calm, languorous, luxurious three-hour meal as much as anyone. But it's obvious nowadays that a lot of business people simply don't enjoy eating lunch. They like the social and business implications of lunch, the warm environment of a nice restaurant, the friendliness of sitting down with people, and the chance to move a relationship or transaction forward. It's the food that annoys them. They order a large salad or, in an effort to accommodate hungrier companions, two appetizers. They always pass on dessert. My solution: speed lunch up. Why waste two hours on the experience when 70 or 80 minutes will do? No one will resent you for it.

7. Conduct faster meetings

Meetings are no different than any other time-intensive activity. If you can speed up your telephone conversations and lunches, you can do the same with your meetings. Again, no one will resent you for it.

8. Commit quickly

There is a difference between making a decision to do something and actually committing to getting it done. I see this all the time. People meet to decide on a course of action. A decision is made and then three or four weeks can go by before anyone actually executes the decision. I'm not sure why this happens so often. It's the same delay mechanism as the one between a request and the response. If you want to impress your bosses, act quickly on their decisions. I doubt if they'll be expecting such a speedy commitment to executing their plans.

9. Say 'Thank You' as soon as possible

It's a simple equation: the impact of a 'thank you' note is in inverse proportion to how long you delay sending it. The longer you delay, the less power it has. At some point, when a lot of time has gone by, you may be better off simply not sending it. So don't delay. Do it as soon as you can.

10. Accept that 90 per cent will usually suffice

When people take two days to finish an assignment they expected to finish in one, it's often because they spent the extra day trying to make it 'perfect.' They want to hand in something 100 per cent acceptable when actually 90 per cent will do.

A music *aficionado* once showed me his $100,000 stereo system. It sounded great but I wondered if he needed to spend all that money. Could he tell the difference from a carefully selected system that cost much less?

'Everybody asks that,' he said. 'A $10,000 system would sound about 90 percent as good and very few people could tell the difference. Striving for perfection drives up the cost. Each percentage point improvement costs about $10,000.'

Likewise in business, striving for perfection on the job can cost you hours if not days of time. I decided a long time ago that I would rather get 100 letters out that were 90 per cent my best than 90 letters that were

100 per cent. I'd rather appear responsive to 100 people than let 10 items fall through the cracks. Massaging a memo until it gleamed like a jewel just wasn't worth the time.

11. Write shorter memos and e-mails

Shorter memos and e-mails are a win-win for everyone. They take less time to write and even less time to read.

DON'T BET AGAINST YOURSELF

I'm always amused when I hear people talking like bookmakers in a meeting. You know the drill. The boss goes around the room asking people to lay odds on whether a deadline will be made, or all the interested parties will show up at the negotiating table, or a project will come in under budget. It doesn't really matter what's at stake. Everyone is invited to venture an opinion. Someone is 2 to 1 for, another is 5 to 1 against, and so on around the room.

It's amusing because, aside from being a slightly colourful way of measuring the relative optimism and pessimism in the room, it's a meaningless exercise – especially if no one in the room is accountable for their picks.

However, the language of risk versus reward can be useful when you are organizing your business day. I can't think of a better way to establish priorities than to assign odds on whether a task will pay off or waste your time. At the risk of making your daily schedule sound like a Las Vegas betting shop, here are three criteria that can give your handicapping a firm basis in reality.

1. What can you contribute?

Setting odds is all about how accountable you are for the success or failure of a project.

The more accountability that rests on you, the better your odds. It means you have control. You're not at the mercy of other people's schedules, prejudices, or ineptitude. If you're reasonably confident about your ability to get things done, your odds of success in any task should be directly proportional to how much you contribute to that task.

When I'm setting up my business day, I always start off with items where I'm contributing as close to 100 per cent as possible to the task's completion: reading and answering correspondence, dictation, reviewing and fine-tuning the rest of my schedule. I wake up very early. Very few people are up at that hour. So I can't rely on the contribution of others. The odds are close to even that I'll get these simple tasks done in the time allotted. If I don't, I have no one to blame but myself.

2. Who controls whom?

I save the rest of my day for tasks where I need other people's contributions. But even then, I'm figuring out the odds of success based on how much or how little control I have over the situation.

Because I run my own company, if I want to meet with a dozen employees, the odds tend to be in my favour that all 12 will show up when I want them to.

On the other hand, if I want a dozen people from outside the company – over whom I have no control – to show up for a meeting, the odds are almost overwhelmingly against me. It's tough enough to get two or three people to agree on time, date, and place for a meeting these days. With 12 people involved, you're almost defeated before you start. And keep in mind, this is just a simple meeting. I'm not asking people to write a cheque. I just want them to show up.

Yet I never cease to be amazed at how much time and energy other people devote to schemes far more complicated and futile than a meeting of 12 strangers. If they objectively gauged the complexity of the task before them and how little control they exercised, they would know success was a million-to-one shot and move on to something else. But passion or short-sightedness or naivety blinds them.

I recall one of our executives concocting a music project that, if it got off the ground, would have required cooperation and financing from television channels, music executives, and concert presenters on four continents. If the young man had two years to pursue only this fantasy, he might have pulled it off. But this project was off to the side of his everyday responsibilities. Whenever we talked, he would always inject an update on how he had met with so-and-so who had introduced him to someone else and he was getting closer to a major commitment.

We're an entrepreneurial company. We don't like to throw cold water on people's ideas. Yet I eventually had to kill the project. I pointed out that making it happen would require a chain of cooperation so beyond his control that he was not only wasting his time but endangering his credibility with me. Until I laid it out for him, he had no idea that he was betting on such a long shot. In truth, he had never even considered the odds.

3. Are you a risk junkie?

Every company wants and needs people to take risks. There's no fun, no magic, and ultimately no glory if you only bet on sure things. Nor can you devote all your time to million-to-one bets. At the end of the day, you'll have nothing to show for it.

What most people need in their schedule is balance. A mix of sure things, short odds, and the occasional flyer.

For the most part, I maintain a crowded and meticulously timed schedule that's calibrated in minutes, not hours. But on any given day, I always schedule one or two long-shot events. It could be a meeting with a friend who may be passing through. It could be a phone call with a client whose whereabouts are unknown. It could be going to a tennis match if our client makes the quarterfinals.

If the long shot comes through, I'm happy. It's as if I've won a big bet. If it doesn't, I'm not terribly disappointed – because I knew the odds were against me. I still have other things to do.

The key is to avoid becoming a risk junkie. If you schedule too many long shots in your day, the odds that you'll achieve even half your tasks are not in your favour. At the end of the day, what do you have to show for it? A host of cancellations and few results.

This isn't a problem for people who understand the risk-reward ratio underlying everything in their day.

PUT PARKINSON'S LAW INTO REVERSE

We all know the wisdom of Parkinson's Law. If you give a subordinate a week to hand in an assignment, he or she will usually take all of that week to finish the job. If you gave the subordinate two weeks to finish the job, he or she would take two weeks (even though the job itself is no more complicated or labour-intensive). It's a seemingly immutable law of the workplace: work expands to fill the time allotted to it.

But I've always wondered if the opposite is true. Does work also *contract* to fill a shrinking amount of time allotted to it?

On the most rudimentary level, I'm sure it's true. Let's say you're packing for a week-long business trip overseas. If the trip has been planned well in advance, you'd probably set aside several hours the night before to pack your bags. You'd take your time, making sure your shoes and suits and shirts matched. You'd double-check everything. You might even lay out what you were planning to wear on the plane. It would be a leisurely exercise – no rush, no panic, nothing overlooked – because you have given yourself the gift of time.

Now, let's shrink the time you have to pack your bags for the same trip. Let's say your boss has just rushed into your office and told you to jump on a plane overseas for a week of business meetings. You only have an hour to get home and pack your bags before you have to hurry out to the airport. If you're like most people, you'll find a way to pack your bags in 20 or 30 minutes (and anything you've forgotten, you'll pick up when you get there). But you'll make your flight and you will look presentable. That's Parkinson's Law in reverse. You've compressed the work to fit the time allotted.

The last two minutes of a close football game is a perfect example of how time can be compressed.

A skilled quarterback marching his team up the field for a score can make those final 120 seconds seem like an eternity for the opposing side. The quarterback does this by eliminating any activity that fails to conserve time. No more huddles to call the next play (which eat up precious seconds). No more running the ball up the middle (which keeps the clock running). Instead, the quarterback passes the ball, usually to receivers near the sidelines. An incomplete pass stops the clock. A completion advances the ball and gives the receiver a chance to run out of bounds (which also stops the clock). If the receiver can't get out of bounds, the quarterback uses one of his allotted time outs (which he has saved precisely for this situation).

In football you see this sort of intense time management only in the waning seconds of each half. If football teams controlled the clock this carefully from start to finish, a 60–minute game would probably take six hours to complete. The players would be exhausted. The fans would be comatose.

It's different in business. The net effect of such intense clock management at work isn't exhausting or boring. On the contrary, it energizes you and gives you an irresistible momentum throughout the day. That's why people say if you want to get something done, give it to a busy person. He or she will make time to make it happen.

What's interesting, though, is why more of us don't do the same thing in our own workday. It's only normal to want more time rather than less when you have a job to do. But it's also obvious that, given Parkinson's Law, we are hardly doing ourselves a favour by taking that extra time. It slows us down. It tricks us into accomplishing a task in three weeks that we might be able to do in one or two.

My point is, all of us could benefit from a little more challenge in how we organize ourselves and what we have to accomplish. Try this experiment:

the next time your boss or most important customer tells you, 'I need this in ten days,' tell him or her, 'I'll have it on your desk in five.' You'll not only surprise your boss or customer, you might even surprise yourself.

Parkinson's Law tells you what happens when you have the gift of extra time. Parkinson's in reverse gives you a greater gift – the gift of speed.

NEVER WRESTLE WITH A PIG

We all know the big secrets of time management:

- Be punctual.
- Plan ahead.
- Write everything down.
- Do what you planned when you planned to do it for no longer than you planned.
- Maintain a list of things to do.
- Don't be upset if your to-do list spills over into the next day. (If you accomplish everything on your list, you're not doing enough.)

But there are variations on these major themes that, when played well, can help you squeeze even more time out of an already busy day. Here are nine I've always taken to heart.

1. Always carry a pen

You can't write everything down if you don't have something to write with.

2. Note when people call you

Some years ago, a friend of mine New York joked about how never got to see his favourite show, 'Cheers,' because his widowed mother in Los Angeles habitually called him at 9 p.m. on Thursday nights when the show aired.

'Doesn't she know there's a better time to call, that she's irritating you?' I asked.

'She knows exactly what she's doing,' he said. 'That's why she calls. She knows I'll be home in front of the TV.'

Smart woman. She knew her son and exploited his schedule.

You can do the same in business if you pay attention to when your regular contacts call you. People follow patterns. Some people make their phone calls in the morning. Others prefer the end of the day. If you make a point of recognizing these patterns, you'll always know the best time to reach people.

This isn't a life-changing secret. But when you consider how much time people waste playing phone tag, trying to connect, and talking to voice mail these days, a little due diligence about people's phone habits can shave minutes off every day. And those minutes add up.

3. Don't double-check what doesn't need double-checking

If you write a sales proposal, you should take the time to proofread it (proofread it twice if it makes you feel better). If you write a report, you should take the time to make sure the figures add up (and check them again if you want). These are two activities that demand double-checking.

On the other hand, if you ask an assistant to do something – mail out a package, set up a lunch date, or return a call – you shouldn't have to be constantly double-checking to make sure that it was done. If you do, get a new assistant.

4. Be an extra day ahead of the curve

Don't plan for Thursday on Wednesday. Do it on Tuesday. That 24–hour head start will give you a slight edge on the rest of the world.

5. Tackle your tasks in order of descending importance

Start your day with the most important items on your agenda. It not only means you execute them when you are most alert, but it spares you from having to worry about them the rest of the day. That worrying, whether you realize it or not, slows you down. Just think about the last time you found yourself daydreaming at your desk or in a meeting, worrying about what you really had to do rather than what you were actually doing at that moment.

For reasons that escape me, a lot of people reverse this rule. They put off the big items on their agenda until the last possible moment. When you consider that all of us in the course of a business day accumulate more things to do, I wonder how these people ever get around to finishing the important tasks.

6. Never pick up someone else's ringing phone (unless you're prepared to pick up someone else's headache)

I realize this flouts the notion of teamwork and cooperation in the work-place. Frankly, if a phone is ringing on someone else's desk. I hope our people have the good sense to pick it up. I know I would automatically without thinking.

But that's the larger point. When you pick up that phone, you should at least be thinking. – about what it costs you in terms of time and about how far you're prepared to go to help the other person on the line. If that sort of thinking makes you cautious, makes you hesitate a little before you pick up the phone, then it's good. If it teaches you to take a message rather than try to solve the caller's problem all by yourself, then it's saving you and everyone else a lot of time.

7. When the day is done, make one more call

I don't know who first said this at our company, but it's a trend I endorse.

When you're through for the day, snapping your briefcase shut, turning off your computer, and putting on your coat, always place one more phone call. It could be a friend you haven't talked to in weeks, or a lead you've been meaning to pursue, or a name suggested by a colleague. It doesn't really matter. Just make the call. It only takes a few minutes, but I guarantee you'll learn something you never knew in every second or third call. That's the nature of business. You learn by talking to people. But first, you have to make that extra call.

8. Never wrestle with a pig. You get dirty and only the pig enjoys it

In other words, don't waste time arguing with people who love to argue for the sake of argument.

I wonder how many man-hours are lost in every organization because people get innocently lured into discussions with colleagues who love to debate the undebatable and argue the inarguable. We all know such people exist. They're adversarial, confrontational, and incredibly talkative. They have an insatiable desire to be 'right' all the time and are incapable of admitting that they are wrong.

You can't win a 'wrestling match' with these people. You can only lose time. My advice: avoid them like a plague.

9. Bad habits drive out good habits

This is a variation on Gresham's Law ('Bad money drives out good money.') I saved it for last to make the point that time management is a skill. You don't need any natural talent to be well organized. Anyone can learn it by acquiring good habits and shedding bad habits. But it's a skill that requires constant practice and you have to practise perfectly.

You can't be punctual some of the time. You have to be punctual all the time. It's a habit (and a good one). If you break the habit with occasional tardiness, it won't be long before tardiness becomes habitual.

Likewise, you can't organize your life by carefully planning some days and winging it on others. You have to work hard planning every day. The good news is that the hard work pays off. After a while, being organized becomes habitual.

3 Fallacies of the Workplace

PEOPLE WHO SAY THEY CAN KEEP A SECRET USUALLY CAN'T (OR THE TEN MOST TOXIC LIES IN BUSINESS)

A colleague showed me a recent survey in which 93 per cent of the 40,000 Americans polled admitted to lying regularly and habitually in the workplace. I think my colleague meant to shock me by all the rampant deception going on at work. But I was more intrigued by the 7 per cent who claim they don't fib. How, I wondered, do these people get through a typical day? How do they maintain any friendships if they always speak what's on their mind?

The fact is, the workplace is a far healthier environment because of all the little lies that we allow to float harmlessly among us. I'm especially in favour of the white lies that spare other people's feelings, the ones where you don't say what you really think of their unfortunate haircut or their ridiculous new glasses or their poorly researched report. Why start a fight or bruise an ego when a few words of mild approval are all that are called for?

However, there is a wholly different sector of lies that are far less benign. These are the cliches and verbal mantras that many people employ to mask their failings at work. These catchphrases are hard to argue with, but you should be alert when you hear them because they often come out of the mouths of people who mean exactly the opposite of what they are saying. Here are ten of the most common and therefore most dangerous lies in business:

1. 'I can keep a secret'

People who can keep a confidence don't brag about it – because the alternative, namely betraying a confidence, is not an issue with them. People who tell you they can keep a secret invariably don't.

This is similar to people who say. 'I always meet my deadlines.' or 'I always deliver on time.' Punctuality isn't an issue with people who are always on time.

2. 'This was a rational decision'

People say this in order to take the personal sting out of a decision that will adversely affect you, as if a rational decision deserves a rational response from you. Don't be fooled. There are no perfectly rational decisions. Every decision, even the ones based on hard numbers, is a series of either/or choices that are founded as much on intuition or personal inclination as anything else. In other words, 'This was a rational decision' really means 'I wanted to do this.'

3. 'I want totally honest feedback'

When bosses say, 'I want to know what you really think,' they probably mean it. It's the moment after you tell them what you really think that the statement becomes a lie – because they don't react to your blunt opinion in a welcoming manner. Whether they resent it or they're hurt by it or they don't believe it, very few of them are grateful to you for saying it. Consciously or not, they will usually punish you for it.

There are plenty of occasions to tell the boss the unvarnished truth. When the boss asks for it is not one of them.

4. 'The cheque is in the mail'

This is the granddaddy of business lies, so egregious and trite that people laugh about it as they are saying it. Of course, the accompanying laugh track doesn't make this lie more palatable. When you hear this, the truth is plain and simple: you have a collection problem.

5. 'You're the only one we're talking to'

This is the lie about exclusivity. When people tell me I'm the only they're talking to about a project, they're probably telling the truth. What's missing from this sentence, however, is the phrase, '. . . but if things don't go our way we won't hesitate to talk to other people too.'

There's nothing wrong with this. We're all adults in business. In any transaction, I realize that I don't have the field all to myself. I just wish more people would state their real intentions.

6. 'It's business. It's not personal'

The truth is, everything is personal. All things being equal in business, people won't shaft you if they personally like you. In fact, they'll go out of their way to help a friend even when all things are less than equal. Likewise, they won't hesitate to decide against you if there is no personal connection.

This phrase is not a lie so much as a contradiction. If it's business, it only means that there was nothing significantly personal between you.

7. 'The customer comes first'

Quite often, this is true. But in even the noblest of service businesses, people shade the truth. They're selective. They treat customers differently, depending on what they think they can get away with. Big customers get taken care of because doing so clearly benefits the business. Little customers get ignored if people perceive there is little risk to their business in doing so.

8. 'I'll call you right back'

This is more a verbal tic than a lie. People say it to end a phone conversation or because they have to take another call. Unless it serves their interest to call back immediately, people rarely deliver on this promise. If you're one of those people who are still waiting for the return call, you shouldn't.

9. 'We judge people on their performance'

If this were true, the workplace would be a perfect meritocracy. The truth is more like, 'We judge your performance based on how much we like you.' People don't get fired for not doing their jobs well. They get canned because someone in authority doesn't like them. It's that simple.

10. 'The boss is clueless'

This is more a myth than a lie. It's uttered by every subordinate who thinks he or she is smarter than their boss. It's also a convenient excuse when an unpopular decision needs explaining. Don't believe it. There are usually sounder reasons for an unpopular decision than the boss's purported ignorance.

TWO FRUIT BASKETS AREN'T ALWAYS BETTER THAN ONE

It's an unquestioned tenet of our mammoth service economy that mistakes will be made. Quite often, no one's to blame. Mistakes simply happen, and sometimes they multiply. Bad weather in Cincinnati delayed the technician's flight to Dallas so he missed his connection to Phoenix and arrived a day late at your Phoenix facility to fix the machine you needed to ship the delivery to Seattle on time. As a result, you missed your delivery date – all because of a little storm in Ohio.

Mistakes such as this, compounding like falling dominoes, are so common and inevitable that any smart service organization has developed a corollary tenet to deal with it. If mistakes will happen then mistakes are also an opportunity – to show the customer or client how earnestly and efficiently you can correct the error.

Every company that deals with the public knows this.

The shirt we mailed you is not the size you ordered? Don't worry. We'll send the correct size by overnight delivery.

Your flight was seven hours late, which ate up a whole day of your vacation? We sincerely apologize. Can we make it up to you with a free upgrade for you and your family on the return flight?

This is one of the hallmarks of superb customer service. How you correct your mistakes and handle the customers' complaints (valid or not) makes as vivid an impression as the mistake itself or the reason for the complaint.

It's easy to forget, but there was a time as recently as fifteen years ago when most enterprises didn't behave this way. If the car you bought was a lemon, that was your problem. If the toaster you bought stopped working the day after the 60–day warranty expired, you had to jump through hoops simply to find the right person to complain to. But the quality movement, especially in customer service, has changed all that. We have always expected mistakes to happen (that has never changed). But now we expect a courteous correction.

In fact, this dynamic is so ingrained that many of us will excuse the most deplorable errors if the guilty party expresses contrition or makes an attempt to assuage us.

A friend of mine was dining at a trendy New York bistro a few years ago with two clients. He ordered a tomato juice, drank it, only to find a cigarette butt at the bottom of the glass. He summoned the maître d' who whisked the offending glass away and offered my friend another tomato juice. My friend's dinner companions were appalled and were a little befuddled that he was not outraged at this revolting service.

The outrage didn't set in until meal's end, when the maître d', with only the slightest acknowledgement of the gross error, presented the full bill, minus the charge for the tomato juice. Ordinarily, this is the sort of situation that a quality service establishment would handle by tearing up the bill (the money involved was negligible – less than $25 per person) or lavishing the diners with effusive apologies, extra-attentive service, and complimentary drinks. But not here. The restaurant behaved as if nothing unusual had happened. Perhaps they would have acted differently if my friend had been a regular or a celebrity, or if he had created an embarrassing scene. Instead, he questioned the bill, which the maître d', defended, paid the bill, and vowed never to return.

I mention this fairly uneventful scene because it highlights an interesting facet of our attitudes to service providers in a service economy. My friend wasn't outraged by the cigarette butt in his glass – although many people would have been. That's because we accept mistakes. Rather, he was outraged by the restaurant's seeming refusal to deal with the mistake. That's because we have come to expect the apology, the make-good gesture, the gratis this or that.

Sadly, I think this attitude has made us much too tolerant of mistakes in the marketplace.

I know this because of a basket of fruit. As a Christmas gift, a friend had signed me up to receive a monthly basket of fruit. Unfortunately, this elaborate Fruit of the Month gift was sent to my New York office – which I visit only 45 days a year. This means I rarely even see the basket let alone sample its contents. My assistant called up the fruit company to change the address to my home in Florida where I could actually enjoy my friend's thoughtful gift.

A simple error, a simple solution, I thought. Not really. Even though my assistant called every month to get the address changed, each month another basket arrived in my New York office. It seems the fruit company's system couldn't handle a change of address very well. It was easier to send out a replacement basket to my Florida home. Thus, every month for the past year, I've received two baskets – one in New York, one in Florida. Whenever we called to alert the company to this waste, they couldn't understand why we were calling. They thought I'd appreciate the two-for-the-price-of-one gesture. Actually, I was appalled by it. For one thing, it meant a phone call each month to remind them that they hadn't really fixed the problem. After each call, they would say the same thing, 'We'll send a fresh basket to Florida.' It wasn't automatic. We had to call each month. They had turned a simple gift into a nuisance.

But what really galls me is the skewed sense of customer service at this company. Oh yes, they're superb at handling the acute symptoms of customer dissatisfaction. Every time we call, they respond.

But I worry about the more chronic problem: instead of throwing a second case of fruit at me each month, why don't they simply change the shipping address? That would eliminate the source of our complaint altogether. Wouldn't erasing the mistake be more impressive than their speedy handling of the complaint? A company that ships two cases for every one ordered is not a company built to last. Eventually, its reliance on fixing mistakes rather than reducing their number will drive it out of business.

YOU DON'T NEED TEN GOOD REASONS TO MAKE A DECISION

In truth, you only need two or three good reasons to tip a decision one way or the other. But they had better be your strongest, most compelling factors, not your weakest.

A friend and I were marvelling at how decisive another CEO has been in recent years. He has the ability to make seemingly snap decisions that could make or break his firm. He doesn't delay, falling back on the customary executive privilege of forming a task force to study the situation and make a recommendation a few weeks later. Instead, he canvasses his aides, lists the pros and cons, and decides on the spot. That speedy decision-making has given his firm a huge head start on his less decisive rivals.

My friend wondered where he acquired the conviction or courage to act this way.

'It's simple,' I said. 'He doesn't dwell on all the arguments for a particular move. He focuses on the arguments that matter. If he has ten reasons why he should or should not pursue a course of action, he accords considerably more weight to the two most compelling arguments than he does the rest. If arguments one and two are against the move, that's the way he leans, regardless of whether reasons three to ten are in favour of it. In his mind, the first two reasons cancel out everything else. That mindset frees him to be decisive. If he always gave equal consideration to all the pros and cons, he would be paralysed. He'd be spending all his time comparing arguments rather than making decisions.'

As I thought about this discussion later on, I realized this man's philosophy represents the secret to being an effective, decisive leader. The people who emerge from the pack to become leaders in an organization are the ones who can focus on the arguments that matter and use them to back their decisions. Their decisions are not only better (because they key in on the strong reasons) but they are quicker (because they don't waste days or weeks considering the weak ones). Over time, as they prove themselves right more often than they are wrong, their decisions begin to carry a weight and conviction that distinguishes them from everyone else. That's how leaders emerge.

Once you recognize this aspect of decision-making, you begin to see how it colours every move in life.

Consider, for example, a major decision that is common to many married couples. You and your spouse have just bought a home. The kitchen that comes with the house is a tired relic of the 1960s. The appliances are old. The cabinets and countertops are a hideous pink. The space is too small and the layout is less than perfect. You'd like to renovate and expand the kitchen, but you're not sure if it's worth the cost. Do you renovate or do you learn to live with it?

If you're like me, you would jot down the pros and cons in descending order, perhaps like this:

1. You need a new kitchen.
2. You can afford it (up to a point).
3. It will make your life more pleasant.
4. It's a good investment; it will increase the house's value and you'll get your money back when you sell.
5. The two of you can't agree on the new style.
6. You're afraid the contractor will rip you off.
7. You're not looking forward to the mess and inconvenience during the renovation.
8. You can't afford the top of the line yet.
9. You may not stay in the house long enough to fully enjoy your kitchen.
10. You could use the money for other things.

Obviously, I've stacked the deck in favour of the renovation. But it's not as if I've strayed too far from reality. When couples consider a kitchen renovation, these are the usual arguments.

To people who are comfortable making decisions, this kitchen renovation is not a problem. But to a lot of congenitally indecisive people this list is not stacked in favour of a renovation. The fact that they need a new kitchen and can afford it does not outweigh factors such as their inability to agree on a style or the possibility that they may someday move to another house. Instead, they go up and down the list, giving equal weight to each of these arguments. They don't distinguish between the weak arguments and the strong.

Among some couples, this sort of back and forth continues for so long, they never decide on anything. They're always considering a new kitchen, but they never actually build one.

It's not hard to extend this homeowner's example into the workplace and learn a little about your decision-making style.

Think about the most recent big decision you had to make. It could have been on the job – for example, giving the green light to invest in a new project. Or it could have been a personal decision – like accepting or rejecting a transfer to a new city.

How did you handle that decision? Did you construct a list of the pros and cons? Did you weigh the pros and cons from strongest to weakest? Did you accord more significance to the strong arguments? Or did your focus keep shifting back to the weak arguments? Did you take a long time to decide? Were you comfortable with your decision? Or did you second-guess yourself afterwards? Most important, did you actually decide one way or the other? Or did you let the matter sit until outside circumstances or other people forced the decision?

If you're not happy with your answers to these questions, it's probably because you're considering too many reasons to decide one way or the other. Remember, you don't need ten good reasons to make a decision. The first two will usually do.

HOW TO RECOVER FROM A BAD DECISION

If the preceding rule is true – that you don't need ten good reasons to make a decision – then the corollary is also true. You don't need a lot of reasons to undo a bad decision. One will do. I noticed this in a meeting with executives from Victoria's Secret, an ultra-successful apparel company that featured two of our top modelling clients, Tyra Banks and Heidi Klum, in their ads and catalogues. As part of the launch of a new line, the company decided that a photo exhibit featuring the works of the young photographers who had shot their recent ad campaigns would be a terrific event at which to feature the models and the clothing. The photos would be sold as they would be in any gallery. The money raised would go to charity. The crowd invited to the exhibit opening night would generate tremendous publicity. And the event could then travel to several cities, repeating the publicity blitz and raising even more money for charity.

It sounded like a good idea on paper – until everyone started getting into the details. Galleries had to be contacted to see if there was room for the exhibit in their schedule. The galleries had to be sufficiently large to handle a big crowd. Then the photographers had to agree to the concept. There was the not-inconsiderable cost of printing and framing these large handsome photos in sufficient numbers so people would buy them. There was the ticklish matter of designating a charity that was agreeable to everyone involved. The list of details, particularly to a group of novices in the photo exhibition game, was endless.

A meeting was called to review the progress on the project. After twenty minutes of reviewing various options, Ed Rezak. the company's head of sales and marketing and the same fellow who had decided that the project was important, looked around the room and asked, 'Does anyone remember why we were so gung-ho to do this?'

The room was silent. No one had an answer.

'Well, I don't remember either,' he continued. 'And I think it was my idea. So why don't we shelve the idea. It seems like a lot of work and I can't see what we would get out of it. We could spend the money and the man-hours elsewhere and probably sell more clothes.'

And with that simple excuse, to the great relief of all present, the decision to put on a photo exhibit was undone.

I suspect a lot of corporate miscues and folly would be avoided if more people had the courage to question in midstream the sanity of continuing to pursue a patently bad decision to its logical conclusion. But there are a lot of forces in the workplace that make it hard to appreciate that a decision was patently bad to begin with or has turned bad in the course of executing it.

The biggest hurdle is the false assumption that you need a lot of good reasons to kill a bad decision. I'm not sure why people believe this. Perhaps its because a lot of thinking went into making the decision – and they feel they need an equivalent amount of thinking to undo it. Not true. There's no law that says you need to counter every argument for a decision with an equally persuasive argument against it. A skilled defence attorney knows that he doesn't need to counter each and every argument that the prosecution make. All it takes sometimes is one dramatic piece of evidence to cast the prosecution's entire case in doubt.

It's no different in business situations that demand your 'verdict.' You don't need ten reasons to change your mind. You just need one. Some moves to get to that point:

1. Step back from the situation

Circumstances change in the life cycle of any decision, and as a result they alter the urgency of that decision. With the landscape of any business situation shifting more rapidly today than it has at any other point in history, it only stands to reason that every two weeks or so, you should step back from a project and ask yourself, 'Is the reason we said yes to this project as valid today as it was when we started?'

I try to prod our executives into this thought process as often as possible. For example, one of our executives was agonizing not long ago about whether to fire one of his employees (which is the equivalent of undoing a hiring decision). His ability to think clearly was fogged up by his personal fondness for the employee. I'm sure there was also the reluctance to admit that hiring him had been a bad decision. No one likes to admit they made a mistake. So I tried to make it easier for the executive to pull the trigger. I asked him, 'Given what you know now about this fellow, would you hire him today?'

That simple question framed the situation in a context he could understand. If he wouldn't hire him, he should fire him. It gave him the one good reason he needed to undo a bad decision.

2. Is there more than one obstacle?

Tough decisions rarely create a smooth path for you. There are always one or two obstacles strewn along the way for you to overcome. But if the obstacles reach three or more, that ought to make you pause and review the decision. I'm not saying you should abandon a course of action simply because the obstacles begin to mount up. But you should take a time out to reconsider the decision. The obstacles could be the one good reason you need to avoid a quagmire.

3. Who started all this?

I've seen a lot of projects get bogged down in problems, and then when people look for a scapegoat, it turns out the executive who got the ball rolling is no longer around. He or she has left the scene of the crime to move on to more promising projects. If the individual responsible for the decision is no longer involved, that should be a red flag. It doesn't mean you automatically undo the decision. On the other hand, it could be all the reason you need to do so.

4. How much time has gone by?

There's no better indicator of the health of a project than steady activity. But if weeks or months go by and nothing positive has happened to keep the decision moving forward, then people begin to question the wisdom of the decision itself.

We see this on occasion in our literary business when authors fall behind schedule in delivering their manuscripts. Publishers rarely leap on this lateness as a contractual breach that entitles them to cancel the book. After all, they are in the business of publishing books, not cancelling them, and they understand all too well that writers miss deadlines. But a publisher's enthusiasm for a book can die if a writer lets too much time go by in finishing the book. At some point, the publisher will seize on this lateness as the one good reason he or she needs to undo the decision to publish.

If activity is a sign of a sound decision, then inactivity is the clearest signal that a decision is in trouble.

THE GOAL IS MORE WORK, NOT LESS

I get confused when I hear people complain about how much work they have on their plate.

The complaints confuse me because I can't see how otherwise intelligent people overlook one of the most obvious paradoxes in the workplace. When it comes to duties of the job, the goal is more work, not less. The most successful people in business, from assistant to CEO, never have a perfectly proportioned workload that somehow is cleared up at the end of each eight-hour day. On the contrary, the most successful people at any company always seem to have more work than they can handle.

And that's the way they want it. They appreciate the 'more work, not less' paradox. They understand that the condition of being slightly overwhelmed on the job comes with significant career perks.

For one thing, it increases your exposure – to colleagues, ideas, projects, opportunities, mentors, future bosses, future allies. That only makes sense. The more you have to do, the more you have to throw yourself into the mix of the workplace. That's how you learn and get better.

This improvement generally doesn't go unnoticed. when people see that you can get things done, they more readily gravitate towards you when they want something done. This invariably means more work rather than less.

Which leads into the most interesting career perk of all: when you're overloaded, you get reinforcements. The senior manager of a large multinational once explained to me how he rose from a lowly accounting position into a leadership position with several thousand people reporting to him. 'The company had a simple work ethic,' he said. 'The management piled on the work until you cried uncle. Then, when you were totally swamped and couldn't possibly take on more duties, they let you hire someone to help you. That's how you get to be a manager here. That's how you can build your own empire.'

It's an interesting dynamic. *More work* leads to *more exposure* leads to *more work* leads to *greater skill* leads to *more work* leads to *more resources* to accomplish the extra work.

It doesn't take much to get this dynamic working for you in your career.

But first you have to stop thinking of work as a finite, close-ended concept, the thing you do when you leave home and stop doing when you return home. That's the hang-up most people have about their jobs. They resist extra work when it invades what they regard as their personal time, their down time. There's nothing wrong with that. Everyone needs balance in their life. But there's also nothing wrong with a little imbalance in favour of work, particularly at the start when you are jostling with your peers and rivals to make the best impression.

Once you make the commitment to being overburdened if not overwhelmed, the next step is extremely simple: volunteer more. Put yourself in a position where people dump assignments on you. Not every task will bathe you in glory or make a big impression. But over time, people catch on. They begin to think of you as someone who's not afraid of work, who's willing to do whatever it takes to help out and get things done. That's not a bad reputation to have. It only invites more work, not less. (But that's good. Remember the career perks.)

After that, there's only one more vital piece to the puzzle. Stay within as narrow a niche as you can manage. Don't say yes indiscriminately to any and every request. Take the ones you can do well; ignore the ones you can't. At some point, as you do more and accumulate experience, you're supposed to make things happen with a greater economy of effort. An assignment that took you three days when you were a novice can be handled with one or two phone calls when you have a year or two on the job. If you find that every new assignment leads you back to the beginning of your learning curve, you are saying yes to too many of the wrong assignments. In that case, you're not moving ahead; you're staying in place and quite possibly falling behind.

If you can't do your job more swiftly and effectively after a year or two, there's no point to, no benefit from, the paradox of more work, not less.

MAKE FRIENDS WITH FEAR, IGNORANCE, AND SLOTH

When I look back on the low points in our business, it amazes me how often our failures can be directly attributed to at least one member of the most dangerous triad in business: fear, ignorance, and sloth.

No matter who you are, you will always have to deal with people who have more talent, greater resources, and better connections than you do, and because of those factors, these people will often beat you at your own game. Given those circumstances, defeat is almost easy to accept. But it's not acceptable to fail because you were afraid, or didn't know something you should have known, or were flat-out slow and lazy.

Unfortunately, a lot of people respond to this trio with a peculiar extreme: denial. They refuse to admit they're afraid of a situation or that they don't know something or that they aren't working as hard as they could be. That's why I say it's crucial to make friends with fear, ignorance, and sloth. If you can recognize them in yourself and embrace them, you can not only overcome them, you can take advantage of them in other people.

For example, fear, by definition, is one of the most inhibiting and paralysing factors in the workplace. It prevents people from making decisions, from putting themselves on the line, from taking risks, even from picking up the phone and dialling someone they know they should be talking to.

But what many people don't appreciate is that fear is one of the greatest positive motivators in business. If I'm being honest with myself, I have to admit that some form of fear has been lurking behind almost every one of our company's successes. It may have been fear of losing a deal to the competition, or being number two in our industry, or not meeting the payroll, or going under. Whatever the case, it was fear that kept me awake at night, that sent a little tingle down my spine and urged me to work harder, and compelled me to demand the same from our employees. I suspect you'd get the same admission from any other entrepreneur.

When you stop being paralysed by fear, you're ready to be motivated by it.

If fear is the most unrelenting factor, then ignorance is the most unforgivable. Ideally, we should all fight ignorance by knowing everything we're supposed to know about our business. But that's not realistic anymore (if it ever was). Information is gathered, distributed, and consumed so rapidly today that none of us can presume to be perfectly informed or, for that matter, even semi-perfectly informed. Even in our modest niche of the sports business, I suspect our company's reputed 'experts' are familiar with only a fraction of all the material in their respective areas. That's scary to some people. To others it's an opportunity.

There are two ways to make friends with ignorance.

The first is to admit it in yourself. Instead of bluffing when you don't know something, learn to say, 'I don't know.' It's an incredibly liberating statement, and people rarely brand you as stupid or ignorant for employing it. One of the first promises we make to our clients is that we will always tell them when we don't know the answer to a question. But we will find someone who does. I can't remember any instances when clients have resented our 'ignorance' or thought less of us for admitting it.

The second way to embrace ignorance is to become an expert at something. It might be impossible to know everything about your chosen field, but it is eminently do-able to isolate a part of that field and develop a thorough knowledge of it. If you can become an expert at something, there will always be people flocking to take advantage of that expertise. I saw this in my early years in the golf business. I had been passionate about golf all my life, but I was hardly an expert at it. I didn't play it as well as my clients. I knew very little about putting on tournaments. I knew nothing about golf course design and development. But if you wanted someone to negotiate a golf endorsement contract, I was your man and that little bit of expertise proved to be a very attractive feature to professional golfers at the time. It literally put me in the sports business.

Of the three factors here, sloth is the most subtle. Very few people in the workplace consider themselves lazy. Whether they work from nine to five with a two-hour lunch break every day or from seven to seven and grab a sandwich at their desk, almost everyone thinks they work hard. It's one of the great delusions. People either think they're a) working harder than they actually are or b) harder than everyone else.

I've always thought one of my more valuable managerial advantages is that I work at least as hard as everyone else in the company (so far no one has told me that I'm deluded about this). It's easier to make great demands of employees when they know you're making great demands of yourself.

What people in our company might not appreciate is that I also get a lot of time off. That's because I don't let them know. Making friends with sloth means finding the right time and place for it. When I work, I'm working. When I'm being indolent, I do it privately outside the work environment – and call it a vacation.

I suspect most people could overcome their delusion about how hard they work if they simply came to terms with sloth and left it where it belongs – away from the job.

IT PAYS TO OVERESTIMATE YOUR COMPETITION

I was in a meeting helping our senior executives map out a strategy for dealing with a pesky competitor who was making inroads in one of our profit centres. After a couple of hours of brainstorming, the group had put together a detailed list of moves we intended to make over the next 18 months, some muscle-flexing, some risky, some expensive, that would put some added pressure on this new rival. Sitting there in the meeting, I was genuinely pleased with the scenario we had sketched out. It had us not only growing the market in this area but increasing our share of that market. I felt it was a productive meeting until someone in the room pointed out what should have been obvious to all of us. He said, 'The only thing wrong with this war-room scenario is that we're acting as if we live in a vacuum, as if our competition won't respond in ways we haven't considered to these moves. It's dumb to think they won't counterpoint when we take a swing at them. Never underestimate your opponent's abilities and cunning.'

Someone else countered, 'Never overestimate them either.'

A few days later, I still couldn't get the session out of my mind. Given the choice, is it smarter to overestimate or underestimate your competition?

I'm convinced the better route is always to overestimate your opponents. I've certainly seen this in sports. You cannot compete in match-play golf counting on your opponent to miss a crucial putt. You have to believe he's going to make it. That's what keeps you alert and hungry and in the match.

It's the same in tennis. If you have just hit a great forehand down the line that looks like a sure winner, you can't stand at the baseline and admire your shot, figuring that you have won the point. You have to go to the net, anticipating that, despite all the odds, the fellow on the other side of the net is going to chase down your 'winner' and somehow get it back. If you overestimate your opponent, you'll either be ready to deal with him when he succeeds against you or pleasantly surprised when he fails.

It's no different in business. When we decided to make a big corporate push three years ago into Latin America, thinking that this was the next big sports market, we had two options.

One, we could go with the conventional wisdom that this was virgin territory, that advertisers and corporations were light years behind us in terms of marketing ideas and sophistication, and, consequently, that our potential rivals who were calling on these customers were equally backward and unsophisticated. That option would have dictated that we devote limited resources to 'invading' Latin America. After all, if there's not much opposition, why should we spend as if there were?

Or we could overestimate the competition. We could give the local talent the benefit of the doubt and assume that they were at least as smart as we were and, given their familiarity with local customs, probably a lot smarter. That option would either scare us away from the market altogether or remind us that we would need to act and spend aggressively to make an impact.

In the end, we chose the latter option. We made a full-bore commitment to the region and have not been displeased with the results.

The question at hand, however, is: when the benefits are so obvious, why do people resist overestimating their rivals?

The most obvious reason is ego. Successful people tend to overestimate themselves in almost every way. Flush with a track record of success, they think they are smarter, funnier, better looking, more charming, more commanding, even thinner than they really are. That ego-inflation is one of the side effects of success. But people can't help elevating themselves without diminishing others. Thus, the underestimate of other people's abilities usually stems from an overestimation of our own.

Another reason is what I can only term denial. People not only refuse to recognize their strengths and weaknesses. Sometimes they turn everything upside down. They think they are strong where they are actually weakest. I've seen this among our executives who angle for more responsibility by telling me how good they are as managers, when there are no facts to support this claim and, in reality, the opposite is closer to the truth. They couldn't lead or delegate or manage a staff if I took them by the hand every step of the way.

This sort of denial is just as dangerous in dealing with rivals as thinking too highly of yourself. It demonstrates a blind spot. If you can't distinguish between weakness and strength in yourself, how will you make the distinction in your competition? You may be underestimating your opponent precisely in the area where he or she is strong.

The third reason is the 'mirror fallacy.' It's the belief that everybody thinks and acts just like the person you see in the mirror in the morning. This isn't necessarily bad, but it can create problems. For example, if you happen to be a very kind and charitable person who's indifferent to money, it's only natural that you mirror yourself in others. You assume that everybody else is kind and charitable just like you. You don't recognize that people can be less than charitable and that money is extremely important to them. In those moments, you are underestimating your opponents – and you will probably pay for doing so.

There's an upside to the mirror fallacy. I saw it in my early years in business. I was ambitious and hungry, for both money and success. These aren't necessarily attractive qualities and they're certainly not shared by everyone in the business world. But mirroring those qualities in other people made me a better businessman. I operated under the assumption that my rivals were working as hard as I was; thus, I refused to slow down. I assumed that my customers were inclined to drive as hard a bargain as I was; thus, I made it a point of honour to negotiate hard on every deal point.

As I say, I'm not sure this showed me in an attractive light at all times.

But that sort of fear and paranoia helped us stay in business and grow.

In effect, my ambition and fear of failure made me overestimate everyone. So I was prepared when my overestimation turned out to be true and at a pleasant advantage when it wasn't.

DON'T BE SEDUCED BY BIG IDEAS

Here are three things I know about ideas in the workplace:

- Little ideas get little respect.
- Big ideas get all the attention and applause and resources.
- The best ideas usually start out as little ideas and grow into big ideas.

I jotted these three thoughts on a yellow pad as I listened to a silver-tongued venture capitalist outline his latest brainstorm. He was looking for investors in a concept that would revolutionize how Americans shop. There was no doubt that the idea was grand, ambitious, and if it worked, hugely profitable. It also required a tremendous amount of up-front investment.

That's when I scribbled my three bullet points. I did it to remind myself of the seductive power of big ideas. They lure you in with their cleverness, their originality, their sweeping vision – and not incidentally, their promise of big returns. But more often than not, big ideas are a mirage. They take an inordinate amount of energy, manpower and money to keep them moving along successfully – and if any of those ingredients disappear for a moment, the big idea can come to a grinding halt.

In reality, the best ideas rarely start out as big ideas. They tend to start out small.

The irony, however, is that there is little motivation in the workplace for people to come up with little ideas. Every reward structure in the workplace, whether it's tangible or psychic, encourages us to wrap our ideas in as big and impressive a package as possible. The big idea draws attention to us. It lets us stand out from the crowd. It brands us as a bold, innovative thinker. And it puts a big chunk of the company's resources under our control. After all, a big agenda requires a big investment.

And yet, everything in my experience convinces me that the best ideas show up at your door in little packages.

I saw this firsthand at our company in the late 1980s when one of our senior executives proposed creating a Grand Prix motor race on the streets of New York City. We had experience running races in other American cities. But taking over the streets of Manhattan suggested a new level of complexity and risk. It was a big, bold, audacious concept. It would require a huge investment from corporate sponsors, which in turn meant a dedicated sales force to sell sponsorships. It would require a battery of lawyers to deal with the demands of the city government and civic groups. It also meant keeping a new office open in Manhattan for at least two years before we would ever see a dollar of race revenue.

I remember at the time that everyone at our company believed that the concept of a motor race in Manhattan was mildly insane – so fraught with complex negotiations with dozens of 'interested parties' and logistical headaches that it would take most of the joy, and perhaps profit, out of producing a successful race. But we were also seduced by the grandeur of the idea. A New York Grand Prix was bold and unconventional. So we gave it the green light.

At the same time, another of our senior executives had a problem with his client, Scott Hamilton. Hamilton, who had won the Olympic gold medal in figure skating a few years' earlier in Sarajevo, had just lost his job as the star attraction in the Ice Follies. Back then a skater without a contract with one of the two big skating shows (the other was the Ice Capades) was a skater without a career.

Our executive's solution was to back Hamilton in his own skating show. It would start out small. We wouldn't incur the expense of hiring, training and transporting a huge corps of skaters as the existing shows did. It would just be Hamilton and a few other stars on the ice. We would test out the concept in small arenas in four towns in New England, and see if people would buy tickets. The idea was packaged in such a small, non-risky way that hardly-any of us gave it any notice that first year. As I recall, we were all amused that our company was now in the skating show business, competing with the venerable Ice Capades and Ice Follies.

Flash forward to 2000. The New York Grand Prix does not exist. It never happened. After three years of planning and hard work, during which we enlisted the full cooperation of the city of New York and signed up corporate sponsorship commitments that exceeded $50 million, we tossed in the towel. Dealing with the various civic groups – from neighbourhood organizations to environmentalists – proved to be incredibly frustrating, and sapped a lot of our momentum.

As for Scott Hamilton's skating tour of New England, it is now called 'Target Stars on Ice.' It's in its 14th season. It visits 60 cities in the US each year, selling out arenas the size of Madison Square Garden, starring the likes of Kristi Yamaguchi, Katarina Witt, and Tara Lipinski – and, of course, Hamilton. It has spun off a Canadian touring company as well as an international edition that regularly visits Japan. It has also eclipsed the Ice Follies and Ice Capades, which no longer exist. It is one of our company's most valuable sports properties.

I believe that a big reason for its existence is the way it was presented at the beginning. It was such a small, harmless idea, it was too small to resist or object to.

Remember this when you propose your next idea. You have a choice in how you package it to your bosses. You can go big or you can go small. You can inflate its potential to the point where everybody is watching you, second guessing you, and, given human nature, perhaps rooting for you to fail. You have set such expectations that it is virtually impossible to deliver on your promises.

Or you can tailor the idea so it barely shows up on people's radar screens. If you fail, you fail small. No one notices. Likewise, if you succeed, the success is small. But that's also why there is big power in little ideas. That small success lets you stay in business. It lets you grow a little bit more each year to the point where you are bigger than anyone imagined.

It's your choice. But in my experience, your chances of success are much greater with the latter.

THE BEST IDEAS CANNOT BE STOLEN

A young executive was complaining to me that some of his colleagues (including his boss) had a nasty habit of catching onto his ideas and claiming them as their own. He claimed he didn't have the temperament to fight people over this, mostly because it ends up making everyone look childish. But he hated that people were getting credit that belonged to him.

I assured him that most people in the workplace, including his superiors, generally have a strong sense about which people *come up* with good ideas and which people tend to *attach themselves* to good ideas. I also assured him that, painful as it was to have someone else get credit for your creation, it was far more preferable to be the individual who was stolen from than the individual who did the stealing.

Unfortunately, the battle over credit for an idea is something that will never disappear from the workplace. Ideas are money. And like money that's sitting out in the open, they beg to be stolen. If you're the type who tends to come up with ideas rather than borrow them, the following points will protect your thinking and, more importantly, your sanity.

1. Does it qualify as an idea?

The first thing you have to realize is that it's possible that not everyone has as high an opinion of your so-called creativity as you do. To them, your brilliant 'idea' may be nothing more than a marginally productive thought that breaks a deadlock or moves a project further. It's the reason people talk to one another: They're looking for help and they want to move forward. That's why they catch on to your 'idea.'

Actually, I've always thought it's amazing what some people claim as an 'idea.' The standards can often be incredibly loose and forgiving. For example, several people in our company were meeting to discuss potential sponsors for a tennis event. A junior executive suggested that we call on Company X because he happened to know the CEO was an avid tennis player. As it happens, we followed up on that suggestion and did, in fact, sell a significant sponsorship position to this particular CEO.

To some people, I suspect that sales lead qualifies as a creative idea. I'm sure it seems that way to the junior executive who suggested it. After all, no one else in the room came up with the CEO's name. And it did help us break through to find a sponsor for an event that heretofore had lacked corporate support. Taken to its logical extreme, I can actually imagine that every time this young man sees Company X's logo attached to the tennis event, he proudly thinks to himself, 'That was my idea!'

I'll grant that the young man made a valuable contribution (and that it should be factored in to his year-end salary review). But is it an 'idea'?

Not really. An 'idea' has to be more than a suggestion that someone else can pick up and run with. At the minimum in business, an idea must be a clever recombination of two seemingly disparate concepts into a larger concept that no one else has considered before. A couple of years ago, one of our more creative executives proposed that we should be in the executive recruiting business. On the surface, this is a bad idea. There's a lot of strong competition (out of the gate, we'd be tenth in a five-horse race). Corporate customers don't think of us in terms of executive searches (we'd have to re-educate them). Also, we're not staffed properly to conduct executive searches.

But our executive chose to ignore these negatives. He was looking at several other factors:

i. We would be a niche player in the business. Our focus would be strictly sports. (That took care of the competitive issue. In sports, we had a nice lead on the field.)
ii. We were always getting calls from sports companies and teams about job openings. (That took care of the customer issue. We already had companies calling us for advice.)
iii. We knew the talent pool of executives as well as anyone. (That took care of most of the search issue.)

The only thing missing was the staff to conduct a complete search and prepare the reports for the clients. Our executive solved that by finding a partner already in the business who was willing to share the workload and the profits with us.

That sort of thinking comprises a solid idea. You take an existing concept (i.e., our current resources), put it next to a seemingly disparate concept (i.e., executive recruiting), tweak it slightly (i.e., limit it to sports), and find a practical way to bridge the two (i.e., find a partner already in the business).

It's not a cure for cancer. But it's the minimum thought process for what I would consider creativity in business. Anything less is not quite an idea, at least not one worth fighting over or stealing.

2. The best ideas are almost impossible to steal

I've always taken some comfort in the belief that the stronger an idea is, the harder it is to steal.

That's because the best ideas, by definition, are so original and unique that they cannot survive without their creator. He or she is the only one who understands the concept fully, who can execute it up to its full potential, and who has a personal stake in keeping the concept going despite all the obstacles.

For example, many people outside the golf community do not know that we are the people who came up with the idea for the World Golf Ranking, which is now the universally accepted ranking of the world's top golfers. I don't advertise the fact, but of all our company's innovations in sport, this may be the one of which I am most proud – because it was good for the sport, good for golf professionals around the world, and will endure for a long time.

The idea's origins were simple. I had always thought that golf needed an international rating system, much like the tennis computer rankings, reflecting the fact that American players were no longer the dominant force in golf and that there were outstanding players in Europe, Asia, and Australia who were going unrecognized and, therefore, uninvited to lucrative American tournaments.

In the early 1980s, I became an evangelist for this notion of a world golf ranking system. I shared the idea with anyone who would listen. I never worried that someone would steal it because, quite frankly (and pardon my arrogance), it never occurred to me that anyone else could bring it to life. I truly felt our company was the only organization that understood it, cared about it, had a professional stake in it, and knew enough people in and out of golf to make it happen.

What made the idea strong was not its originality (tennis and skiing already had world rankings). Rather, it was perfectly suited to my interests and our company's capabilities.

So if you're worried about someone stealing your idea, it's probably not as strong as you think it is.

3. Some ideas deserve to be stolen

Not every idea is strong. Not every idea is suited to your ability. If you can accept those two facts, you can accept the notion that the next best thing to protecting an idea is sharing it with someone who needs it more than you do.

This is particularly true with bosses. In fact, I've heard some cynical types argue that bosses exist in large part to steal their subordinates' best ideas. There's more than a grain of truth in that. That's one reason bosses become bosses. They have the ability to sit in a meeting, listen to a dozen or more concepts, and pick out the two or three that are brilliant and kill the rest. It's like any other form of larceny. The best 'thieves' have a keen eye for the most valuable merchandise; they don't waste time on stuff that won't return top dollar.

Once you realize that about your boss, it might make it a little easier to accept his or her appropriation of your ideas. Ideally, you should be tossing ideas at your boss for the express purpose of having them stolen. It's part of the care and feeding of bosses. If you're not feeding your boss at least a dozen good ideas a year, you're not taking care of your boss – and you're certainly not taking care of your career.

One caveat: it's crucial that your boss remembers that these ideas came from you. Bosses have an amazing tendency to 'rewrite history' when it comes to someone else's idea. What begins as *your idea* becomes *our idea* and often ends up as *my idea*. If you can stop this revisionist thinking in the middle at 'our idea' you will usually be rewarded for your efforts.

DON'T LET BRAINSTORMING KILL YOUR CREATIVITY

I always worry a little when someone at our company says we need a meeting to brainstorm ideas. It's not that I don't recognize the value of brainstorming, but I do have some serious doubts about the quality of ideas that come out of such sessions.

Just because you gather people in a room to come up with creative solutions to a problem, doesn't mean that they will actually do so. You can't schedule creativity. And you certainly can't legislate it by telling people around a conference table, 'Okay, be creative.' Creativity doesn't work that way. It happens, if it happens at all, in spontaneous and unexpected bursts of insight. You're fooling yourself if you think you can predict it. The best you can hope for is being able to recognize it when it's staring you in the face.

Then there's the self-fulfilling nature of brainstorming, which I think can be insidious and counterproductive. If you gather people in a room to brainstorm a solution to a problem, they will always come up with a solution. It's built into the process. People can rarely admit failure. And they certainly can't own up to it when it involves creativity. I've never heard anyone who considers himself 'creative' admit that he sat in a room with intelligent colleagues, thought about a problem, and couldn't come up with at least one idea.

As a result, brainstorming sessions always produce ideas. They might not be good ideas. They might not be the right ideas for the problem at hand. But they're the only ideas you have and, by God, you're going to act on them. In a lot of cases, considering all the time and resources wasted on bad ideas, you would have been better off not having the brainstorming session at all.

That's my big gripe with brainstorming. It's an abuse of the creative process in the workplace. It puts too much pressure on people to come up with a big idea when, in fact, big ideas don't come along that often.

As a result, I've learned to expect a lot less of my associates' creativity. I've also learned to expect a lot less of my own.

For example, I used to expect to make a sale at every meeting. If I didn't, I considered the sales call a failure, I'd lash myself, thinking 'I had a live one in my hand. I can't believe I didn't sell something to him.' But over time, I realized that sales didn't work that way. I came to accept the fact that I couldn't close a deal on every call. I was doing well if one out of ten prospects bought from me. I also lowered my expectations. A sales call was a success if I found someone in the room who liked me and might do business with us in the future. A sales call was a success if I got a new lead or learned something about the company's buying habits that stopped me from wasting my time pursuing them.

It's the same with creativity. I've lowered my expectations. I've learned that you can't expect yourself or your people to come up with big ideas all the time. Big ideas don't come along that often. And even when they do, you probably don't know it. The size and dimension of an idea – i.e., it's bigness – isn't apparent until you act on it and see how it plays in the marketplace. Until then, it's just an idea, no different from hundreds of other ideas.

The key is to be creative in some way every day, to keep flexing the right muscles.

My personal goal now is to have one creative thought a day. It doesn't have to be a big idea that changes my life or the fabric of our company. It merely has to be some thought that, if only by a fraction of an inch, moves our business forward or prevents us from falling backward.

In practice, it's not difficult at all. Being creative is sometimes nothing more than taking someone else's flawed idea and making it slightly less flawed.

People in our company were discussing what to do with the unused lodging capacity at our Nick Bollettieri Sports Academy in Bradenton, Florida. One solution was to try and sell the properties as condominiums to our various athlete clients. After all, the athletes might be attracted to a warm-weather property attached to a world-class sports training facility.

Although I liked the idea of selling condos to get a return on our investment, I didn't think that our athlete clients were the right target market. As athletes, they would be busy competing around the world in their chosen sport for most of the year. They could only take advantage of the facility for a few weeks out of the year. It wasn't a good investment for them. Instead, I thought we should be targeting corporations. They also might be attracted to a warm-weather venue at a world-class sports facility. But they could use the corporate condo 52 weeks a year, offering it as a perk to their employees or to their customers.

That suggestion was my creative thought for the day. It wasn't big or bold. It merely identified flawed logic and corrected it.

4

Office Politics

FIND OUT WHO'S ON YOUR TEAM

Most people have a good idea who their enemies are at work. The boss who hates them. The colleague who envies them. The subordinate who wants their job. These are some of the most vivid and common stereotypes in the workplace.

And if they're smart, most people employ some variation on Machiavelli's 'Keep your friends close, your enemies closer' in dealing with these intra-corporate rivals.

But all this emphasis on Machiavellian manoeuvering and shrewdness distracts people from an even more important assemblage of people who can alter your life: your friends.

It's really quite remarkable how little thought people give to the team of friends they have on the job. They may keep a watchful eye on every step their enemies make. But when it comes to their true friends, they are indifferent or unthinking.

I noticed this once when I called on a customer at his office. A colleague of his in the Office of the Chairman that they shared, a longtime rival obsessed with corporate intrigue and infighting, had finessed him out of a major investment of company resources. He mentioned it at the start of our meeting but seemed remarkably composed for someone who had just lost out in a power struggle involving billions of dollars.

I told him I was impressed with his 'serenity' under the circumstances.

That's when he showed me his list – a list of all the people on what he termed as 'my team.'

The list, he explained, comprised all the people, high and low, at the company whom he regarded as his teammates. He was the team 'captain.' There was only one criterion for membership: you had to like this fellow and have his best interests at heart. The list included forty or so people, from the chairman/CEO who hired him to the information systems manager who kept his computer running at cutting-edge speed to his assistant of 20 years who kept his life in order.

Very few people on the list were aware that they were on this man's 'team.' It existed largely in his mind. But the fact that he had a list was a great source of his peace of mind.

'There's a lot of infighting going on at every level of any company. And you're never going to win every battle,' he said, 'That's why I remind myself who my friends are. As long as my team has more depth and character than my so called enemies, I'm not worried about my fate.'

I thought that was a singularly sane attitude. But I was more interested in his list. It seemed like an ingenious invention, not only for peace of mind but for dealing with almost any problem at work.

When you assemble your team, here are the people you should include:

1. People who want you to succeed

In any organization, there are the handful of people who are clearly for you and the vast majority whose intentions are vague or not overtly friendly. Your team should only have people in the first group. You can usually identify them because they are genuinely happy when something good happens to you. They don't feel competitive with you. They don't get a twinge of jealousy when it seems that you are achieving slightly more success than they are. They simply enjoy your good fortune as if it were theirs. These folks are not rare, but neither are they common. Get them on your team.

2. People whose talents complement yours

People rarely gravitate to other people whose talents overlap their own. They prefer people with complementary skills. There's no friction or no ill will when people perceive themselves as compatriots rather than competitors. There's also the additional benefit that people with complementary skills actually can help you where you most need help. They let you do what you do best and you return the favour. Having friends on your team is one thing; having friends who enhance your ability to get things done puts your team in a higher league altogether.

3. People who watch your back

Every captain needs a few team members who can play defence. They may not be the source of great ideas or great contacts. But they alert you to company gossip. They tell you when trouble is looming or when some-one is talking about you behind your back. This, too, is good to know.

4. People who give you good leads

There's no better way to gauge a person's attitude towards you than by the tips and leads they give you on a regular basis. It is the essence of generosity and goodwill. If people are willing to share what they know without hesitation or fear that it will put them at a disadvantage, you'd be a fool to kick them off your team.

5. People who stay in touch simply to stay in touch

You never have to worry about these people's agendas. They simply want to keep in touch. These are pure friends. They may not be 'starters' on your team, but they are a valuable part of your bench.

6. People who can run (rather than run away) with your ideas – and let you do the same with theirs

Ideas can turn people into territorial and proprietary monsters. So when you find a friend who doesn't have a problem sharing his or her ideas with you, or for that matter, giving them away to you, draft them for your team. If you have one of these on your side, you're doing better than most people.

7. People who hang out with you after work

By definition, these are people who like you. After all, they're willing to spend time with you off the job, when they are no longer obligated to do so.

8. People who sing your praises to others

Everyone needs a personal publicist, someone who'll say nice things about them without the slightest prompting, simply because they believe them to be true. Such people are so rare and are obvious choices for team membership. On the surface, these criteria appear to be relatively benign. But they may be harsher than they seem. I guarantee they will appear more disturbing if you can't assemble a healthy list of names employing them.

CONTROL YOUR 'STORY' BEFORE OTHERS CONTROL IT FOR YOU

When the Tom Cruise movie, *Jerry Maguire*, came out a couple of years ago, it brought an unprecedented level of attention to the job of representing big-time athletes, which is what we do at IMG, the company I founded nearly 40 years ago. After the movie became a big hit. People started referring to me in the media as 'the original Jerry Maguire.' I didn't dispute it. It was a good sound bite. It told my 'story' – what I do, what I've accomplished, and where I stand in my chosen field – and it did it in four simple words. As self-marketing slogans go, you couldn't do much better than that.

But over time, when I thought about it, I became a little annoyed with this sound bite. It told an interesting 'story' about me, but it wasn't necessarily a 'story' that I believed or wanted to tell. If Jerry Maguire was the stereotypical fast-talking, finger-snapping, always-hustling sports agent, I preferred to think of myself as the head of the monolithic well-oiled sports marketing firm that Jerry left.

It got me thinking about how all of us in business define and market ourselves with simple story lines about who we are and what we've done. Sometimes those stories build us up and render us more vividly and more interestingly to the people we want to impress. Other times, the stories diminish us or only present a small part of the picture. It all depends on how well you understand the nature of marketing yourself via a simple story and how well you control it before others take it away from you.

Here are four of the more basic story lines in the workplace:

1. 'I succeeded where others failed'

This is the story line of people who have overcome great obstacles. For example, a CEO I know was at a loss about what to do about a talented executive who didn't fit in anywhere at the company. He didn't want to let him go, but he didn't have any where or him to go. Finally, in exasperation, he assigned the executive to turn around a floundering division far from the company's core that, over the years, had perplexed several of the company's ablest managers. Through some miracle of chemistry and circumstance, the assignment was the perfect tonic for the executive. Within three years he had turned the division around into a huge cash cow for the company. That single success, totally redefined the executive. Suddenly, his story changed from 'Doesn't fit in' to 'Succeeded where others failed.' It enlarged his image and identity so completely that he became the CEO's first choice whenever he needed someone to handle another 'turnaround'.

2. 'I was there first'

This is the story of pioneers, people who are slightly ahead of the curve, who spot trends before everyone else and are willing to act on their hunches. An investment banker I know rose quickly to the top of his firm because of a simple but bold hunch about the future of telecommunication companies he had when he was a lowly market analyst. The companies he identified over several years generated enormous fees for the firm and his career ascended with each triumph. He became known for his ability to spot opportunities before anyone else. It didn't matter if he never repeated that triumphant insight for the firm. As a defining story, 'I was there first' is a statement that can make a career.

3. 'I'm a nice guy'

This is the storyline of mediators and consensus builders, people who will do almost anything to eliminate conflict in the workplace. It's a great slogan if your job is to keep people contented. But if you want to go farther within your organization, you may have to find a more daring story to define yourself.

4. 'I have the client in my hip pocket'

This is the story line of salespeople with only one arrow in their quiver. If you have to rely on your strong relationship with one client to impress people, you probably don't have enough clients. 'He has a dozen clients in his hip pocket' is a much more impressive story line.

These are by no means the only 'stories' in the workplace. But they demonstrate that how you tell your particular 'story' can have an impact on your career that's sometimes out of proportion with your actual achievements. With that in mind, isn't it better to define yourself before others define you?

IT'S NICE TO HAVE FRIENDS IN LOW PLACES

I met with the chief of a small but profitable division at a major media company. The chief was a bright, engaging man who had recently taken the job as a favour to his CEO after successful tours of duty in several bigger divisions at the same company.

The man was trying to convince one of our clients and me to commit to a project with him, even though the financial guarantees he was offering were nowhere near what two other companies had on the table.

Like a true salesman, though, he wouldn't let the fact that he was the low bidder deter him. Although he couldn't match the competition dollar for dollar on guarantees, he was offering hundreds of thousands of dollars in promotion and free advertising. His company owned TV stations and cable channels. These TV outlets didn't always sell out all their spots for commercials and he was confident that he could place commercials for our project whenever this so called 'remnant time' was available. This was the ace up his sleeve.

He had charts to show us how he had finessed endless air time for a previous project – and the sales and excess royalties this marketing muscle had generated.

Remembering his long service at the company and his relationship with his CEO, I said, 'It must be nice to have friends in high places.'

He said, 'No. It's nice to have friends in low places. The commercial slots open up at the last minute. Senior executives don't decide who gets them. It's usually a technician who slips a videotape into the machine. And I know the people on the technical crew. I started out with them.'

He had a point. Many of us spend so much time looking up – to our bosses, to decision-makers, to people with alleged 'power' – that we often overlook the people in the trenches below us, the folks who have the discretionary power that, at critical moments, can seal a deal or kill it.

I see this dynamic all the time when I travel. If I'm the victim of a ticketing crisis at an airport counter, the fact that I might know the CEO of that particular airline is irrelevant. At that specific moment in time, the only person who can help me is the ticketing agent standing in front of me. The agent can either pull a few strings or make me squirm.

So I behave accordingly. In the few brief seconds I have to make the agent my 'friend,' I acknowledge his or her discretionary power ('I hope you can help me . . .'), I defer to it ('What do you recommend?'), and I challenge it ('I'm sure you'll come up with something . . .'). Unless the agent's hands are completely tied, he or she usually rises to the occasion. That's an agent's job. That's when it's nice to have friends in low places.

This dynamic, of course, is rampant in the workplace as well. But I'm not sure people exploit it as well as they could.

For example, everyone knows that easy access to a company's president is one of the keys to success. (It's not absolutely necessary, but it certainly makes life easier when you need a quick decision or fast escape route from a problem.) Likewise, everyone knows that in order to get through to the president, you ought to make friends with his or her secretary. The secretary is the gatekeeper, with incredible discretion over who sees the boss and who doesn't. It's a fundamental that should be imprinted on the cerebral cortex of any salesperson or career-minded individual.

Yet how many people actually do it?

If I canvassed my secretaries in London, New York, and Cleveland, I'd wager that only a small fraction of our employees have ever introduced themselves to them, let alone befriended them. I have no idea why. Perhaps they think the gesture is too obvious. Perhaps they think it's manipulative, that my secretaries will suspect their motives. Perhaps they think if everyone else is doing it, how special can it be?

Whatever the reasons, very few people act on this most basic self-advancement strategy. I'm not suggesting that getting to know my secretary will instantly improve your access to me. The payoff is even better than that. My secretaries are very efficient people who are in daily contact with almost every part of our company. As a result, they know the nooks and crannies of our company in a way that few other people do. In my mind, the greatest service they can provide has nothing to do with access to me but rather with knowing shortcuts within the company that may be mysterious to everyone else. In terms of problem-solving, they may be our company's greatest resource.

I suspect the same can be said of most well-tenured highly-placed executive assistants at other large organizations. The only remaining mystery is why so many people don't appreciate these assistants – and get to know them. To do that, though, they have to reset their sights. Instead of looking up, they have to look around and down. Only then will they appreciate the power of having friends in low places.

YOU ARE BEING JUDGED AT EVERY MEETING

As a general rule, it takes time to win respect and admiration at most organizations. It can take your colleagues weeks or months to decide that you're a nice person. It can take you months or years before you get the chance to hit a business home run. But if it's instant recognition you crave, there's no better way than to do something absolutely brilliant in a meeting.

Like it or not, meetings are the forums where you are most often judged by your superiors and peers. That may not be obvious from the collegial bonhomie that prevails in many meetings. Everyone is ostensibly there to share information and form a consensus rather than to show off or triumph at someone else's expense. Yet as someone who has spent a great deal of time running meetings, I can assure you that your performance is being judged. Failure to heed this is like forgetting that your school-teachers and professors graded you on 'class participation.'

I remember a few years ago, we had a young executive who was called upon in a group meeting to talk about the income projections of one of our biggest clients. This fellow was the athlete's account executive. He was supposed to be the expert on the athlete's finances, contracts, and business affairs.

I guess this was one of the first times he was asked to speak in front of thirty of his superiors and peers because he totally choked. He was unable to answer the simplest question about this athlete's business.

I sat there stunned, thinking 'This is the guy we have looking after this athlete?'

But the really bad news is how that performance has negatively affected that executive's career. His ineptitude in the meeting is indelibly imprinted on my mind. Perhaps I'm not being fair, but years later I still have this impression that this fellow is not star material.

It's hard to recover from that kind of disaster. Worse, it was totally unnecessary.

The executive didn't identify that he had to be at his best at this meeting. He didn't prepare. He didn't anticipate questions. He didn't rehearse. He didn't do anything so that his answers would come out automatically, no matter how nervous he was.

A lot has been written about how to make meetings run smoothly. But the meetings you attend should also let your career run smoothly if you:

1. Beware the ad hoc meeting

Most of us have enough good sense to be thoroughly prepared for the major meetings, the meetings called weeks in advance where we are expected to make a formal presentation. If you can't get 'up' for these events, you'll never understand the importance of meetings.

However, some people don't have the same respect for ad hoc meetings, the internal meetings hastily called that morning or the night before. Perhaps they think that a meeting convened on the spur of the moment doesn't require them to be brilliant on the spur of the moment. On the contrary, these are the easiest forums to display your brilliance. When everyone else is napping, you should be wide awake.

Surgeons like to say there is no such thing as minor surgery, only minor surgeons. The same goes for meetings. There are no minor meetings, only minor participants.

2. Don't hide

Ed Artzt, when he was chairman and CEO of Procter & Gamble, once surveyed a dinner meeting of senior managers at company headquarters in Cincinnati. When he spotted a top executive in charge of a struggling division sitting in the back of the room, he quipped, 'I guess you can tell people's business results by where they are sitting.'

Never try to hide in a meeting. If you want to hide, you're better off not going at all. Pick a position that says you want to be at the meeting.

3. Know your sightlines

There are all sorts of theories about the optimal seating position in a meeting. They vary because seating arrangements vary.

At the standard rectangular conference table setup, the power is at the head and foot of the tables. Round tables (since King Arthur's day) are the most democratic. Everyone can see each other. There are no power positions. All positions are equal. Informal living-room arrangements around a coffee table are fairly democratic too (although I've noticed that the highest-ranked people always get the most comfortable seats).

If there is a lesson to be learned from these various arrangements, it is this: pick a spot where you can make eye contact with as many people as possible, especially the person running the meeting. If you're in the leader's sightline, you're more likely to get his attention and get a chance to speak. And when you speak, you'll also be able to see how everyone is responding to your remarks.

Experts in meeting dynamics tell me that the dominant players, when speaking, tend to look at people more than other participants do. Eye contact is a great advantage in any public forum. Use it.

4. Resist the urge to dominate

If you're invited to a meeting, you deserve a chance to be heard. Chances are you will be asked for your opinion or expected to speak at some point in the meeting. Don't abuse it. That is, don't be so long-winded that the meeting suddenly revolves around you. You may enjoy your protracted stay in the spotlight, but I doubt if anyone else will. The longer you speak, the greater the risk that the leader superior will cut you off.

5. Defend your people and yourself

There's no way to predict the impressions that people take with them from a meeting. But I do know this: people always remember an argument. They can vividly recall how one attendee attacked another and, more important, how that person defended himself. Sometimes that's all people talk about after a meeting.

That's an irony not everyone appreciates. Having someone attack you or your people in a meeting is sometimes your greatest chance to make a strong impression. Everyone will be alert. Everyone will be watching you. Don't let the attack go unchallenged. Don't let the moment pass you by.

WINNERS KNOW WHOM TO TRUST AND WHOM TO AVOID

Some years ago we were doing a lot of business with a broadcasting organization. I became well acquainted with one of their mid-level executives. This gentleman, who was in his mid-40s, always impressed me with his acumen and his character. But I was puzzled by his diminished status at the organization. He was clearly brighter than his bosses, many of whom were several years younger than he was.

At one point I actually asked him how he got shoved off the fast track.

He surprised me with his candour. He told me, 'There are two reasons. One, I'm not ambitious. Clawing my way to the top is not that important to me. Two, I'm not a good judge of character. I trust everyone. And sometimes people have disappointed me.'

There's a ton of wisdom and self-knowledge in that remark. If there is one quality that separates the winners from the also-rans in business, it isn't brains or ambition. It is the ability to gauge correctly another person's character. The winners know who to trust and who to avoid, who will support them and who will slow them down. They look at an organization's personnel as if it were a cast of characters in a play. Then they pick out the heroes and villains – and proceed accordingly.

I don't think anyone is born with the ability to judge character. It is an acquired skill. You have to mentally note what is and isn't acceptable behaviour. Then you must examine people with a cold, critical eye to see who meets your standards and who fails.

But first you must set your standards. Here, for starters, are six character flaws that can help you identify some of the most dangerous people in the workplace.

1. People who never do what they say will

A small percentage of people are always true to their word. The majority of people usually keep their promises. Then there's the small percentage who rarely do what they say they will – and don't consider this a problem. This last group is severely flawed and dangerous.

There's no way to avoid these people in business. But it shouldn't take more than one experience to learn that you cannot rely on them. If they disappoint you once, shame on them. If they disappoint you twice, shame on you.

2. People who push their work onto you

Some people are geniuses at avoiding hard work. Either through ignorance or strategic incompetence, they are constantly shunting their responsibilities onto someone else. It's easy to identify these flawed individuals. If you delegate something to them, they always return it to you half done. They bounce the problem back to you.

People like this can kill your career. In effect, they are asking you to do the work of two people.

3. People who are late and don't apologize

If consistent punctuality is a positive sign, then habitual tardiness is a negative. Still, if you know someone is always late, you can work with that. You can factor their tardiness into your schedule – and give them the appropriate slack. It's a nuisance. But far worse are the people who are never on time but refuse to acknowledge it or apologize for it. This is more than poor manners. It's a personal attack on you. In effect, they are telling you that, in their mind, their time is more valuable than yours. Avoid them. You won't change them, and you will always be, in some way, at their mercy.

4. People who tell you, 'I'm too busy'

This is almost always a canard. People who are truly busy don't admit it (and they certainly don't boast about it). If it's true that to get something done you should give it to a busy person, then the corollary also applies: don't expect much help from people who tell you how busy they are.

5. People who reject your ideas (because they didn't think of it first)

I'm not sure which person is more dangerous – the one who steals your idea because he knows it's good or the one who buries it because it came from you. At least with the first type, the idea gets a chance to be tested.

Every organization has its share of people who suffer from 'not invented here' syndrome. If your best ideas are consistently getting bad reviews from one audience, don't discard the ideas. Try another audience.

6. People who won't let you off the hook

There's something to be said for being rigid and demanding, for expecting everyone to keep their word. But nothing is absolute. Total inflexibility is a flaw.

One of the pleasures of doing business with friends is that you always have a cushion for unforeseen error. Friends will let you back out of a promise if, through no fault of your own, circumstances arise that prevent you from keeping it.

If a business associate is so unyielding that he cannot bend when you are in trouble, he is no friend. As a general rule, you only need one incident to learn this about someone.

DON'T BE AFRAID TO TACKLE THE IMPOSSIBLE

I always shake my head when I hear junior executives, male and female, complain about the 'glass ceiling' that keeps them in their junior positions. They don't appreciate how most corporate structures are designed to help them get noticed and get ahead. Meetings are a great showcase for your ability to think on your feet, but so are sales calls, budgets, reports, proposals, one-off projects, crises, quotas, projections . . . All of these are opportunities for a junior executive to make a strong impression on the bosses deciding his or her fate. Once you appreciate the myriad opportunities, you can put some distance between yourself and the pack by spicing it up with one or more of the following strategies:

1. Tackle the impossible

Every company has its share of corporate politicians who hold their finger in the air to see which way the wind is blowing and then volunteer for all the easy 'sure-win' projects. Most bosses aren't fooled by this.

In our company, I like to say that a chimpanzee could close million-dollar deals for Tiger Woods or Pete Sampras when each is the number-one player in the world. I am more impressed by the executives who can generate new income for the players that Woods and Sampras are beating. It shows a resourcefulness that goes beyond answering the phone and taking the order.

Be careful not to volunteer for every sure-win assignment that comes your way. Over time, you'll get a reputation as someone who likes the easy way out. Do the unexpected. Tackle some impossible cases. If you fail, no one will hold it against you, particularly if none of your peers was even willing to try.

2. Stay close to home

I once read an article about municipal layoffs during one of New York City's perennial budget crises. It reported that city employees who work *outside* City Hall – that is, the valuable employees on the streets who deal face to face with the public – were considered more expendable than the paper pushers *inside* City Hall who work near their bosses.

The inherent unfairness of that situation reveals something important about organizations: most bosses will reward the above-average people they see every day ahead of the great people they hear about occasionally. This is standard out-of-sight-out-of-mind thinking. I don't endorse it, but you ignore it at your peril.

I had a friend who passed up a giant promotion at his company because he wouldn't be given the office next to his new boss. He wasn't too concerned about his title or his compensation, but he was adamant about the office location.

When I asked him about it, he said, 'Most of the good relationships in this company start with people bouncing ideas in the hallway or around the water cooler or simply popping into one another's offices to shoot the breeze. I can't do that with my boss if I'm way down the hall or on the other side of the building. I'll be in his division, but not in his inner circle.'

3. Don't be afraid to make an enemy or two

I know a CEO who judges his executives' potential for advancement by how many enemies they make. His reasoning: he likes friction and controversy. He wants people who have one or two enemies within the company because that indicates a certain boldness of spirit, a willingness to try new things and rub people the wrong way.

I'm not sure I fully buy into his logic (and I'm positive that's one corporate pyramid I wouldn't enjoy climbing). But there's a germ of wisdom here.

It's one thing to be abrasive and obnoxious. It's another to be so cautious and benign that no one notices you. Somewhere between the two is a strategy for success. By all means, be bold enough to make an enemy or two along the way (it comes with the territory). But when you have done so, be smart enough to know who they are and never let them out of your sight. Better yet, make the effort to transform them into friends.

4. Be the logical successor

It's an axiom of good management. All bosses are expected to have heirs apparent – backup people who are as good if not better than they are. Bosses are only doing half their job if they fail to develop a visible number two who could effortlessly step in and replace them if they got run over by a truck.

Look around you. Who among your peers would you say is your boss's logical successor? What are you doing to make sure that it's you rather than someone else?

LOSE YOUR LEARNING DISABILITY

I was at a social dinner some years ago when the subject turned to the many marriages of the man hosting our dinner. With a mixture of pride and bewilderment, the man confessed that he had been married five times, all to fashion models.

One of the guests at the table gently observed, 'It sounds like you have a learning disability.'

I believe until that moment the man never fully recognized the pattern of his marital life. Obviously, he knew that he was attracted to a certain type of woman, but I don't think he appreciated that (based on the evidence) the marriages were doomed to failure. Why else would he continuously make the same mistake?

Romantics might claim the man was an 'eternal optimist.' But I think the guest at the table was more on target: when it came to models and marriage, the man had a learning disability. What was instantly obvious to a disinterested observer escaped him completely. And, because he was oblivious to the lessons of his personal history, he was doomed to repeat it.

The same dynamic crops up in business. If we're honest with ourselves, all of us would admit we are 'learning disabled' in one area or another (or more). The fact is, few of us learn from experience as quickly or as well as we should. When we are confronted with a familiar situation, we often fail to recognize that familiarity. Worse yet, on those occasions when we do spot the familiar pattern, we don't adapt or re-tailor our response. Instead, we resort to a familiar, predictable response. This failure to adapt, to alter behaviour that has been consistently disastrous in the past, is the essence of a learning disability.

For example, as the CEO of a growing organization, I've promoted lots of people into new positions over the years. Of course, moving someone out of a position means you have to fill that vacated spot. I didn't appreciate that ego and human nature rarely guide people to replace themselves with a superior candidate. They'd prefer someone good but not too good, someone who will make them look good by comparison. That was one of my learning disabilities. I thought, 'Who better to pick a successor than the person who knows the job best?' It seemed perfectly logical. It took me years to realize that asking the promoted employee to choose his or her successor was a sure recipe for mediocrity or failure.

When I think about the most common learning disabilities in the workplace, the bulk of them revolve around the subtle interplay of human dynamics, i.e., office politics. For example:

1. Constantly review your trust fund

In any organization, there will always be people you can trust and people who will burn you. Figuring out who they are should be easy to do, in theory. Just follow the formula: 'Fool me once, shame on you. Fool me twice, shame on me.' In other words, there's no excuse for trusting someone who has betrayed you more than once.

The learning disabled, however, get fooled three times and more.

In most cases, it's because they have short memories. They don't remember the last time a colleague let them down or the time before that. Hence, they cannot see a pattern developing.

My solution is to constantly review my 'trust fund.' If someone has a history of being trustworthy and honourable, it's easy to overlook a lapse or two. Nobody's perfect and there are all sorts of legitimate reasons for why people mess up. But you have to be vigilant. You don't want to wake up one morning to find you're depending on formerly dependable people.

I remember doing business some years ago with a European businessman. He always did what he said he would do. But a series of financial setbacks changed him. Gradually, he became more slippery in his business practices. He would unilaterally change contractual terms midstream. He was slow to pay, and when he did pay, there was always some money missing. Given his long track record of honourable behaviour, it could have taken us a year or two to notice the change.

But trust is one area where I'm not learning disabled. I'll give anyone the benefit of the doubt once, even twice. But, I monitor my trust fund. I don't get fooled three times.

2. Always count your votes

An executive I know, a happily married mother of three, explained how her family votes on a decision. 'You never want the kids ganging up on you as a voting bloc,' she says. 'So each of the children gets one vote while each parent gets two. Two kids and one parent can get their way, but not three kids without a parent.' Like a politician, she knows where the votes are and, whenever possible, she rigs the odds in her favour.

More people could use that common sense in the workplace. They go into meetings, where important decisions will be made, without counting their votes. They don't bother to learn how many attendees support their position, who they are, and why other people don't. In many cases, they don't even realize that a 'vote' will take place. They assume they will get a fair shot at presenting the merits of their case and that merit alone will determine the outcome. If they don't carry the day, it's because their argument wasn't strong enough. They have no clue that their case was lost before the meeting began.

The first few times this happens to you, you can blame it on naivety. But if you're constantly on the losing end in major decision-making sessions, you have a learning disability in corporate politics. You're in the middle of an election and don't know it. Candidates for office don't rely on their position papers to win votes. They campaign and talk to voters. They stir up their supporters and try to turn around their detractors. So should you.

3. Don't get caught between a rock and a hard place

I used to know a marketing vice president whose career almost collapsed because he unwittingly got caught in the crossfire between his company's founder and the company's new CEO.

The founder, who had retired from day-to-day management of the company but still owned a controlling interest, was not completely enamoured of the new CEO. But rather than discuss his differences with the CEO directly, the founder preferred to needle him in meetings. Unfortunately, he used this marketing VP as the go-between. If the CEO took a specific position, the founder would ask the marketing executive, 'What do you think?'

This was a classic no-win situation. Whatever the VP answered, he was guaranteed to displease either the founder or the CEO.

I sympathized with him. Getting trapped between two 'bosses' happens in our business, too. We've had customers try to pit us against our clients. We've had clients pit us against their family and friends. We've even had clients try to pit us against other clients. What I couldn't sympathize with, however, was how long it took the VP to notice he was caught between a rock and a hard place.

In my opinion, he should have refused to play the founder's game after the second or third meeting. But that was his learning disability. He felt flattered that the founder solicited his opinion and always ventured an opinion. He would have been much better off saying, 'I don't know' or something innocuous like that. It wouldn't have been insubordination. It would have meant he was learning.

DEVELOP A KNACK FOR GOOD TIMING

We all know people with exquisite timing. They are always in the right spot at the right moment with the right idea. To the untrained eye, I'm sure these fortunate folks appear as if they operate under a lucky star.

But in my experience, luck has nothing to do with exquisite timing. No one can be lucky all the time. At some point, even the most envious observer has to concede that consistent good timing has something to do with skill – and it can be learned.

I came to appreciate this fact some years ago watching Ian Player (the brother of our client Gary Player) at work. Ian was the head warden of the largest game reserve in South Africa's Natal province. Ian's crisis at the time was caused by the poachers who were depleting and endangering his reserve's population of white rhinoceros.

Ian set out to save the remaining white rhinoceros by capturing them and sending them to zoos where they could rebuild their numbers. Every morning Ian and his crew would venture into the bush in a big truck, armed with rifles and tranquillizer darts. When Ian spotted a white rhino, he would shoot the dart into the beast's hide and follow him. This exercise required perfect timing. Ian had to sense the precise moment when the rhino was getting wobbly, at which point he could drive the truck up and push the rhino into the truck. If Ian drove up too soon, the rhino would attack him. If he drove up too late, the rhino would collapse and be too heavy to drag into the truck.

Fortunately, Ian became very adept at this. He knew everything about the white rhino's movements and quickly developed the perfect combination of patience and decisive action that let him save the species.

That's the image I have of Ian Player: forever watching, forever patient, forever waiting for the decisive clue, until it was time to strike.

That image of vigilance, patience, and action comes in handy in business. Consider, for example, the not-so-recent phenomenon of world champion athletes who are 15 or 16 years old. As managers of athletes at that tender age, our responsibilities are largely commercial. We do deals and negotiate contracts. The true responsibility for the young athlete rests with his or her parents. They're the ones making the everyday life decisions that determine the welfare of their child.

But there comes a time – usually around age 15 – when teenagers get rebellious and want to assert their independence. They defy their parents. They turn to strangers and dubious friends for advice. That's a very precarious moment for anyone, not just highly compensated athletes.

It's particularly precarious for our people who handle athletes. They have to be vigilant for signs of discord between parent and child – and ready to step in. But their timing has to be perfect. If they intercede too soon, both parent and child will take it as an intrusion and resent it. If they sit back and until they're absolutely sure it's all right to step in, it might be too late. The damage may be done.

This situation may seem unique to our client management business. But its parallels occur in business all the time.

For example, let's say you've had your eye on one of your competitor's big accounts for your own portfolio. If you approach the account too soon, when the customer is happy with the service he's getting from your rival, you'll be brushed off. Yet if you wait until the customer is totally dissatisfied, it might be too late. Other competitors might have stepped in with the proposal you should have been making.

As I say, luck has nothing to do with it. You need (1) vigilance, (2) patience, and (3) the courage to act decisively when you see what you've been looking for.

Vigilance means keeping your eye on the situation at all times. A lot of people don't have the discipline to do this. They get an idea, act on it, and if it doesn't work out immediately, they stop paying attention to the situation. They simply forget to go back when the timing is more propitious.

Patience may be the toughest quality to master, because it runs counter to the equally prized quality of speed and decisiveness in business. When everyone in your organization is functioning at warp speed, it takes great discipline to *not do something*. Yet in my experience, when business people's timing is off, it's usually because they acted too soon. They didn't wait.

As for the third quality, if you can teach yourself to be vigilant and patient, finding the courage to act decisively should be almost automatic.

YOUR SUCCESS DEPENDS ON HOW YOU TAKE IN AND SEND OUT INFORMATION

Some years ago a friend accepted the job as the chief operating officer of a large industrial company where he would be groomed to succeed a notoriously difficult chairman/CEO. It was a risky move for my friend, but if you had asked me to bet on his success at the time I wouldn't have hesitated to back him. He was the consummate chief operating officer type: a quick study, great on follow-through, terrific on details, not burdened by an oversized ego, and a good judge of character and talent. All these attributes made him the perfect number two.

Within eight months, though, he was out. He and the chairman never hit it off, although there were no overt personality clashes and no one could figure out exactly where things went awry.

A few years later, I had a chance to spend some time with the chairman. I asked him about my friend and what went wrong.

'I liked him well enough,' said the chairman. 'But he was too much of a "systems" guy for me. He was always bombarding me with memos and reports. I didn't want to read. I wanted a partner, someone I could talk to each day and bounce ideas around. But he seemed to be much more comfortable shoving paper at me.'

Over such a seemingly petty difference, a career went off track. The two men had opposite styles of processing and disseminating information. The chairman was verbal. He liked to talk and listen. My friend was literal. He preferred to read and write. It's hard to imagine that these complementary styles clashed so violently. After all, most successful partnerships at the top thrive because of complementary talents. One is Mr Outside, the other Mr Inside. One is a salesman, the other a manager. One is decisive, the other more advisory. One is broad brush, the other nitpicky. And so on.

But over the years, I've learned that how we process information is one area where complementarity does not pay. When it comes to giving and receiving information, you have to be in harmony with your bosses, clients, and peers.

I've seen boss/subordinate relationships fall apart because the boss wanted daily action reports and the employee chafed at this obsessive supervision. Likewise, I've seen employees get upset because the boss didn't talk to them every day to see how they were doing. In both cases, the relationship was strained because of different requirements for giving or receiving information.

I've seen client relationships founder over pretty much the same thing. Some clients get upset when their manager calls them every day to update them on his or her activity on their behalf. To these clients, that's too much communication. We shouldn't call unless we have something solid and final to report. Conversely, with other clients, if they don't hear something every day from their representatives, they assume that no one at our company is doing anything for them. If we're not communicating, we're not working.

It may not be fair, but it's a fact that people ignore to their detriment. How you take in and send out information is a near-flawless predictor of how you will thrive in a business relationship.

The good news is that it's not tough to figure out if you clash or coordinate with the people that matter to your career. Basically, people fall into two camps. In taking in information, they are either readers or listeners. In sending it out, they are writers or talkers.

It's that simple. Talkers won't thrive with readers, and listeners will not get along with writers.

I see it in myself. I pride myself on being a good listener. But if I'm honest with myself. I'm a reader. I love seeing stuff in writing. I have fairly involved meetings or phone conversations with associates every day of the year. I will patiently listen to them describe every detail of what they're dealing with. And if you asked me to repeat what I heard, I could give a reasonable facsimile of what was said. But I almost invariably end the conversation saying, 'Do me a favour. Could you give me a one-page memo summarizing what you just told me?'

It's not because I want to make work for our executives. I simply need it in writing because I don't feel I have a complete grasp of a situation unless I can read about it. That makes me a reader.

I know this about myself. But it's amazing how many of my colleagues, people who have worked with me for years, don't fully appreciate this. If they did, they would be bombarding me with written bulletins – and getting more of my attention.

Then again, they might not. They may not be inclined to write it down for me because it's not in their makeup.

Just as some people are readers rather than listeners, the flip side is that some folks are talkers, others are writers. Some people are comfortable thinking out loud. The more they talk, the more likely they are to stumble on a good idea. And so they talk until they hit paydirt. Others are more scholarly. They need to sit at a keyboard to organize their thoughts and present them coherently.

One is not better than the other. The key is knowing which category you fall into and whether it clashes with the people who matter most to you.

If you're a reader surrounded by colleagues who are talkers, there's a good chance you're missing out on a lot of information. While your colleagues are talking amongst themselves, you are falling out of the loop because you don't process information the same way. While you're waiting to see it in writing, your colleagues are moving on.

Nowhere is this distinction more important than in your relationship with your boss. As with my friend above, a writer is not going to get along well with a listener for a boss. So making the boss/subordinate relationship work requires two steps.

First, you have to determine how your boss processes information. The clues are easy to spot. Is your boss the scholarly type who is constantly reading? Does he or she write elegant, persuasive letters and proposals? Does he or she respond immediately to your written communications (where someone else might ignore them for days or weeks)? If so, your boss is a reader.

In that case, let's hope you're a writer. You don't need clues to know who you are. You just have to be honest about your inclination to write. Do you enjoy it or hate it? Do you feel confident expressing yourself on paper? When you have to persuade someone, do you automatically put your thoughts down in writing, or do you do it face-to-face?

Answer these questions and you'll understand why your relationship with your boss (or your peers and clients) is thriving or strained.

PS. If you and your boss are clashing as communicators, don't waste time trying to change. Get a new boss. You are who you are. So is your boss.

IT'S OKAY TO RUB PEOPLE THE WRONG WAY

The CEO of another company once asked me for some objective advice as he was hiring a new chief for his most important divisions. The contest had come down to three candidates, all of whom had negatives and positives.

Candidate no. 1 had ascended to a divisional presidency at another company, but a new management would not be renewing his contract. His résumé was impressive. He also got high marks for being very friendly and popular with his subordinates and colleagues. All in all, a nice guy but a bit lacking in imagination and flair.

Candidate no. 2 was stronger on all fronts than no. 1, but he was happily employed. It would take a lot of money and promises of career development to lure him away.

Candidate no. 3 was the strongest in pure business terms. He had a stellar track record of performance and innovative thinking. However, he was a prickly fellow. He had made some enemies along the way, although none among his superiors and clients.

The CEO couldn't make up his mind. Should he go with the safe bet in Candidate no. 1? Should he break the bank to lure Candidate no. 2? Or should he risk offending some of his other executives by bringing in the edgy Candidate no. 3?

In an unusual move, the CEO put the decision up for a vote by the people in the division. Not surprisingly, they went with Candidate no. 1, in large part because everyone liked him. Nobody had a bad word to say about him.

That's when the CEO asked for my thoughts. My first reaction was disbelief. I couldn't believe that the CEO was relinquishing one of his chief responsibilities – namely, hiring senior people. I also couldn't believe that he was turning this major decision into a popularity contest.

But my biggest concern was the complete absence of scepticism about Candidate no. 1's credentials.

'Wait a minute,' I wanted to shout. 'Isn't anyone here curious about why he's available and why his old company isn't renewing his contract? Doesn't that worry anyone even a little? Doesn't that say something about his abilities? In effect, you're hiring someone else's reject!'

I was also concerned about the fact that everyone liked him. When everyone in the room is in complete agreement. I worry. It means someone is not asking the right questions or thinking hard enough about a decision.

The same can be said about people who are liked by everyone. I worry when I hear someone is that much of a 'nice guy.' I thought the CEO should be questioning the underlying reason for the candidate's universal popularity. If he had, I suspect he'd find out that Candidate no. 1 had sailed smoothly through life without ever making a tough decision, or challenging his superiors, or articulating his own vision, or for that matter, stepping on anyone's toes. While these may be admirable qualities in a friend or a vacation partner, it's not necessarily the right stuff to lead a valuable division.

In the end, I encouraged the CEO to take a closer look at Candidate no. 3. In my mind, the fact that he had made enemies along the way (although, crucially, none among his bosses or clients who signed his pay cheques) said something positive about him. It meant he was willing to step on people's toes, at some personal expense, to achieve a corporate goal. It meant that he knew what he wanted and was willing to shake things up. As the cliché goes, 'You have to break some eggs to make an omelette.'

To his credit, the CEO took my advice, met again with Candidate no. 3, found him to be strong-willed but not obnoxious, and ultimately hired him.

In our constant search for consensus and harmony in the workplace we are sometimes less than fair to the prickly, edgy, combative people in our midst. We resist them or avoid them altogether (and warn others to do likewise) because it's easier to deal with more agreeable types. That's perfectly understandable. But in doing so, we do ourselves and our organizations a disservice. Every organization can use a few strong-minded warriors who rub people slightly the wrong way – not only to fight the ugly battles that the more diplomatic among us avoid but also to challenge their superiors and peers. They keep everyone on their toes.

Don't get me wrong. I'm not advocating that you make a place in your company for mean, surly people with major attitude problems. You'll always regret it, no matter how talented they are. But I am advocating more tolerance and appreciation for people with robust personalities and, at the same time, a healthy scepticism about people who are always nice.

Personally, I've always enjoyed doing business with strong-minded people who are slightly rough around the edges, especially if they are at other companies (rather than ours) and I'm trying to sell them something. If nothing else, I know these people won't waste my time. They're decisive, whether they're saying yes or no. That's certainly better than the endless humming and hawing of someone who's trying to be nice.

Not long ago, when one of our younger executives complained to me that he was having trouble getting a decision out of his friend at one of our major customers, I told him, 'Go to your friend's boss. Your friend is afraid of offending you. His boss won't be. He might not tell you what you want to hear, but he won't string you along.'

I have to believe that kind of blunt personality always serves a valuable purpose in any business.

KNOW WHEN TO SAY, 'IT'S NONE OF YOUR BUSINESS'

We used to have an executive in our company who was an incorrigible snoop. He had an insatiable need to know what everyone else in the company was doing – what project they were working on, with whom they were meeting, where they were travelling to. He wasn't sneaky about it. In fact, he was almost charmingly open when he pried.

One of his favourite tactics was to ask a senior executive's secretary about her boss's whereabouts. He would always phrase the question to imply that he already knew where the executive was: 'Joe's in Atlanta today, isn't he?'

The secretary would correct him: 'No, he's in Dallas for the week.'

'Really!' this snoop would reply. 'What's he doing there?'

And then the secretary would proceed to fill him on everything her boss was up to.

I have no idea what he did with all the 'intelligence' he gathered this way, but he was amazingly persistent and democratic with this approach. He would pry into anyone's affairs – subordinates, colleagues, senior executives, even assistants on my staff. Even more amazing was how long it took people in our company to figure him out. For a number of years, he snooped unchallenged. Very few people had the savvy or the gumption to tell him. 'That's none of your business.'

I've always thought that some of the most awkward moments in business occur because people can't say, 'It's none of your business.' I'm sure we all know people who are naturally curious by nature. But even the most curious people know what's appropriate and what's not. They know the difference between innocent curiosity and outright rudeness or invasion of privacy – and they usually don't go over the line.

For example, the snoop at our company was engaged in relatively harmless curiosity rather than corporate espionage. As I say, I don't know what he did with all the ephemera he gathered and I've never detected any damage to us as a result of his prying. But I suspect if he started asking some very detailed questions in quasi-confidential areas, most of our people would have cut him off immediately or, at least, suspected his motives.

Unfortunately, the world doesn't make it easy for us to gauge when someone's curiosity is appropriate and when it's not. There are grey areas in even the most sensitive discussions that can cause trouble or make us look bad – and not all of us have the wisdom to appreciate that.

As a general rule, there are two topics for which 'None of your business' should always be on the tip of your tongue: someone else's money and your personal life. Of all the topics that are nobody's business, these would seem to be the most obvious. But I am astonished at how aggressively people pry into these areas, how much people reveal on these subjects, and how few of us fully appreciate the consequences of doing so.

Consider the subject of money. All of us know that certain types of money discussions are taboo. In an era when people will gladly tell you how much they paid for their house or their jewellery, we still know that another person's salary is none of our business. Even with our best friend or our sister, we don't pry. But there are grey areas that confuse us, even on the subject of compensation.

Not long ago one of our literary clients called up his agent in our New York office with an innocent-sounding request. We had just negotiated a fee for this writer to write the text of an illustrated book. For the work that needed to be done, the fee the publisher offered was fair and the writer agreed to it. As the writer began working on the book, however, he started having second thoughts about the illustrator's contribution to the project. So he called our office and asked us to find out what the illustrator was being paid. He didn't feel it was right if he was earning less than the illustrator. I suppose you could argue that this wasn't a totally inappropriate request. As agents, we want to get the best deal for our clients. But in another sense, the request was outrageous. In effect, our client was prying into the illustrator's pay cheque.

The fact that the request involved someone else's money should have put our agent on red alert. The agent should have told the client, 'You've accepted the fee. What the illustrator gets is none of your business.' But our agent didn't do that. Acceding to the client's request, she called the publisher who, in so many words, told her, 'Butt out!'

I can't help thinking that everyone would have come out smelling better if our agent had told the client, 'It's none of your business.' The client would not have looked like a whiner and meddler. The agent would not have gone on a fool's errand. And the publisher would have been spared an awkward confrontation.

Your personal life is another area that theoretically is nobody's business – and yet a lot of people allow the line between their professional and personal affairs to get blurred.

I can see how this happens in a normal working environment, where bosses and subordinates are working eight hour days together. Over time, as you develop a warm, friendly relationship with people at work, it's understandable when they become curious about some aspects about your personal life. They may know where you vacation with your family, whom you're dating, what you do on the weekends. In my opinion, this is precisely the sort of information that's nobody's business – because you never know what your associates will do with that seemingly trivial knowledge.

A few years ago I met with the CEO of another company and two of his senior staffers. One of the staffers wasn't as well informed as he should have been on one of the topics under discussion. The CEO snapped at him. 'Maybe you'd know more if you didn't spend your evenings on the phone to your girlfriend in Chicago.'

I was taken aback by the CEO's remark, not merely because of its crudity but because of the betrayal it implied. The staff person obviously trusted the CEO; at least he regarded him as a enough of a friend to confide some details of his personal life. But the CEO abused that trust when he used that information to berate his subordinate in front of me. The normal boss-subordinate relationship was weakened by the fact that the two men were also friends. I can't help thinking that both men would have been better off if they had kept personal details out of their professional relationship, that at least one of them had regarded this information as nobody else's business.

5

Acquiring a Power Base

DON'T LET YOUR BRAINS BECOME YOUR BIGGEST LIABILITY

I once sat in on a meeting with the owner of a company as he listened to his vice president of business development recommend a heavy investment in a new venture. The vice president made his case brilliantly. It was well documented and he arrived at his conclusion with exquisite logic. The way he presented it, it sounded like a sure thing.

At the end, the owner turned to his vice president and said, 'Tim, that was one of the best presentations I've ever heard. The only problem is that if we go ahead with it, we'll be competing with our biggest customer, who probably won't like that and might fire us.'

End of discussion. But the vice president persisted, arguing that the best minds in the company supported him.

The owner cut him off, saying, 'That's why you're not rich. You and your buddies are too smart.'

The owner's last remark was said in jest, but it had the ring of truth. Given the choice, I would always rather have more brains than less. But there comes a point when sheer braininess is more a liability than an asset in business. The smartest people often come up with some of the most ingenious ways to undermine themselves.

1. They surround themselves with other smart people

Inherently, there's nothing wrong with this; it's certainly better than being surrounded by fools. But it can lead to a dangerous sort of cliquishness in a company, where the smart people only agree with each other and shut out anyone else. You see this a lot in highly technical areas of an organization, where the technical wizards only speak to one another in their own private jargon. This single-mindedness makes them very good in their narrow area, but it undermines them with other parts of the company. When they want to branch out with a bold idea, they often don't have the contacts, the allies, or the communication skills to get the job done.

2. They boast about their brilliance

Bragging is never attractive, but it's downright stupid to brag about how you outsmarted someone else.

An advertising salesman I once knew at a sports magazine had the good fortune of selling a huge block of pages to a major advertiser. As part of the deal, the salesman promised to try to get a major article on the company into the magazine. It was an outrageous promise, because the editorial departments reflexively chafe at any interference from the business side.

But this salesman was smart. He spent months manoeuvring inside the company, until the article was assigned, written, and ready to run. Then he turned stupid. He publicly boasted about how he finessed the editorial department into running the piece. Of course, this eventually reached one of the magazine's top editors who, irked at the slightest appearance of favouring an advertiser, immediately killed the piece. That would never have happened if he had kept his clever scheme to himself.

Smart people can't help but outsmart themselves when they rub their brilliance in other people's faces.

3. They ignore feedback

This isn't the exclusive domain of smart people. Everyone can be blind to the warning signals that their idea isn't working or they're on the wrong track. But the smartest people tend to be a little too confident about their facts and their insights, to the point where they won't tolerate any opinion that contradicts them, especially if it comes from people who are not their intellectual equal.

The irony is that in most organizations the most sensible people are always inviting second opinions about what they're doing. The super-bright people tend to shut this sort of feedback out.

4. They overcomplicate everything

Most situations are as simple as they seem – one plus one almost always equals two – but smart people have a tough time accepting this. It's as if the one-plus-one-equals-two equation is too easy for their giant intellect.

And so they try to think of reasons why the answer might be three.

We once had an executive who could come up with eleven reasons why a project wouldn't work for every reason why it would. No one doubted his ample intellect, but it took me a while to see how undermining it could be.

I once made the mistake of bringing him along on a sales call (I thought I might need him to explain some technical matters). I made my pitch for an event sponsorship. The customer agreed on the spot. And then I watched in horror as my associate outlined all the things – weather, insurance, crowd control, television coverage – that could go wrong at the event. He couldn't accept the simple reality of the situation, that the customer liked the concept enough to buy it. He had to complicate it by demonstrating that he knew all the risks involved. Although I could admire the perverse agility of his mind, which created a scary scenario that almost undid the sale, it was a brilliance that I thought belonged in someone else's organization.

5. They pick the wrong fights

I guess this is the most effective way smart people outsmart themselves. They think their intelligence gives them a licence to flout convention. They expect people to excuse all their personality defects simply because they are right more often than they are wrong.

This perverse streak is most evident in the way smart people deal with authority.

Some years ago I had frequent dealings with a bright young man who had had a meteoric rise to the managing director's job of an apparel company that was part of a holding company controlled by a friend of mine. My friend was the one who suggested I initially talk to this young man. At some point, my friend took some stands about the apparel business which this managing director violently disagreed with. He voiced his displeasure by disparaging my friend to anyone who would listen, including some people in our company.

I remember thinking at the time that this managing director might not be as smart as he thought he was. No matter how solid his record of accomplishment, he wouldn't be managing director for long if he forgot that my friend was the ultimate boss, the kind who could say, 'You're fired.'

But authority seems to bring out the worst in smart people. They can't yield to it, so they fight it. As a result, they often end up in battles they can't win. That's what happened to the managing director, who took on the boss and ultimately lost his job. You'll never convince me that this was smart.

THINKING IN HYPOTHETICALS SHARPENS THE MIND

In almost any important business situation, I'm playing games of 'What if . . .' in my mind.

If I'm trying to decide whether to pour our company's resources into a new area, I ask myself, 'What if the competition put its money into this first? Would I feel relief or regret?'

If I'm wavering about hiring someone, I think, 'What if someone else offered this person a job? Would I let him or her get away?'

If a friend is urging me to invest in his project, I wonder, 'What if we could remove our friendship from the equation? Would the concept still be appealing?

Thinking in hypotheticals sharpens your mind and lets you to approach problems from unusual angles. The approach is also useful when you need to reassess your career. I know if I were at some sort of impasse in my job, I would be madly constructing 'What if . . .' questions to determine where I really stood in the organization and how I felt about it. The following nine hypotheticals would be a good place to start.

1. If you could have anybody's job at your company, which one would you take?

I can't think of a better litmus test for gauging your ambition. If you want the CEO's job, that says something about how high you're aiming in your career. If you merely want your boss's job, that says something too.

If you're happy where you are, I salute your good fortune. On the other hand, if you don't want anyone's job, you might want to reconsider what you're doing showing up at work each day.

2. If you could work for anyone in your organization, who would it be?

If your answer is someone other than your current superior, what are you planning to do to change your situation?

3. If you could eliminate the most time-consuming part of your job, would you miss it?

This is the most accurate way to measure your on-the-job satisfaction. If you would honestly miss doing your main job, you are at least properly employed. If the opposite is true, both you and the company are suffering.

4. If you could erase your biggest flaw, would anyone notice?

This is a good test for eliminating some of your personal insecurities. If you can honestly say no one would notice or care that you somehow corrected a major personal failing, how big a flaw can it be?

5. If you lost your biggest personal asset in business, would anyone care?

This is the converse of the previous question. It's a good indicator that you may be overestimating your contribution to the organization. If no one would notice or care that you somehow lost your principal business talent, how valuable can it really be to the company?

6. If the company published a depth chart for your department (or for the entire organization), what line would your name be on?

This hypothetical is like truth serum about your future. It also begs at least two other questions: how has your position changed in the last year or two? Who leaped over you and whom did you pass?

If your position hasn't changed, that doesn't bode well for your prospects for advancement. And if other people have forged ahead of you, that bodes even less well.

7. If you could assemble a board of directors that existed only to guide and advise you, who would be on it?

The more important question is the follow up. Once you've assembled the list, how many of these people are you consulting on a regular basis? If nothing else, you'll learn whether you're taking advantage of the collective wisdom of the people who know you and care about you.

Then there's the other obvious follow up: what do you think this board would be telling you?

8. If you were a publicly traded company, what price would you be quoting for your stock?

Would it be at an all-time high or low? More important, would you be buying, holding, or selling?

9. If you were offered your job today, would you still take it?

This is the ultimate reality check for people in a career crisis. If the answer is no, you need to start thinking in terms other than 'What if . . .'

YOUR RÉSUMÉ DOESN'T ALWAYS REVEAL THE TRUE YOU

A friend and I were discussing the hundreds of résumés that cross our desks each year. I remarked how frustrating it was for me to see all these excellent résumés and know that there weren't any openings at our company for these young people. I worried that our company was letting a whole generation of talented people go elsewhere or, worse, to our competition.

My friend stunned me with his view of the situation.

'I don't see it that way at all,' he said. 'The only frustrating thing about all these résumés is their incredible sameness! All the candidates have good grades, perfect references, interesting extracurricular activities, MBAs from top schools, even some on-the-job experience. Just once I'd like to see a résumé that told me something about that person's character, about who he or she really is. Just once I'd like to see the résumé that's in their mind, not the one on paper.'

I see his point. There can be a tremendous disparity between the achievements people hold dearest in their mind and the achievements they actually put down in writing.

I see this in my case. I haven't had to write a résumé in 40 years, but I approve the biographical material that is sent out about me and our company. The data is almost like a résumé: played golf in college; trained as a lawyer; met Arnold Palmer; created sports marketing industry; built an international company with 2500 employees in 31 countries . . .

Those are the achievements on paper.

But if I was being totally candid, I might admit to being prouder of an entirely different set of accomplishments.

- Perhaps it's the fact that I managed Palmer, Player, and Nicklaus for ten years when it was such an obvious conflict and what that says about my people skills.
- Perhaps it's the fact that our senior executives have been with the company an average of 23 years and what that says about their loyalty to me and vice versa.
- Perhaps it's a favour I did 12 years ago for a friend's son that gave him a start in business.

All of these items could give a stranger a much richer insight into my character. And yet none of these items would normally go into a résumé – because it's hard to articulate their significance and pointing them out comes close to boasting.

It's no different for any other job candidate.

Let's say that you saved your best friend from drowning or that for 86 Sundays in a row you have helped run a soup kitchen for homeless people simply because you felt you needed to do that. Those are character traits that are quite extraordinary, but they are not something that you can inject very easily into the standard-issue résumé.

And yet, if I were a prospective employer, those are precisely the qualities that I would like to know about an individual and that might help me choose between seemingly equal prospects.

Of course, highlighting these achievements on paper is virtually impossible. 'Saved best friend from drowning' somehow looks out of place on the same page with your 3.8 grade point average. And writing down that you run a soup kitchen can backfire on you. It can make you appear a little too calculating and self-congratulatory, as if you are doing that good deed, in part, so it looks good on a résumé.

It's not much easier to inject these achievements into an oral interview – even when the interviewer looks up from your résumé and says, 'Okay, tell me what you're really like.'

So how do prospective employees expose their proudest accomplishments to prospective employers?

The first step is to be subtle about it but not shy. Prospects should be smart enough to realize that, like my friend above, employers are hungering for this sort of information.

The second step is to realize that these qualities are usually best heard not directly from you but from other people. That's what references are for. If I wanted an employer to know I saved my best friend from drowning, I'd list that friend as a reference (and identify him simply as 'friend'). If I wanted an employer to know of my voluntarism at the soup kitchen, I'd list the kitchen's director as a reference (and identify him simply as 'soup kitchen director'). I guarantee those sort of references will provoke some curiosity from your interviewer – certainly more so than listing three bosses or three professors.

There's nothing sly or manipulative about this, not if it helps worthy people shine a light on their true achievements and makes it easier for employers to get a better reading of a candidate's character.

GET PAID FOR THINKING RATHER THAN DOING

A few years ago I tried to promote one of our more talented television production people into an executive position. This young man had done outstanding work for us for years, going around the world, setting up broadcast operations at remote sporting events. On every assignment he seemed to surprise us with something new – a technical improvement in the broadcast, a better relationship with the event's sponsor, a new idea for the following year's event. At some point, it became obvious that this fellow had a greater value to our company than lugging cables and setting up camera positions at sports events. We could use him to help develop programme ideas, talk to sponsors, and sell the concepts to television channels around the world.

To my surprise, he declined my offer. He was young, healthy, and single. He enjoyed the peripatetic lifestyle of televised sports production, setting down roots in one part of the world for a few weeks, then picking up and moving on to another location. The hard work and running around suited his temperament.

At first, I was puzzled by his resistance. But then I realized that a part of this young man was afraid of the promotion. If he took it, he would no longer be judged and paid for his technical contributions to the job. He would be judged for his creative contributions. Instead of doing a particular task, he would now be spending most of his time thinking.

Eventually one of our senior managers took him aside and pointed out that this was a pivotal opportunity. What turned the young man around was the distinction between doing and thinking on the job. Our executive told him, 'Anytime you can move from a doing role to a thinking role at a company, you have made yourself more valuable.' Of course, what our executive didn't tell him (and what the young man apparently knew already) was that you are also more vulnerable because you have to maintain a certain level of thinking to stay valuable. If you're paid for thinking, you have to produce. If you're paid for doing, sometimes just showing up is enough.

I don't mean to glorify people who use their heads for a living (certainly not at the expense of the equally valuable people who use their muscles and technical skills for a living). But in a sense, the transition from doing to thinking is the pivotal moment in most careers. For an assembly line worker, the transition is becoming a shop manager or line boss. For a policeman walking a beat, the transition is becoming a detective or desk sergeant. For a salesperson covering a territory, it's becoming a sales manager and being responsible for other salespeople. For an advertising copywriter, it's becoming creative director and being able to judge other copywriter's work.

Over the years I've noticed a couple of interesting facets to this transition.

The most successful people I know have spent a lot of time doing backbreaking work in their company's trenches before they were invited to use their brain for a living. That experience gives them credibility when they offer their thoughts about a subject. It also vests them with authority so the people who are currently doing the backbreaking work in the trenches obey and respect them.

But, there's always the danger of overdoing it after you make the transition. We've had people go totally overboard with the thinking part of their responsibilities to the detriment of everything else. Ensconced in their new position of authority they feel they have a licence to think for everyone else. Thus, they delegate everything they can, even the tasks they are better off doing themselves. They inject their opinions where they are not wanted. They interfere in areas that are running smoothly without them.

I see this in myself sometimes. I've always felt that if I had nothing to do but think about how to deal with a certain area of our business, that area would perform better.

My ultimate fantasy would be to hole up at my home in Orlando for three months where my only job was to think about our company. It wouldn't take me long to dictate memos to dozens of executives, outlining an idea I conjured up in my study or suggesting a strategy for one of our clients who happened to be competing on television over the weekend or attaching an article I clipped from a magazine. After three months of this, I can easily see me sending five memos a day to everyone I know at the company. I can also easily imagine everyone in our company quickly tiring of this and thinking, 'Gee, I wish McCormack would get out more and stop thinking.'

My point is, once you make the transition from doing to thinking, there's no law that says you can't shuttle back and forth between the two. Ideally, you should strike a balance between the two that works for you. Over the years, I've developed a rhythm where I spend two weeks 'doing' (i.e., maintaining a heavy travel schedule, meeting with customers and clients, and managing the company) and one week 'thinking' (reflecting on my activities, talking to our executives, arranging my priorities, etc.).

The people who find that balance are generally the ones who are the most successful 'thinkers.'

KNOW YOUR SUPER BOWL SUNDAY

I once invited the head of a chain of flower shops in New York to join me and several other business people on a golf trip during the second week in

February. We would escape New York's harsh winter and spend a few days in bright sunshine on a beautiful golf course with some interesting people.

'The date's no good,' said the flower entrepreneur. 'That's the week of Valentine's Day. That and Mother's Day are my Super Bowl Sundays. We do a third of our sales on those two days alone. You wouldn't want me in your group. I'd be so distracted I'd probably hurt someone with a golf ball.'

Of all people, I should have been sensitive to the fact that the man had peak periods in his calendar year which he aimed for with total dedication. I had seen it all my life with our athlete clients. Their training schedules – in fact, their entire lives – are designed to help them peak for the major competitions in their sport. Golfers and tennis players peak for the four Grand Slam events. Skiers and figure skaters aimed for the Olympics and world championships.

I had learned that the best athletes would tolerate none of our commercial distractions during these periods. They were so focused on and being at their best, they simply tuned out any 'noise' that wouldn't help them perform better. Frankly, many of them were so monomaniacal about this, they weren't much fun to be around. And we gradually learned to approach them with all our business opportunities after the peak events, when their metabolisms and mental states had calmed down.

In fact, I build my calendar year similarly around peak events.

When I was starting out, my year seemed to peak around the Masters golf tournament in April in Augusta, Georgia. My clients, Palmer, Player, and Nicklaus, virtually 'owned' the tournament back then (between them, they won six Masters in a row from 1960 to 1965). It was impossible to overestimate my delight in attending the Masters.

But it was also a crucial week in my business. The entire golf community was gathered in a small town in Georgia during Masters week. I would have been a fool if I didn't capitalize on it. So I scheduled as many meetings as possible during the week. Over time, I learned that I could accomplish more in a casual ten-minute chat with a key person along a fairway at Augusta than I could in a half-dozen formal meetings back home.

Back then (and it hasn't really changed that much since), I seemed to end all my phone conversations with golf people saying, 'See you at the Masters.' The situation was ideal and I peaked for it.

Today, the fortnight around Wimbledon is the centrepiece of my calendar year. It's a demanding two weeks of non-stop activity for me – mostly pleasant, some exhausting – that I aim for with military discipline. Wimbledon is my Super Bowl Sunday.

But a strange thing happens as you build your business: Your Super Bowls accumulate. Every October, for example, I gear up for a full week of business in Scotland around our Alfred Dunhill Cup team golf event. The following week I oversee the Cisco World Match Play Championship in London. After that, there's the Trophée Lancôme golf tournament outside Paris. And so on. If I wanted to, I could be at a major sports event around the world every week of my life – and I could construct a full week of activity around each event.

But that would be suicidal. No one can be at his or her best week in and week out. Martina Navratilova is as focused and well-conditioned as any athlete I've ever met, and even she couldn't fine-tune her game to perfect pitch every tournament or, for that matter, every Grand Slam. If a nine-time Wimbledon champion has to pick her spots carefully, business people should, too.

The key is constructing a year-long calendar that has a clear pattern of peaks and valleys.

First, you have to identify the moments when you have to be at your best. In sports, that's usually obvious. If you're a professional tennis player, you want to be at your best at the major grand slam events, such as Wimbledon or the US Open. But you have to single these moments out and aim for them, so you can make your best performances when it really does matter.

I learned this from the sports psychologist Jim Loehr, whose principle of periodization is one of the cornerstones of training and exercise physiology. Loehr says that no athlete can be at his or her best all the time and that periods of rest are just as important as periods of stress. You must select the times you want to be at your best and then weave in cycles of rest, so that for every period of stress you have a period of recovery.

The stress-recovery cycles vary with each athlete. Some athletes can only function at their best for two or three weeks (you see this in tennis stars who are mediocre at meaningless tournaments but somehow excel at the major events). Their stress cycles have to be very short, and their recovery cycles are long. Others are more durable. They can peak for six- or seven-week cycles before they need a recovery period. But no one can stay at his or her best for too long.

The concept applies to how I structure my day. I get up very early – around 4 a.m. I take care of dictation and paperwork for three hours before breakfast. Then I'll go into a normal business day. I take a nap sometime in the afternoon, which recharges me for the rest of the day. That's my recovery period.

It's also how I structure my year. I now have eight or nine peak periods during the year when I work in intense bursts for one or two weeks. These are high-stress weeks for me. But I make a point of getting away for several days immediately afterwards. That's my recovery period.

I think it's the single most important organizational concept for thriving and surviving in business. I can't understand people who don't analyse their schedules and highlight the peaks and valleys in their business year. And I'm thoroughly befuddled by people who work at peak intensity on one project and then immediately dive into another intense project without taking time to catch their breath. They have no idea how they're cheating themselves.

Look at your schedule. Where are your Super Bowl Sundays?

Do you have any?

Or too many?

If it's the former, you're dooming yourself to mediocrity. You can't hit the heights if you're not aiming for a few high points.

If it's the latter, you're dooming yourself for the opposite reason. It's just as bad to overextend yourself as not to extend yourself at all.

DON'T LET YOUR VALUES WORK AGAINST YOU

An associate and I called on the managing director of a large company to persuade him to sponsor a new international women's sports event. After laying out all the facts of the sponsorship package – the date, the venue, the athletes competing, the television coverage, the customer entertainment opportunities, etc. – my associate looked the managing director straight in the eye and said, 'There are lots of companies that could sponsor this event. But we're looking for a company that wants to do more than just use the event as a marketing tool. We're looking for a company that believes in women's sports and is eager to make this event grow every year. We're not looking for just a sponsor. We're looking for a partner who "gets it".'

This is not the way we usually sell a sports concept. More often than not, the cold hard facts are all we need.

That's because selling is still a matter of having a product or service that the customer wants at a fair price and being able to deliver everything you promise. Product. Price. Promise. Those are the basic ingredients for successful selling.

But as selling becomes more competitive, as the marketplace becomes glutted with more and more suppliers vying for a finite amount of customers in a particular field, other ingredients besides product, price, and promise enter the customer's decision-making matrix. And one of those warm and fuzzy ingredients is values.

People don't think too much about the values of the people they're selling to. But they should. No matter how superior your product or service may be and how logical the transaction looks on paper, it probably won't happen if your value system is at odds with that of the customer.

Not long ago I introduced an American CEO to a British entrepreneur. The two men ran remarkably similar companies in their respective countries, and it seemed to me that they should be doing business together. So I arranged for my British friend to visit the American CEO at his headquarters.

When I asked him how the meeting went a few weeks later, my British friend focused on one incident. He told me how the American CEO pointed out with great pride an expensive piece of sculpture that he had had commissioned at company expense for his boardroom. Then the CEO added that he had had the artist make a smaller copy of the artwork for his home.

My British friend was almost embarrassed at hearing of this use of corporate funds for personal gain. It demonstrated a value system that made him extremely uncomfortable – and guaranteed that the two companies would not be working together.

On such examples of human frailty, entire relationships can rise or fall.

It's not difficult to assess a potential partner's values. Just look at how the person behaves in quasi-ethical situations.

On the golf course, for example, how does he or she deal with 'gimme' putts, how accurate is his or her score, and how elastic are his or her interpretations of the rules. Some folks are honest. Some cheat. You don't need too many clues on the course to know whether you want someone for a partner off the course.

You also learn a lot about people's values by how they deal with gray areas of a contract.

A marketing chief I know at a profitable but not extravagantly rich apparel company hired a supermodel as his company's spokesperson. In the contract, she was paid a huge annual fee for appearing in the company's advertising and also for committing 20 days a year for promotional appearances. The marketing chief should have suspected something was not right by how strictly the supermodel's representatives interpreted a 'promotional day.' A 'day' counted as any 24–hour period in which she was required to do something for the company, whether it was a single five-minute radio interview or a whole day of interviews.

But what tipped the marketing chief over was the cost of the supermodel's personal hairdresser, which the company was contractually required to pay. The marketing chief didn't anticipate that the hairdresser would insist on a fee of $10,000 a day. And the supermodel would not budge on the price or agree to use someone else.

In the end, the marketing chief paid all the bills. (What choice did he have?) But the experience left a sour taste in his mouth. The supermodel could have been flexible on this contract point. She could have been reasonable. But being reasonable wasn't a value she valued.

The campaign was a success, but when the supermodel's contract was up for renewal, the marketing chief looked elsewhere.

EVERY NUMBER ONE NEEDS A LOYAL NUMBER TWO (OR HOW TO BE A GOOD LIEUTENANT)

With all the emphasis on leadership today and the overt striving to be the boss that such an emphasis inevitably breeds, it's easy to forget that not everyone can be the boss. Do the maths. Whatever the size of your organization, there's room for only one person at the top of the pyramid.

That doesn't mean that everyone who is not the boss is a failure. On the contrary, to the shrewd, self-aware manager who doesn't lose sight of his or her career objectives, it's an opportunity. All you have to do is aim slightly lower. If you can't be number one, what's wrong with being number two?

Of course, not everyone is blessed with the right circumstances or appropriate personality to play the role of good lieutenant. To make this work, you need a magical confluence of factors, involving you, your boss, and your subordinates. For example:

1. Number one must need a number two

A lot of bosses don't feel they need lieutenants. (They're wrong, of course. Every boss can benefit mightily from a well-chosen number two.) The American presidency is liberally dotted with Presidents who ignored or barely tolerated their Vice Presidents and instead relied on their staff, their cabinet, or their political cronies. It's no different in the workplace. Some bosses would rather have a coterie of subordinates running around underneath them, each with his or her special niche and each uniquely beholden to the boss. These number ones are simply not comfortable with the idea of a number two sitting so close to their throne.

It's good to know this about your boss before you aim to team up with him or her. Some bosses prefer to lead solo. It's highly unlikely that you can do anything to alter the equation.

2. Number one must like you

This should be obvious, but it sometimes gets lost in the mating dance of number one and two. Smart bosses seek out partners who complement them in terms of talent and temperament. If they work in broad brush strokes, they want someone who's detail-oriented. If they're abrasive, they want someone who's calm and soothing. If they're impulsive, they want someone who's reflective and rational.

If you fit that description perfectly, you're still only halfway home with number one. Some years ago, a CEO I know was being urged by his board of directors to name a number two who would be his eventual successor. The search committee came up with an unassailable candidate. He was strong in every area where the CEO was deficient. The two men had remarkably similar backgrounds, even to the point where they shared a passion for fishing and jazz. On paper, they were a perfect match. Unfortunately, no one bothered to ask whether these two strong-minded individuals actually liked or respected each other. It turned out they didn't. Some mysterious personal chemistry made it impossible for them to work in close quarters together day in and day out.

There's a fine line between complementing someone and clashing with them. If the two of you genuinely like each other, it doesn't matter whether you complement or clash. You'll work it out. If the two of you don't like each other, nothing else matters.

3. Number one needs your constituency

Ideally, a good lieutenant brings to the partnership everything that the boss does not. This is crucial in terms of temperament, talent, and areas of interest. You don't need numbers one and two to both be easygoing, good at building morale, and keenly interested in that startup project down the hall.

But there's one complementary area that often gets lost in the process: A good partnership should also have complementing constituencies. If this were presidential politics, you might call it complementary voter bases. A presidential candidate from the Deep South looks for a running mate from a different part of the country so the ticket appeals to two different voting blocks rather than one.

It's not much different in the workplace.

I know a man who was recently named a district chief of one of the regional phone companies. This was a big promotion for him. He had gone from managing an office of 400 salespeople to overseeing more than 5000 people. He knew he needed a strong number two to avoid being overwhelmed by the job. Because he was from sales, his first impulse was to tap another salesperson as his lieutenant. That's only natural. Salespeople have a great rapport with people who 'can ask for the order' and 'close the deal'. They think they're a special breed.

But he ultimately chose a colleague from the technical side of the company.

The technician's argument was simple and clear. 'Listen,' he told his new boss. 'This district, for better or worse, has two separate workforces. There are the salespeople who bring in the accounts. Then there are the people who run the lines and can actually tell you how you get a dial tone. You've already got the support of the sales force. What you need is more credibility with the technical force. That's why you need someone like me.'

In the race for number two, you will rarely make a perfect complement to the boss. But don't discount your constituency. If you have credibility with people where the boss does not, highlight it. You will make an impression that few people ever consider.

LOSING YOUR BOSS'S LOYALTY IS NEVER ABOUT BUSINESS

When it comes to loyalty between bosses and their employees, I think employees begin the relationship with a big head start. That's because bosses, as a general rule, are loyal to their employees from day one. After all, they've proved their commitment to the employee simply by the act of hiring that individual. Everything that follows in the relationship either affirms that initial commitment or slowly chips away at it.

That's why it's sad to see a relationship between a boss and a subordinate fall apart. A situation that began with great promise and nothing but positive intentions ends up at a breakpoint where two people can no longer work together. What's even sadder in many cases is that the subordinate usually has no idea that the break is coming or what he or she has done to cause it.

Ironically, when the rupture comes, it usually has less to do with the employee's on-the-job performance (the sales he's generating, the accounts he's servicing, etc.) and more to do with the personal interplay between boss and subordinate. Loyalty is a delicate mechanism and there are lots of indiscretions, lapses in etiquette, and oversights that can upset it. Here are six to be aware of:

1. Arguing with the boss

As a boss myself, I know that bosses like to be argued with some of the time. It helps, of course, if you're right and the boss is wrong. With the facts on your side, you're rarely at risk. And making your boss aware of these facts, rather than keeping them to yourself, is the essence of loyalty.

But that is not a licence to argue constantly with your boss, no matter how comfortable you feel in the relationship. Eventually, that attitude wears thin, and the boss is left wondering why you are perennially challenging his opinion.

It should be obvious that arguing with the boss is a risky policy. Frankly, I don't think any employee seeks it out. But there are other errors employees make that literally force them into it.

2. Not having a backup to Plan A

A friend of mine recently fired one of his division chiefs. The young lady was one of his prize hirings, so the abrupt dismissal surprised me. When I asked him about it, he said, 'She was always arguing with me.'

'Why would she do that?' I asked.

'In hindsight, she had no choice,' he said. 'If there was a problem, she would always come up with a solution. But she never had a backup. Other managers would always come to me with Plan A, Plan B, and maybe Plan C. She only had Plan A. If I didn't like it, she had no choice but to argue with me. She had to defend Plan A because she didn't have Plan B. I got tired of the struggle and let her go.'

If you find yourself in a constant tug of war with your boss, don't blame the boss. It might be something that you're doing that leaves the two of you no other way of communicating.

3. Agreeing with the boss

This is the corollary to arguing with the boss. Constant agreement can be just as tiresome as constant bickering.

Even the most egomaniacal bosses know they're not infallible. Not every idea they float in a meeting deserves a 'That's a great idea!' response. After a while, that predictable yes-man reaction will only make them question an employee's honesty.

4. Trespassing on a boss's relationships with other people

One of the best things about having a boss is getting to know the boss's friends. But it's also one of the trickiest aspects – because you can trespass on those relationships without realizing it.

Let's say I have a friend at another company in New York whom I see several times a year and talk to by telephone at least once a week. Because of the frequency of my contact with this friend, it's inevitable that he and my New York assistant get to know each other if only because they talk on the phone and greet each other when my friend stops by my office. That's perfectly fine.

Now, let's say that my assistant asks my friend for a favour. That, too, is perfectly fine – as long as my assistant informs me. To do anything less is sneaky and disloyal. It's also hard to fathom or excuse.

Invariably, whenever I have felt 'betrayed' by a subordinate *vis-à-vis* my contacts, it is not because of something they did but because they never told me about it.

5. Preferring your priorities over the boss's priorities

One of the chief duties of being the boss is establishing priorities on the job – not only in how resources are allocated and money is spent, but also in how and to whom tasks are assigned and the order in which they should be tackled. Setting priorities is one of the boss's greatest privileges.

That's why it amazes me when subordinates think they can tinker with my prioritizing. If I ask a subordinate to address Task A first, Task B second, and Task C third, I'm not being arbitrary. I probably have my reasons for setting those specific priorities (and even if I don't, I would expect employees to heed my wishes; anything less is insubordinate).

In a boss's mind, when people alter set priorities, they are, in effect, discounting the boss's thinking on the subject and saying they know better. Unless they have a solid explanation for going their own way and tell the boss about it, they are seriously damaging the relationship.

6. Repeating the same mistake three times

This is the easiest way to lose your boss's loyalty.

The first mistake is a chance occurrence. The second time may be coincidence or an accident. The third time puts the boss on high alert. The fourth time (if you're still around to make it) is proof that the mistake is either wilful or beyond correction. Either way, I don't know many bosses who will tolerate it.

6 Promotions, Demotions, and Other Career Hiccups

PROMOTIONS ARE NOT ABOUT FAIRNESS

You probably think that promotions are earned, that they are rewards for past performance, that they are distributed fairly and democratically, that they happen in orderly fashion (like the succession of heirs in a royal family), and that they're good for your career.

Not true, although I can see why people think this way. It comports with our belief in fair play. Superior performance is eventually recognized and rewarded. If we do our job well, we will be blessed with advancement. If we're loyal to our superiors, we will be carried along with them as they rise. If a promotion is up for grabs, it's in the organization's best interest to give everyone an equal shot at the job.

Unfortunately, none of this accords with the reality of promotions as I know them and have dispensed them.

I'm not being cynical here, nor am I suggesting the other extreme that promotions are only bestowed upon fawning employees who cater to their bosses' vanities and tell them what they want to hear. The terrible truth is that promotions don't adhere to any predictable pattern. Each promotion is a one-off, a unique non-recurring event with its special cast of characters and logic.

The only thing promotions have in common are the accumulated myths and fallacies surrounding the process itself. Failing to appreciate these is a big reason so many people are disappointed by the promotion process.

Fallacy no.1. The person must fit the job

I suppose this was true in some not-too-distant era. If a job was open or a desk was vacant, you found the most qualified individual to fill the position or sit at the desk. You never wanted to reduce your head count.

That's not true in the stripped-down third millennium. Today if you can't find the right person to fill a job, either you rethink the job or it wasn't worth filling and you eliminate it.

As a result, promotions now follow precisely the opposite logic. Instead of fitting the person to the job, companies now fit the job to the person. As a manager, I think this is a positive development. I know we adhere to it in our organization. Except at the most junior levels (where the jobs are specific and fairly rigid), I can't think of one executive promotion where the promoted individual went into the new job with exactly the same responsibilities as his or her so-called 'predecessor.' In most cases, there is no predecessor, no departure, no slot that needs filling. Rather, the circumstances behind the promotion are a) we're growing, b) we have identified a talented individual who is ready for more responsibilities, and c) we customize a new job that incorporates his or her old duties and adds a few new ones. Sometimes the new spot is so different, you can't even call the change a promotion. It's more like giving the person a new career.

That's the logic behind most promotions today in dynamic organizations. Companies don't promote good people into someone else's old job. They give good people new jobs that suit their talents.

You ignore this at your peril. If you're still waiting for the spot immediately above you to open up for you, you may be waiting for a train that no longer stops at your station.

Fallacy no.2. All promotions are fair and open competitions

Companies like to advance the notion that every promotion is the end result of fair and open competition among worthy candidates. The reality is that most promotions are slightly rigged in someone's favour. That's human nature. You expect family-run businesses to be dominated by sons, daughters, nephews, and cousins. Bosses are supposed to promote their protégés. Mentors are supposed to look out for the mentored.

But even when there is no close personal connection, managers still play favourites. They'll give the edge to people with whom they've worked in the past. They'll favour people whom they think are being groomed by top management.

Fallacy no. 3. Bosses promote in their own image

This is a minor fallacy, because in many cases it's true. Bosses do hire and promote people who resemble them. They not only favour people with similar backgrounds and college and club affiliations, they also prefer people who share the same personal qualities – from work ethic to sensitivity to other people to the way they dress and talk.

On the other hand, there are clever bosses who appreciate the need for more people who complement rather than duplicate them. A company that only promotes clones is a company with a dull, predictable future.

Thus, if you're counting on your resemblance to the boss to give you a career boost, you may be in for a surprise. Those individuals who march to a slightly different tune may already be a step or two ahead of you.

Fallacy no. 4. Past performance is always rewarded

This is the cruellest fallacy because superior performance should be rewarded. I don't think it's because most bosses and organizations are stupid or unfair. If a company doesn't promote its top performers, it's hurting itself too.

But circumstances can confuse the issue. I know I've sometimes delayed promoting worthy people because they were too valuable to remove from their current position. I've also seen people at other companies promoted into new spots largely because they were available (for example, their division was merged with another or their primary project was cancelled).

Neither scenario is fair. But if you don't factor such circumstances into your chances for promotion, you're overestimating your odds for success.

Fallacy no. 5. All promotions are good

Not true.

Accepting a promotion to a job that doesn't suit your abilities is not good.

Neither is moving up to spot where you clash with your new colleagues.

Neither is taking a loftier position where all your predecessors have failed. (What makes you think you'll break the mould? What are you doing to change the job so you don't fail?)

Neither is taking a corner-office job that completely removes you from day-to-day hands-on contact with your clients and competitors. Eventually, you lose your edge.

I could go on, but you get the point. With promotions it's wise to remember the maxim: when the gods want to punish us, they grant our wishes.

DON'T BE DEMOTIONALLY CHALLENGED

Without a doubt, getting fired is the biggest shock in business. Whether you see it coming or it's a total surprise. I don't know anybody who truly believes it will happen to them – until it does.

The good news about getting fired, though, is that it's not the worst thing that can happen to you in business.

The worst thing is a demotion.

Getting fired is definitive and final. It leaves you no options. It forces you to act.

A demotion, on the other hand, is neither final or definitive. It's paralysing. If getting fired is hell, a demotion is purgatory. It leaves you twisting in the wind, a little angry and confused about your newly diminished role yet also grateful that you still have a job.

A demotion appears in many guises. Whether you believe it or not, if you've been pushed down a rung on the corporate ladder, or if your pay has been frozen while everyone else has received a raise, or if a client has assigned part of his business to someone else, or if you've been forced to accept a pay cut, you've been demoted.

A lot of people – I call them the 'demotionally impaired' – have trouble accepting or appreciating that they've been demoted. The shock is so painful that they automatically go into denial. They tell themselves that they still have a job and steady pay cheque. They still have their dignity and their friends at work. They come up with euphemisms to explain or excuse the hiccup in their career. Most often, they blame it on a structural change at their company, for example, a management shakeup in which they were betting on the wrong party and lost. They also tend to look around them to convince themselves they aren't alone. Other people have been demoted too.

While this sort of denial may bring temporary relief, in the long run it's not good.

What demotees fail to see, of course, is that they've taken a career hit and they're leaking water. If they don't do something to repair the damage, they'll eventually sink. In my experience, no one recovers from a demotion by denying it and not doing anything about it.

For most people, the immediate response to a demotion is to dust off their résumé and start looking for a new job. In their minds, their employer has just slapped them in their faces, insulted them, told them that their performance has been found lacking, and that they should step aside for better people to take their places.

That's a logical emotional reaction to demotion. But as an employer who has demoted people over the years, I'm not sure it's the response I'm trying to elicit. My goal is not to force them to work elsewhere (if that's what I wanted, I would have fired them). My goal is to get them to work better.

A lot of people miss this, ironically, because they have trouble dealing with the humiliation and loss of face that comes with demotion. I say ironic because loss of face is one thing that doesn't matter in a demotion, and yet it's the hardest part for many people to overcome. They think that everybody knows they've been demoted, that they're walking around with a big D on their chest. That's rarely the case. Demotions are not public floggings (or at least they shouldn't be). In my experience, they're invariably done privately and quietly. It's just between employer and employee. As I say, in many cases, the employee doesn't fully realize the demotion. If the employee doesn't know, what chance do people inside or outside of the company have of knowing?

If an employee can get over the loss-of-face issue, a demotion can turn into a valuable wake-up call. The strategy is actually quite simple.

The first step is ride it out. In other words, don't do anything rash or emotional. Don't quit. Don't lash out at the boss. Don't fire off your résumés to a dozen companies, announcing you are unhappy and available. Most important, don't cry about it to anyone who'll listen. Keep it to yourself. The fewer people know that you've lost a stripe or two, the more freedom you'll have to manoeuvre to regain them.

Step two requires a little self-effacement. It means admitting you were wrong. It also means admitting your boss is right. When bosses demote people, they're not telling them they're worthless. They're merely telling the employee in the most convincing way they know that he or she is lacking in one or more areas. Until these deficiencies are corrected, the employee's value is diminished. Hence, the loss of pay or status or power.

Step three is the simplest of all. Once you identify what went wrong, fix it.

This is the strategy followed by one of our now-more-successful executives when he was demoted several years ago. After a decade of rising steadily in our company, he had become distracted and unproductive. His personal life was a mess. His motivation was at rock bottom. He would show up at the office at odd and unpredictable hours. Yet he was smart, talented, and, despite his infuriating work habits, I liked him. He was worth reclaiming. So we cut his pay in half.

Not surprisingly, this depressed him. He was ready to quit until, unbeknownst to me, wiser heads in the company counselled him to stick it out. This was a temporary setback, they said. If you straighten yourself out, you'll get back to your old pay level within a year – which is exactly what happened.

A lot of people say that getting fired – by a boss, a client, or a customer – is the best thing that can happen to anyone – once. (I don't recommend making a habit of it.) It tests your mettle and ingenuity. It can teach you who your real friends are. It often gives you a lift out of a career rut. If you play it correctly, a demotion can achieve the same effect.

STAY IN THE GAME WHEN YOU'VE BEEN DISMISSED OR PASSED OVER

Some years ago a group of us gathered to give comfort and aid to a friend who had been unexpectedly dismissed from his senior position at an American corporation. The friend, who had spent his entire career at the company, was depressed and vulnerable and needed our thoughts on what to do next.

A lawyer in our group said he should fight for the best severance package. If he was taken care of financially, the next step wouldn't matter as much.

Someone else suggested that he should take a few months off to regroup and consider his options.

Still another said that he should get out of his industry altogether. His executive skills were easily transferable to other fields and it would give him a fresh start.

I wasn't as confident with my advice. The best I could come up with was that whatever course he chose, the first step after the dismissal was the most important. It would determine everything that followed and there would be no turning back, no second chances. If he wanted to leave the industry, he should make a clean break and not hope secretly that he would someday come back triumphant. That decision, in turn, would decide whether his severance negotiation would be hostile or amicable. That, in turn, would determine his finances and impact on whether he needed a job immediately or could afford a sabbatical. The key, though, was the first decision.

Since that time I've become considerably more sure of how to handle a career setback such as a surprise dismissal. Unless someone's career was at a standstill in a dead-end field, I always advise people to stay in the field they know.

In 1990, ABC Sports opted not to renew its golf analyst contract with our longtime client, Dave Marr. The network was cutting back and Marr, a former PGA champion and 20-year veteran in the broadcast booth, was deemed expendable. I sat down with Marr in Jamaica at year's end to review his options. He was a droll man, with an endless supply of Texas homilies, and he knew golf. He could write a book, go on the lecture circuit, produce golf instructionals. But he really enjoyed broadcasting. Unfortunately, there were only a finite number of analyst spots on American television and they were all taken.

Marr had two things going for him. He was good and he wanted to work. In a way, that made my job simple. I told him he should take an analyst's job with the BBC. The money wouldn't be as good as what he was used to from an American network. But the critical factor was to stay in the arena.

The BBC was prestigious. Working there would in no way be a loss of professional status.

More importantly, the BBC covered all the major golf championships. This meant that Marr would be present and highly visible at all the big gatherings of the golf community. This would keep people aware of him. They would see that he was alive and well and still performing his profession. After that, who knows? Change is a constant in business, especially in sports television. Broadcasting arrangements undergo realignment. Contracts expire. New television channels appear. People switch jobs. The key was to stay in the arena in a visible, productive capacity.

Marr followed our advice and within four years was not only working regularly at the BBC but was also back on American television with NBC and Turner Broadcasting.

When a career stutters, the smart move is to construct a situation where you stay in the arena, even if you have to swallow your pride on the money. If you do your job well, the money will ultimately take care of itself.

Of course, some career hiccups are so filled with high emotion that it's almost impossible to think straight let alone see the wisdom in staying in the game.

Of all the career crises, perhaps the worst is losing out in a race with one or two colleagues for a promotion at your company. It's worse than getting fired. At least with getting fired, you know what you have to do: find a new job. Losing a promotion leaves you twisting in the wind, not devastated by unemployment but slightly confused about your next move.

There are generally three responses to such a career setback: get mad, get even, or get better.

Getting mad usually means suffering the slight in silence as you slowly twist yourself into a bitter, unproductive employee. It's not a mature response, but it's not surprising under the circumstances. Getting mad is usually Step One in an endgame that leads to your departure.

Getting even usually means jumping ship to a competitor. If you can channel that desire for revenge into your new job, this response can be a great career move. 'I'll show them they were wrong' can be a powerful motivating force.

Getting better is a little more complicated. For one thing, it means swallowing your bitterness. It means accepting the fact that your bosses don't have as high an opinion of you as you do. It calls for a candid re-assessment of your track record. But most important, it means trusting your instincts and staying at the company, no matter how many friends are telling you that you got the shaft and you have to get out.

The reason is obvious but it escapes many people: if you don't stay at the company, you won't be around to reap the rewards when the bosses realize they were wrong to pass you over.

A friend made this mistake some years ago. He was the No. 2 man in his division and appeared to be the logical successor when the No. 1 spot opened up. But the parent company's directors passed him over and chose the No. 3 man instead. There were several reasons for this, not the least of which was that the No. 3 man had lobbied long and hard for the job, something my friend refused to do.

Although I was hardly an objective observer, I remember thinking that the directors had chosen the wrong man. I guess my friend thought so too, because he left the company shortly thereafter.

A few years later I happened to meet the parent company's chairman, the man who had made the fateful decision that derailed my friend's career. I casually mentioned my friend's name, in an effort to make small talk and establish areas that we had in common.

The chairman looked stricken for a moment and then said, 'Passing him over for the top spot is probably the biggest mistake I ever made. The fellow we chose is a total washout.'

I suppose it was gratifying to hear the chairman admit that he had misjudged my friend's potential. But I was saddened because I realized that nothing good would ever come of this admission. My friend was no longer at the company. There was no remedy for the injustice that had happened to him, because he was no longer in the game.

EVEN THE MOST TARNISHED REPUTATION CAN BE SAVED

Several executives and I were debating the concept of reputation in business. We all agreed that a sterling reputation was probably the most valuable intangible in business. But when it came to the question of whether you could ever recover from losing a good reputation, that's when we parted ways.

The other executives firmly believed that, once lost, a good reputation can never be totally reclaimed.

If you do something larcenous that brands you as slippery or crooked, you'll always have that cloud hanging over your head.

If it becomes widely known that you betrayed a confidence, that image of you as someone who can't keep a secret spreads quickly and sticks. No matter how much you protest that you've learned your lesson, people will always be wary of sharing their secrets with you – because they can't tell if you've changed. Keeping a confidence is not an overt act; it's a virtuous deed accomplished only when you do nothing. And people don't pay attention to your acts of omission; they only notice the sins you commit.

Even on small matters such as a reputation for always being late, these executives believed that it was impossible to turn that image around. No matter how punctual you become, people will always remember the times you kept them waiting. Your punctuality now can never erase your tardiness then.

I did not agree. I don't think these executives appreciated how elastic and manipulable a reputation is. In my experience, there are three phases of a reputation:

1. when you establish it
2. when you maintain it
3. when you need to save it

In a perfect world, our reputations would never go beyond phase two. But people get careless or stupid in these two phases. They don't pay attention, and suddenly they discover that, fairly or not, their hard-earned reputation is in jeopardy. That's when they find themselves in phase three. The good news, however, is that the same methods that helped you gain a reputation work just as well in regaining it once it's lost.

To appreciate this, you need to take a closer look at the critical stages in a reputation.

1. Establish it

In broad terms, the reputation you establish at the beginning of a career is defined by what you say yes to.

Young people don't begin their careers knowing what they want their reputation to be. They let it evolve and, if they're smart, they do so by playing to their strengths. They only say yes to projects and opportunities that showcase their special talents.

We see this all the time in our classical music division. Let's say we discover a young piano virtuoso who dazzles people playing Beethoven. If the pianist and we as his managers are properly focused on establishing a distinct and strong reputation for him, we will insist that for the first year or two his concert schedule has him going around the world playing pretty much the same Beethoven programme in every city. We want the pianist playing to his strengths. The audience in Vienna doesn't know that he played the same pieces two nights before in Paris or Boston. All they know is that it is some of the finest Beethoven they've ever heard. That's how reputations are established – by saying yes to what you're really good at.

It's no different in the workplace. An employee gravitates to what interests him at first, and what interests people is what they love or can do really well (these are often one and the same). That's what determines what company you choose to work for, what division within that company, and what specific assignments you agree to tackle. Saying yes to the right assignments is how you establish a solid reputation. Very quickly, people begin to perceive you as someone who can get things done or has a unique expertise in an important niche. Saying yes to the wrong assignments, where you don't have the opportunity to shine, is how you stall that process.

2. Maintain it

If establishing a reputation is defined by what you say yes to, then maintaining it is all about what you say no to. Once you establish who you are and what you stand for, you don't want to stray too far from that image, particularly into areas where you are not performing at your customary high level. It confuses people. Suddenly, they're thinking, 'Maybe he isn't as good as we thought.' Make this mistake several times and you can wipe out your reputation.

Again, the classical music model is instructive here. The opera world is filled with stories of young singers with fresh, beautiful voices who make spectacular debuts in the world's opera capitals singing their three or four signature roles that are guaranteed to knock people off their feet. That's how young singers get noticed: singing to their strengths. But then something happens: impresarios and conductors, always in search of the next big voice, tempt the promising singer with fat contracts to sing new roles in repertory that may not always be right for them. The temptation is often hard to resist. But in the case of singers, a wrong choice not only damages their reputation, it can destroy their voice. With few exceptions, the successful enduring operatic careers like those of the tenor Luciano Pavarotti, the soprano Kiri Te Kanawa – belong to the singers who are most disciplined about saying no. They know their vocal limitations and they enjoy their reputation for being able to deliver the goods. They don't say yes to anything that will tarnish either.

This doesn't mean that the great singers don't tackle new roles that require them to stretch a little. The great ones do this regularly. But when they try something daring, they usually do it in a smaller city, slightly out of the public eye. If the experiment doesn't work out, they don't repeat the mistake. If it's a success, they move on to the major venues. That, too, is how you maintain a reputation: take your risks where no one can see you fail.

3. Save it

To save a lost reputation, you must first determine how it was lost.

Not long ago we started doing business with a company whose founder had just returned from a five-year prison term for tax fraud. As blows to reputations go, prison time for cheating on your taxes is one of the tougher ones to recover from.

The founder's son was called in to try to save the family business, a chain of automotive supply stores. I asked him how his father's catastrophic downfall had affected the business.

'It hurt us at first,' he said. 'Sales were down 30 per cent the first six months I was in charge. But then they started coming back. I learned something from that. Customers needed us and they were willing to buy from us because they didn't think our company was corrupt. It wasn't our corporate reputation that was sullied. It was my family's reputation that took the hit. My family's name, not our company image, needed rehabilitation.

'So, I did some drastic things. I removed any sign of my father from our stores and offices. It hurt personally, like I was abandoning him, but it had to be done. Then I put myself in our advertising. If it's a family business, people ought to see which member of the family is running the show now.

'But the most important thing is I never deny or try to hide what my father did. I don't revel in it, but I always acknowledge it. Even five years later, I can still see it in people's eyes when they're negotiating with me. They're wondering if I'm going to pull a fast one on them. So I go out of my way to be above reproach. If there's any grey area, I concede the point in the other side's favour. I've learned that people are incredibly forgiving if they see you're trying. And what I'm trying to do is get back to the basics of good, honest business that established our reputation in the first place. It takes time, but it's working.'

If a family's reputation can recover from financial fraud, then any reputation can be saved.

A CRISIS DOESN'T END UNTIL YOU LEARN FROM IT

You learn a lot about people by how they deal with a catastrophe. Some folks panic and make foolish decisions. Some are paralysed by the calamity and do nothing to respond to it. Still others deny it, hoping that ignoring the problem will make it disappear.

Then, of course, there are the people who are somehow enlarged by a crisis. They take a disastrous turn of events as a personal challenge. Like a champion athlete who performs at his or her best in the big games, they become sharper, calmer, more alert, and more decisive.

Where do these people come from? What separates them from the rest of the crowd?

Examine them closely and one fact emerges: they didn't get that way overnight. If you ask them, they'll tell you that they've faced many crises in their careers and they weren't always as composed in the beginning. To them, each crisis was not only a challenge but also a learning experience, a chance to get slightly better and not repeat past mistakes.

These people know that there are two phases in every crisis: the one where you manage it and the other where you learn from it. To succeed you have to do both.

A celebrated athlete I know has amassed a considerable fortune since his playing days ended in 1991. But I recalled a time in the early 1980s, at the height of his career, when he had nearly lost everything he had worked for. I was curious not only about how he had recovered from this calamity, but how he had built upon it and multiplied his net worth.

He said that being nearly wiped out was, in a perverse way, one of the best things that ever happened to him. He made three mistakes, but he dealt with them and learned from them.

His first mistake was entrusting all his finances to a so-called friend who was out of his league with large investments.

His second mistake was not paying attention to what his financial manager was doing. The net result was that this athlete had a large part of his assets tied up in risky real-estate schemes where the return on investment could be considerable but was nowhere near as safe and predictable as Treasury bills or bonds.

His third mistake was that he panicked. When the real-estate market collapsed, he saw his $15 million net worth reduced on paper to $3 million. So he fired his manager (a smart move) and cashed out his holdings at 20 cents on the dollar (not a smart move). He figured it was better to retain something than lose everything. In hindsight, of course, he cashed out too soon. His real-estate holdings eventually recovered. If he had held on, he would have actually made a profit on his investments.

Yet this great athlete considered the calamity as necessary and pivotal – because he dealt with it and learned from it.

For one thing, it made him more aggressive about his salary. He had always been one of the two or three highest-paid athletes in his sport. The catastrophic loss of $12 million altered his negotiating posture at contract renewal. He became adamant about being the highest paid athlete, and for several years his contracts set eye-popping standards.

It also forced him to hire better financial advisers and taught him to keep a closer eye on his interests.

He also learned about the pernicious effects of selling out at rock bottom. In later years, particularly during the stock market collapse of 1987 and a couple of rough years in the early 90s, he had the wisdom not to panic when his paper wealth dropped 40 percent. He had the experience and confidence that his investment strategy was sound and that his net worth would recover. And so it did.

In hindsight, this athlete's behaviour in a crisis sounds wise, mature, and obvious. We would all respond similarly, wouldn't we?

I'm sceptical.

Consider, for example, a crisis that I'm very familiar with in our business: getting fired by a client.

It's interesting to see how people in our company respond when they suddenly lose a client. By the standards outlined above, you'd think they would deal with it and learn from it. But it doesn't always play out that way.

For one thing, people have funny ways of dealing with the loss. Their initial response is denial. They try to save face via spin control. They tell people that the client wasn't really that valuable and that they were glad to see him go, that they were on the verge of firing him before he fired us.

Then panic sets in, and they realize they have to make up the financial shortfall by finding one or two new clients. Sometimes this desperate attempt to replace lost revenue results in brilliant recruiting of new clients; other times the results are less brilliant.

I guess that qualifies as confronting a crisis and managing it.

What's interesting to me, though, is how rarely people respond to a client loss by trying to get the client back. To me, that is the most calm, mature, and logical response. Yet it's amazing how often people take a client defection lying down. It never occurs to them to call up the client and find out what went wrong and what they can do to remedy the situation.

That would be dealing with a crisis and learning from it. But it's the two-step move that many people fail to make.

A few years ago one of our most promising tennis clients defected to a rival firm. The executive handling the athlete was devastated by this defection. But experience has taught me that athletes, especially the young ones, can be fickle. An athlete who is willing to leave one manager for another may be willing to leave again at a future date.

So I encouraged our executive to stay in touch with the player, to treat the defection as a business decision rather than a personal insult. The agent and player would be seeing each other dozens of times during the course of the year on the tennis tour. If our man talked to the player, he could learn why he left and what we could do to improve in his eyes – and bring him back into the fold. It was certainly a better strategy than sulking and avoiding the player.

It turned out that the player's main complaint was that our executive didn't return phone calls promptly. That's an interesting fact to learn, but it might not have come out if our man hadn't persisted in talking to his ex-client. It's also a flaw that's easy to correct. Two years later, the player came back to us.

That's why it pays to appreciate the two phases of a crisis. If you face a crisis but don't learn from it, you will not only fail to correct it but you will eventually face it again.

Rules for Dealmakers

IF YOUR CLIENT IS CHANGING, YOU SHOULD TOO

A friend who runs a successful financial advisory business was lamenting that one of his biggest accounts had started taking a large part of his business 'in house.' The client claimed that some of the service my friend provides could be done much more cheaply by people already on the client's payroll.

'If this trend continues,' my friend observed, 'I'll lose the business altogether. The challenge now is: how do I stop this disturbing trend?'

This is the age-old problem for anyone who provides a specialized service: over time, as the client watches you provide your unique service, the mystery of what you do begins to evaporate (or at least the client thinks it does). Eventually, it occurs to the client, 'Hey, this isn't brain surgery. Maybe I can save some money doing it myself?'

Unless you're a trained, accredited professional (like a doctor or lawyer), it's hard to avoid this development. People tend to underestimate the complexity of your job. They think it's simpler than you claim it is. It shouldn't take as much time as you say it does. And it doesn't require all that much brainpower. With that rationale in place, it isn't very long before your clients begin to believe they can duplicate your accomplishments without you.

You can combat this thinking by trying to maintain the aura of mystery around what you do for as long as possible. But I don't recommend this approach. More often than not, it annoys the client – because it requires that you shield the client from your activity on his or her behalf. In my experience, shutting out clients from their business or intentionally keeping them out of the loop is rarely impressive or ingratiating. More often than not, it makes them suspicious.

My experience suggests the opposite approach.

People who provide a personal service should go overboard to include clients in everything they do for them. This is especially true at the beginning of a relationship. Show them every document you write or receive on their behalf. Invite them to every meeting. Alert them to bulletins and rumours in your industry. Seek their opinion of matters that you would ordinarily consider too minor to bother a client with. If your service is truly unique, you won't need the artifice of mystery. You'll have something more valuable: the client's trust. When you have that, clients will literally tell you how much or how little they want to be involved. They'll give you permission to keep them out of the loop.

After that, of course, you have to deliver. In my experience, whatever field you're in, clients want three things (in descending order of importance):

First, they want *results*. They want to see a return on their investment, that you've put money in their pocket or improved the quality of their life.

In the absence of results, clients want *activity*. This is sometimes more important than results. Over the years we've had clients who know they are tough to sell. They know that landing a big endorsement deal for them is a long shot. That's why it's important to keep them in the loop of every call we make for them. They need to know that we are trying.

Finally, clients want *unconflicted advice*. They need to know that your advice is pure and untainted by any other business agenda. If there is a bias, it should be on their behalf, not against them.

If you can construct client relationships that accommodate these three needs, you'll never have clients wondering why they need you.

This advice may be a little late in the game in my friend's case. If the client is taking business in house, he's already wondering, 'Why do I need you?' and coming up with his own answers.

In that case, you need to rethink exactly what you are providing this client. Clients change over time, and so do their needs. You have to change with them – or risk losing them.

We've certainly seen this in our athlete management business. When an athlete comes to us at the start of his career, he needs a lot of things from us. Among other things, he needs our *negotiating skill*. We know our way around a sports contract; he doesn't. He needs our *contacts*. We know who's spending money in sports; he doesn't. He needs our *selling skills*. We can be proactive; a competitive athlete doesn't have the time to make sales calls. He also needs our *credibility*. We have a track record that says we'll deliver on our promises; he doesn't.

But that changes over time as the athlete becomes more successful. At some point, even the most commercially disinclined athletes become more comfortable with contracts, assemble their own Rolodex of contacts, and learn how to sell themselves. At that moment, as the athlete's mindset and sophistication is changing, the nature of the service we provide has to change too. In many cases, as the athletes' careers become more complicated, as the commercial distractions and temptations increase, our most valuable service is to help *simplify* their lives – to let them concentrate on their performance on the field, which is what has made them commercially attractive in the first place.

For example, in recent years we've endured some major defections in our golf division. Big names such as Nick Faldo, for whom we generated enormous incomes, decided they wanted more control over their business affairs. In Faldo's case, he hired away one of our executives to take our services 'in house.' I can't help noting that the move had a disastrous effect on Faldo whose game disappeared the moment he left us.

I'm not gloating over this. Actually, I'm chastising myself. If I had to do it over again, I might agree that, at this point in his well-established career, such a golfer (with five major championships on his résumé) doesn't need us to negotiate a better contract or open new doors. Simplifying careers is now the real service we provide. If it lets an athlete concentrate on his sport, I can't think of a more valuable service.

Learn from this. If your client is changing, you should change too.

WHAT'S YOUR TALKING-TO-LISTENING RATIO?

If you're like most people you probably think you're a better listener than you actually are. In fact, you think you are twice as good a listener as you really are. I know this because of a private experiment I conducted a few years ago.

I was intrigued by a sharp fall-off in our American salespeople's ability to close deals. So I devoted a good part of a month to accompanying them on their sales calls. I wanted to see whether they were doing something wrong or if it was simply a down cycle in the marketplace.

I paid close attention to our salespeople's ability to listen. I literally timed how much of each meeting they spent talking and how much time they allowed the prospect to talk. Afterwards, while the meeting was fresh in each salesperson's mind, I'd ask them, 'What percentage of that 60–minute sales call do you think you spent talking?'

With a consistency that was almost shocking, each salesperson underestimated the number of minutes he or she spent talking and, conversely, overestimated the time he or she spent listening. If I timed one fellow talking for 20 minutes, he would guess that he had spoken for ten minutes. If I asked how much listening he thought he did, he would estimate 40 minutes when it was actually 20. No matter who I asked during my month-long experiment, the disparity was always a two-to-one ratio. Our salespeople always thought they listened twice as much and talked half as long as they actually did.

It got to the point where I could actually write down their answers on a slip of paper beforehand and show them that I knew what they were going to say. I wanted to impress upon them that all of us can do a better job listening. And proving to them that their talking-to-listening ratio was consistently out of whack by a factor of 2-to-1 drove the point home forcefully.

The oddest thing about listening is how easy it is to do. It doesn't take any brainpower or physical exertion to sit in a chair and keep your ears open. And yet, if my highly non-scientific experiment is any indicator, listening is literally the toughest thing for most of us to do.

It doesn't have to be that way if you follow some basic rules.

1. Know your talk-to-listen ratio

Before you can become a better listener, you have to appreciate how bad you currently are at listening. So do what I did: time how much you talk and listen in a series of meetings. That will tell you your talk-to-listen ratio. If it's anything greater than 1:1 – that is, if you're talking more than you're listening – you surely have some improving to do.

2. Ask more questions

This should be obvious. Asking questions forces the other side to speak (and simultaneously forces you to be silent). So, the simple solution is, remind yourself to be interested in other people and ask them to talk about themselves.

But a lot of people don't make it easy for you. Let's face it, there will be times when you will find yourself across the desk from an important person who, at that particular moment in time, doesn't sound very interesting. Maybe the topic is dull. Maybe the two of you have nothing in common. Perhaps you're both tired or distracted. Whatever the reason, sparks aren't flying between you.

In moments like these, it's easy to forget your talk-to-listen ratio and attempt to take over the dialogue – if only to keep yourself awake. Wrong move.

It's much smarter to change the subject.

I once met with the chief operating officer of a large media company with whom we had never done one penny of business. It was an eagerly anticipated meeting – for me and for him. But as we sat down to lunch, I could feel myself being dragged into the dullest of boilerplate conversations. As I have done thousands of times over the years, I explained (briefly) what our company does and then gently tossed the dialogue over to him to describe his corporate objectives. But the more he talked, the more depressed I became. Nothing that he said gave me any hope that we could ever work together. Our paths, at least as he described them, were too divergent.

The normal impulse in such dispiriting moments is to try to recapture control of the discussion. But I took a different tack. With the lofty corporate discussion going nowhere, I got personal. 'Do you like sports?' I asked.

It's not a question I normally ask, largely because I don't have to. I'm in the sports business. The people I meet tend to be in it. Our mutual interest in sports is a given. But this simple question induced a miraculous change in the man. Suddenly, he was describing his college athletic career, which was impressive, and his rapacious interest in all things athletic. It gave me a totally different picture of the man – and a dramatically improved view of how to do business with him.

It wouldn't have happened if I didn't keep my commitment to listening more.

3. Figure out the perfect ratio

There's no perfect ratio for talking *v.* listening. But you can always be sure that you will never harm your cause by talking less.

You see this all the time in job interviews. A candidate can spend the entire interview listening to his future employer talk, revealing virtually nothing about himself, and still make a highly positive impression. If you ask the interviewer how it went, he'll say, 'Great!' – because he did all the talking. If you ask the interviewee, he might not have the same take at first – because he did all the listening. But that impression will change if he gets the job – again, because he listened.

4. Behave as if you were on a talk show

One of our clients, the four-star chef Gray Kunz, was on *The Charlie Rose Show* not long ago with three other superstar chefs. He was brilliant and articulate and loquacious – so loquacious in fact that he came close to drowning out the other chefs and appearing like an overbearing egomaniac. But then he saved himself by making a self-deprecating remark about how much he was talking. Folding his arms across his chest and nodding to his guests, he said. 'I'm through. You talk now.'

It was a charming display of self-awareness and street smarts. I wish more people could do the same. I suspect there would be a lot more real communication occurring in all our meetings if every once in a while each of us sat back, folded our arms, and announced, 'I'm finished. It's your turn to talk.'

It would certainly improve the talking-to-listening ratio.

PEOPLE WILL LOVE YOUR PRODUCT IF YOU LET THEM SAMPLE IT

A few years ago a friend of mine who was running a thriving automotive services company got caught up in an auction to buy a small but promising company in a related business. At least six other companies were bidding. Knowing that the competition might get feverish, my friend asked to me advise him on strategy. I was supposed to watch from the sidelines, keep quiet, and raise my hand only if I thought the bidding was getting too rich. My friend knew that auctions inspire deal lust in even the most poised and rational of executives. I was the control valve on his sanity.

The bidding, which took place over several days, escalated rapidly to the point where only my friend and an arch-rival remained in the hunt with equivalent bids. The price tag was already at the absolute maximum that my friend was prepared to pay. But he was willing to continue bidding in case the other party backed out. Sensing this stalemate, the bankers handling the sale asked the two contenders to submit one final best bid in a sealed envelope. This gambit often inspires bidders to raise their offer dramatically. When people bid blindly, they tend to bid badly.

I advised my friend not to fall into this trap. Based on the value he had assigned to the company, he was already offering the most he wanted to pay. If he raised the bid and won, he would be overpaying and strapping his company with expenses that might hurt in other areas. If he lost, at least he would have the comfort of knowing that a competitor had over-paid. In my mind, he couldn't lose by submitting a sealed bid that was the same as his final open bid.

In the end, he took my advice – and lost the auction. The other side, in a desperate attempt to insure victory, had upped their offer by nearly 30 per cent.

This episode taught me something very interesting about bidding wars. The craziness and irrational behaviour doesn't only take place during the auction process. It lingers after the bidding has ended – when the losers lick their wounds

I had expected my friend to be relieved if not elated about the outcome. After all, he had averted a potentially ruinous deal and, at the same time, pushed a rival into it. He had walked up to the edge of foolish and irresponsible behaviour, and he had made the wiser choice. He should have been proud of himself and his business discipline.

Instead, he was dejected.

Successful people like to win. But the corollary is that they really hate to lose. And they will go to great and sometimes irrational lengths to avoid even the appearance of losing.

It is impossible to overestimate people's fear of losing and how dramatically this fear can alter any business situation. As a salesperson, if you can harness this power, you can sell almost anything.

Economists call this impulse 'loss aversion,' referring to the fact that most of us hate to admit or recognize a loss. Loss aversion is the reason that most managers will cling to a money-losing decision, even when all objective evidence indicates little if no chance of recouping the loss. They can't admit the mistake and so they continue throwing the proverbial good money after bad.

I see it all the time in my business routine. For example, the first time I invite a couple to be my guests at Wimbledon, they are delighted at the invitation. If I invite them the following year, they're grateful again. If I invite them a third year, I'm creating a pattern that can easily turn into an annual ritual. If I fail to invite them one year, they might reasonably wonder at the change in our relationship. An invitation that started out as my gesture of friendship has, through repetition, turned into their right.

They may also be stung at the loss of the tickets. After all, tickets to Wimbledon have one level of value if you've never been to Wimbledon and have no chance of going. They have a much greater value if you've been to Wimbledon, expect to go each year, and suddenly lose that privilege. That, too, is loss aversion.

It doesn't take a genius to see how this translates into more effective salesmanship. If you want people to value and buy your product or service, you cannot merely tell them about your product or service. You have to let them sample it, enjoy it – and then taken it away from them. Threatened with that sort of loss, people can behave irrationally and buy things they never previously thought they needed.

I saw this a couple of years ago when Lexus kindly loaned our company three of their top-of-the-line sedans for our use during the two weeks of the US Open tennis championships in New York City. One of our executives so thoroughly enjoyed driving the car that he refused to give it back at the end of two weeks. Instead, he bought it at virtually full price from the dealer who loaned it to us.

The executive could have walked into a Lexus dealership at any time, taken the car out for a test drive, and bought it. But he didn't. Until he sat in the car, he didn't even know he wanted one. And only when he was faced with the loss of the car was he impelled to buy. That is classic loss aversion in action.

Once you recognize this dynamic, you'll see it all the time in the marketplace. That's why so many merchants are willing to give customers 30–day-return guarantees on any merchandise. They know that once you get the merchandise home and use it, you won't want to part with it.

If a customer doesn't think he needs your product or service, don't waste time extolling its virtues. Let him use it. Then ask for it back.

TIME IN FRONT OF THE CUSTOMER IS THE BEST TIME OF ALL

Not long ago I desperately needed to talk to one of our New York sales executives. So I called his office a few minutes before noon.

'I'm sorry, Mr McCormack, he just stepped out for lunch,' said the executive's assistant.

'Where can I reach him?' I asked.

'I'm not sure,' said the assistant. 'He was joining one of his clients and then picking up a customer at her hotel and taking her to lunch. He didn't say which restaurant they would be going to. But I'm sure he'll be back by 2:30.'

At 2:30 I called again.

'He's not back yet,' said the assistant.

At 3:30 I called again.

'Still not back,' said the assistant.

'Well, can you have him call me when he gets in?' I asked, trying hard to hide my irritation with the executive's astonishingly haphazard work habits.

'Sure thing, Mr McCormack,' said the assistant. 'I'll have him call you the minute he returns.'

At 5:15 p.m., the executive finally returned my call.

After we discussed the reason for my original call, I couldn't resist asking the man if he enjoyed his five-hour lunch.

'As a matter of fact, I did,' he said. 'The woman just wrote a seven-figure cheque for our client, so we wanted to surprise her with lunch anywhere she wanted. She picked a fancy place that has a tasting menu that takes at least 3 hours to serve. Then we had to finish off with brandy and cigars. I know it's not very practical at lunch time. But the way I figure it, Mark, how often do you get to spend quality time with a customer and a major client. I spend so much of my trying to get meetings, travelling to meetings, arguing over contracts, servicing deals, and handling paperwork, that when I get a few hours to actually listen to a customer and do some persuading myself, I have to milk it for all its worth. Today was one of those days.'

The man painted such an enticing picture, I almost regretted that I couldn't have joined him for lunch. But he was also making a very important point about how salespeople manage their time.

Every salesperson needs time for prospecting. These are the hours spent making cold calls, chasing down leads, and lining up meetings. Much of this is a total waste of time, but it's absolutely necessary. Nothing else happens without it.

Every salesperson needs travel time. Unless you conduct all your business over the phone or by mail, you have to spend hours in a car or on a plane, putting your face in front of the customer.

Every salesperson needs persuasion time. These are the golden moments actually spent in the customer's presence – when you listen to the customer, learn his or her needs, build trust, and present your case. These are the hours when you actually sell.

Every salesperson needs contract time – time to dot the i's and cross the t's of the sales agreement.

Every salesperson needs service time – time to deliver the goods, fulfil promises, and follow up on customer concerns. This is the heart and soul of any sale. If you don't spend enough time on this, you'll be spending more and more of your time prospecting for new customers.

Finally, every salesperson needs back office time – time to take care of all the paperwork and niggling details that come with each sale.

No two salespeople divide their hours on these essential tasks in precisely the same proportion.

I've known salespeople – not very good ones – who spent the majority of their time prospecting; they were so busy chasing down leads that they forgot the purpose of selling is to close the deal.

Likewise, I've known fairly effective salespeople who, after making a sale, would spend the bulk of their time haggling over the contract. I can only wonder how much more income they would have generated if they had devoted their limited hours to persuading customers rather than arguing with them.

All the essential tasks of selling are important (that's why they're essential). But the third task on this list should be in a category all by itself.

The time you spend going one on one with a customer, learning about him or her and making your case, is the rarest time of all – and therefore the most precious. You'd be a fool not to take as much of it as you can get – even if it takes the entire afternoon.

THE BEST ROUTE IS THE MOST DIRECT ROUTE

There's a terrific scene between John Travolta and Gene Hackman in the movie version of Elmore Leonard's comic thriller, *Get Shorty*. Travolta plays a street-smart, extremely confident loan shark trying to switch careers into producing movies. Hackman is a fourth-rate producer trying to raise money for a hot movie script. Hackman thinks he has a chance of getting a big actor named Martin Wier to play the lead. He's encouraged because he showed the script to Wier's psychotherapist's personal trainer. (Got that?)

Travolta, bemused by the arcane ways of Hollywood, can't understand why Hackman is taking such a roundabout route to the star.

'That's the difference between you and me,' he tells Hackman. 'I say what I mean. If I want something from someone, I ask them straight out. If I want Martin Wier, I go get Martin Wier. I don't mess around with his shrink's trainer.'

I remembered this scene the other day when I received a letter inviting me to speak to a professional society in Cleveland (where our company is headquartered). The letter was originally addressed not to me but to one of our senior executives in Cleveland. The executive passed it on to me with a note saying, 'I have no idea why he wrote to me instead of you.'

I thought the same thing.

But the incident points up a common practice in selling today: people are afraid to be direct.

They're afraid to announce their intentions and say what they want from the customer. I can understand this. Salespeople don't want to seem to be too pushy. They'd rather let the customer take his time making a decision than press too hard and too soon for the order. After all, the customer may be turned off by this hard-sell approach.

Salespeople are also afraid to approach the customer directly. They prefer to use third-party intermediaries, especially if these intermediaries have a better relationship with the customer.

Again, I can understand this. If you are totally unknown to a prospect, there's nothing wrong with leveraging someone else's credibility to get your foot in the door. Having someone else vouch for you is a legitimate time-honoured sales technique. It's also a great buffer and ego protector.

After all, if the customer doesn't buy into your idea, he's not just rejecting you; he's rejecting you and the third-party. It's nice to share the pain.

But salespeople are doing themselves a big disservice if they rely too heavily on the indirect approach. Given the choice between approaching a customer directly or indirectly, the former is always the better choice.

For one thing, the direct approach eliminates confusion at both the seller's and the buyer's end.

If you go straight to the decision maker, it's just the two of you. You don't have to worry about subordinates and their conflicting agendas which may derail your deal.

More importantly, the direct approach is refreshingly clear to the buyer. I know if someone approaches me through intermediaries, I always wonder why he's doing that. Is he insecure? Is he bogus in some way that I can't see? Is he illegitimately borrowing the third party's credibility? And what's in it for the third party? If I say yes, who am I saying yes to? The seller or the third party?

The direct approach also simplifies the final terms of a sale. When you use other people to contact a customer, you are, in effect, inviting these people to participate in your deal. If you succeed, they will usually want a finder's fee or a commission or a permanent piece of the action. In my experience, adding this third element to a transaction, no matter how effectively it may smooth your path at the start, rarely works as smoothly at the close. More people in the mix means more issues. More issues always means more risk that the deal will blow up.

If that doesn't convince you, consider how much time you can save by being more direct. Masking your intentions and hiding behind others is time-consuming. Before you can sell to the customer, you have to convince a friend to help you. For every meeting where you're speaking directly to the customer, there's usually two or three behind-the-scenes meetings to get you there. That's not efficient. If salespeople spent as much time calling on decision-makers as they do constructing circuitous routes to reach them, we would all profit handsomely from the move.

It's not tough to figure out why the indirect approach became so popular. For decades, part of being a salesperson meant learning to deal with the accumulated and often maddening layers of management in corporate America. Closing deals in this bureaucratic environment often meant developing finesse moves that either sidestepped the bureaucracy or used it to your advantage. The clever, circuitous approach was one of those finesse moves.

But it should be obvious to anyone that the last 15 years have been an era for eliminating layers of bureaucracy. Isn't it time to adapt our sales approach to this new lean environment?

NO ONE LIKES SURPRISES

Being direct is an even greater virtue once you actually get in front of the customer.

How easy life would be if at the beginning of every sale both buyer and seller would put all their cards out on the table. The seller would announce. 'Here's what I want to sell and how much I want to make on it.' The buyer would say, 'Here's what I want and what I'm willing to spend.' Taking that element of suspense out of the process would surely make a salesperson's life less dramatic – fewer highs for sure, but also fewer lows – and probably more productive.

Unfortunately, it doesn't play out that way too often. Customers rarely tip their hand, and salespeople, perhaps in response, rely heavily on the element of surprise. They want to trick or trap the customer into revealing his hand.

I can understand why customers play it close to the vest. They're afraid they'll get taken to the cleaners by a slick salesperson otherwise.

But I can't understand why salespeople like the element of surprise. Customers don't buy when they think they've been tricked or manipulated into a decision. Selling doesn't work that way. In any sale, there's rarely that one high-impact moment when the salesperson says or does something so miraculous that the customer shouts 'Eureka!' and hands over his money. The best salespeople know they have to do a lot of small simple things that have an impact when taken together.

A few years ago an entrepreneur I know was being importuned by several investment banks to take his company public. After the various firms came around to 'kick the tyres,' two finalists emerged. On the face of it, the two firms were identical. They were both top-shelf firms of indisputable prestige and ability. Their people were smart and polished. They were in the same ballpark on the money they would raise and the fees they would rake in. So the decision really boiled down to who had the most convincing presentation and sales pitch.

What clinched it for one firm over the other was the element of surprise or, more accurately, the absence of surprise.

At the final meeting, the losing firm made the grave error of bringing in their rainmaker chairman. It was the first time my friend had met this wealthy and powerful financier, who was apparently there to close the deal by giving a stirring speech about capitalism and greatness. This speech was a proven hit; it had inspired many other entrepreneurs to sign on the dotted line. Unfortunately, the entire effect was lost on my friend, who didn't like new faces and last-minute surprises.

Instead, he went with the other firm precisely because they were steady rather than dramatic. As he explained it, 'They were always on time for meetings. They never cancelled an appointment. They always returned my phone calls. Their reports were meticulous. They treated my staff with the same deference they showed me. They were confident but not arrogant. They were willing to say "I don't know" when they didn't know something.'

None of these reasons alone was enough to tip the scale in their favour in this entrepreneur's mind, but taken together they added up to a lot more than one surprise appearance and a dramatic speech.

The lesson here should be obvious to any salesperson. All things being equal, the salesperson who consistently executes all the small details well has a much better chance of closing the deal than the salesperson who relies on one big statement or gesture.

You wouldn't be taken in by someone like that. Why would you expect your customers to fall for it from you?

YOU CAN'T GET YOUR PRODUCT ON THE SHELF UNTIL YOU KNOW WHAT YOU'RE REPLACING

When I started selling sports marketing ideas to corporate customers, it didn't take me long to develop a list of reasons that prospects didn't want to buy from me. They had all sorts of euphemisms and polite language to decline my invitation to give me their money, but basically their reasons were:

- They didn't have the budget.
- They didn't have the authority.
- They didn't have the guts to make a decision.
- They didn't have the brains to understand my proposal.
- They didn't like the idea.
- They didn't like me.
- My proposal was bad.

It didn't matter what idea I was pitching or who the prospect was, if there was a 'no' in my near future, the reason for it always fell into one of these categories. These selling conditions remained unchanged for years.

More recently, however, I've noticed that customers have found a new reason to say no: they don't have the shelf space.

I first noticed this about ten years ago when an entrepreneur I know started up a fat-free cookie business. Working in her kitchen at home, the entrepreneur's wife had developed a fat-free chocolate brownie that tasted remarkably close to the real high-calorie thing. (This couple were pioneers of the fat-free phenomenon.) They made all the right moves. They found a bakery to mass-manufacture the brownie. They tested it among their friends and neighbours (and got unanimous thumbs up for the brownie's taste). They designed smart-looking packaging that somehow made the brownie look like both a gourmet treat and a diet item.

It was the husband's job to get the cookie into stores. His first sales call was to a neighbour who was the head buyer of a local supermarket chain. He brought along samples for the man to taste, showed him the packaging and advertising plans, explained his pricing strategy. The buyer bit into the brownie and smiled. 'This is remarkable,' he said.

The entrepreneur smiled too, believing he was about to write his first order on his first sales call.

'I have one question for you,' said the buyer. 'Which cookie should I take off my shelves to put your brownie on?'

'I don't understand,' said the entrepreneur. 'Are you telling me you don't have room on your shelves?'

'I'm telling you that we sell 5000 cases of Oreos a week in our stores. If I replace Oreos with your brownies, are you going to sell better than Oreos?'

The question surprised the entrepreneur. This was America, the land of endless bounty, where every supermarket stocks 14 different brands of detergent (all of them exactly alike) and ten brands of ice cream! Was this buyer telling him that he couldn't find room for a breakthrough product like his fat-free brownie?

In fact, the buyer was. In a world where the customer may like your product, understand why he needs it and what it can do for him, and has the authority to place the order, salespeople now have to consider another reason customers say no. Let's call it the replacement factor. The logic goes like this: if I buy your product, I have to give up something else. Is your product going to perform better than whatever it's replacing?

As the cookie entrepreneur learned that day, if salespeople don't have an answer for this question nowadays, they're dead in the water. There are too many new products and services out in the marketplace chasing a limited amount of 'shelf space.' Salespeople have to know what they're replacing before they can sell the replacement. Or they have to convince the customer that replacement is not the issue.

That is what the entrepreneur did. After this sales call, he realized that he wasn't replacing Oreos. Oreos were caloric. His cookies weren't. Instead of replacing a famous brand, he was creating a new category: fat-free cookies. He eventually used this pitch to get his cookies into thousands of convenience stores across the United States and sold his company to Campbell Soup Co. for a multimillion-dollar sum. But that's another story.

In a way, I shouldn't be surprised by the power of the replacement factor in making buying decisions. We've been using it internally in our company for some time.

For example, a few years ago we considered acquiring a literary agency to represent authors in our UK operations. This would have been a departure from our bread-and-butter sports activities. We were far along in the negotiations when one of our senior executives said, 'Hold on.' He pointed out that once you added up the cost of new salaries, benefits, and overhead during the three years it would take the authors to write their books and generate some income, our investment in a new literary agency would be close to $1 million. 'Wouldn't that $1 million be put to better use in our golf and tennis divisions where we already have established businesses,' he asked. In effect, he was citing the replacement factor: we were taking money from good businesses and putting it into an untried venture, with no guarantee how well the replacement would do. Since no one could refute him, the deal died quickly thereafter.

Once you realize the replacement factor in the buying decision, you can steer yourself toward opportunities where replacement isn't an issue.

I'm sure that's a big reason our television operations around the world have been growing so rapidly in recent years. It wasn't so long ago that if you wanted to get a sports programme on television in the United States, you basically had three customers: the sports divisions of the three major networks. That was it. And the networks had a limited amount of air time available for sports programming (i.e.. they had limited 'shelf space'). If you wanted to get your idea on the air, you had to convince the networks to take an existing programme off the air. It wasn't always an easy sale.

Today in the US, there are four major networks and a half dozen thriving cable outlets as well, including ESPN and ESPN 2, all interested in buying sports programming. The 'shelf space' is not unlimited, but it's close enough. It certainly makes it easier to get sports programmes on the air.

We see the same dynamic in Europe and Asia, where dozens of new television channels have created a lot more 'shelf space' for our 'product line.'

If you sell for a living, the lesson here should be clear: If the buyer likes your product, likes you, has the budget and authority to buy, and still says no, you probably haven't properly addressed what you would be replacing. It's on the buyer's mind. It should also be on yours.

NOT ALL DEAL POINTS ARE CREATED EQUAL

A bunch of us were in a meeting with the marketing chief of a major apparel company to discuss an event he wanted to create. The marketing chief was looking for a company to find corporate sponsors for this event, and we were in the room to convince him to toss the assignment our way.

Ordinarily, we have to sell ourselves and our abilities in these meetings. We show our corporate video, brag about our past triumphs, tease the client with a few ideas that he hopefully has not heard before, and drop a hefty formal proposal on his lap which he can take back to his office and share with his colleagues.

But this meeting was different. The marketing chief knew our company well, so we didn't have to go through the routine of presenting our credentials. More important, we didn't have to go through a hard sell.

In fact, for the first 45 minutes of the meeting the marketing chief turned the tables on us. He was the one who showed up with an elaborate proposal describing the event. He was the one who had prepared a slick video about the project. He was the one outlining a week-by-week schedule for launching the event the following year. He was the one extolling the importance of this project to his company. For all intents and purposes, he was selling the concept to us.

After he finished his spiel, an amazing thing happened. One of our executives raised his hand to ask, 'Why are you launching this in February?'

The marketing chief appeared dumbfounded by the question. It was clear that there was no specific start date for the project. It would start when a partner like us jumped on board.

As for me, I couldn't believe my ears. The marketing chief had just spent 45 minutes successfully firing us up about the project. In effect, he was saying. 'Here it is, folks. If you like it as much as I do, the assignment is yours.'

At that precise moment (assuming it's a good idea and we want the business), the appropriate response would have been to congratulate the marketing chief on his brilliance and say, 'Let's get started.'

But instead one of our executives threw a wet blanket on the proceedings by bringing up a minor detail. I have no idea why he did this.

Whatever the reason, his response nearly derailed the meeting. When someone tries to elicit your enthusiasm for a big idea, your first move should be to see the big picture and embrace it.

Experienced salespeople and negotiators know this intuitively. They know that every transaction has a fragile momentum, especially at the start. If you want the transaction to happen, you have to be careful not to disturb that momentum.

That's certainly my negotiating philosophy. I've always thought that 90 per cent of the deal points in any transaction are decided in the first 10 per cent of the negotiation. You need the remaining 90 per cent of the time to settle the last 10 per cent of the details.

In my mind, only three considerations carry any weight in a negotiation:

- Do I like the other party?
- Does the other party like me?
- Do I like the idea?

If the answer is yes to one or two out of three, we've got a problem that may never be resolved by negotiating.

On the other hand, if the answer is yes to all three, we've resolved 90 per cent of the negotiation right there. Little if anything can disrupt the momentum of the deal. Even the thorniest details will be resolved – because there is a will to resolve them. More often than not, the last 10 per cent is routine and inevitable.

Unfortunately, a lot of people don't appreciate the simplicity of this approach. They give equal weight to every deal point in a negotiation. Negotiating with people like this is exhausting. You have to begin at square one on every point because every niggling detail is a potential dealbreaker.

Adopting this approach as your negotiating style is also exhausting. It means you can never be sure that you're in business with someone until the agreement is signed, sealed, and delivered. While you're sweating the details of one transaction, it's quite possible that another dozen opportunities have passed you by.

Remember this the next time you step into a negotiation. If you want to make something happen, you have to manage the momentum of the transaction – by embracing the concept and the other party with enthusiasm and letting them do the same to you.

On the other hand, if you want to kill the deal, all you have to do is bring up a minor detail.

LOVE OR LEAVE THE LOW-HANGING FRUIT

A senior sales executive at another company was moaning to me the other day about the high turnover among his sales force.

'I've tried everything,' he said, 'but it's difficult to keep people from walking. We pay as well as anyone. We have the perks, the healthy travel budgets, the sales conventions at fancy resorts, all the goodies that attract good salespeople. But we're in a cutthroat business. The weak salespeople get weeded out in a matter of months. The good ones stay for a few years, long enough to pick the low-hanging fruit off our tree. But when the going gets tough and they have to stretch a little to find new prospects, they walk. They think it will be easier at another company.'

I didn't have a ready-made answer for this executive, nor did I have any words that would make him feel better about his dilemma. Frankly, every business person who manages salespeople faces the same problem. It's human nature. Salespeople are always going to gravitate to the easy sales, the so-called 'low-hanging fruit.' If you give salespeople a quota, they'll take the path of least resistance to achieve it. Can you blame them?

After years of dealing with this, I'm convinced the fault lies not with salespeople but rather with their sales manager. After all, we're the ones who set the quotas and approve the salespeople's priority lists. We're the ones who let them pick off the low-hanging fruit.

The solution is obvious: redefine what low-hanging fruit is and make your salespeople want to call on these prospects. You don't have to do this with smoke and mirrors. If you're clever, you can make almost any prospect seem like an opportunity rather than a dead end.

In my mind, customers who are doing business with a competitor are the ripest fruit for plucking. They meet all the criteria for an ideal customer – except one. They know your business. They clearly have the need for your product or service. They have the budget. They have the desire and willingness to spend it. The only problem is they're not spending it with you.

Whatever the reasons for this – perhaps they don't know you exist, or they don't have a warm relationship with you, or they think you're over-priced – they can all be overcome. You can make a sales call to let them know who you are. You can do them a favour to warm them up. You can slash your prices to get your foot in the door.

It's the sales manager's job to make salespeople see the situation in this glass-half-full light. Under these circumstances, a manager who can't make salespeople fight among themselves to call on these ripe customers should be the one taking a walk.

Then there are the customers who are already buying from you.

In theory, they are the ideal customers. They have the need, the desire, the will, and the budget to spend – and they're already spending it with you!

But for reasons that continue to elude me, a lot of salespeople stop calling on these customers after the initial sale. Perhaps they pigeon-hole the customer into one purchasing niche; they don't think the customer would be interested in a totally different concept. Perhaps they think the customer has a finite budget, and that selling him something new will come at the expense of the initial sale. Perhaps it's the thrill of the hunt; once a salesperson has bagged an account, he needs new prey to chase.

Perhaps . . . but more likely, it's because selling a second and third time is hard work. It means plunging deeper and deeper into the customer's affairs (which takes time), learning the intricacies of his business (which takes mental effort), dealing with new people (which takes patience), and coming up with attractive solutions (which takes creativity). Time, effort, patience, and creativity are not the path of least resistance to a successful sale.

But all of these obstacles can be overcome by the simple fact that a customer who has bought from you once will probably buy from you again – and again, and again. A sales manager who doesn't remind – no, religiously hound – his team about this should also take a walk.

The most fascinating customers are the ones doing it themselves.

If you're selling any sort of personal service, your prospects have four options: They can 1) hire you, 2) hire someone else, 3) do it themselves, or 4) not do it at all. The third option intrigues me. It has all the potential to turn into low-hanging fruit.

After all, prospects who are doing it on their own clearly need your service. They just happen to think they can do it in house. As a salesperson, I'd rather deal with that hurdle than try to turn around a prospect who doesn't believe he needs any service at all. Yet a lot of salespeople see this as an overwhelming obstacle. They think that people doing it them-selves are cursed with Not Invented Here Syndrome.

We see this quite often in our sports-marketing business. A lot of well-heeled companies believe they can handle this type of activity – using sports events and star athletes to market their product or service – in-house. I understand why. Sport comes with a high fun quotient, more than you find in other businesses. If I were a marketing executive charged with creating a sports event or signing up a celebrated athlete as a spokesperson, I'd want to handle it all on my own too.

But as a sales manager, I see this as an opportunity. If we can't convince an organization with in-house sports marketing department that we can do the job with more panache and less cost, we have a bigger problem than finding new customers.

CUSTOMERS NEED EVEN MORE MANAGING
AFTER THE SALE

A fellow executive was complaining not long ago about his customers.

'I don't understand them anymore,' he said. 'In the old days, all you had to do was deliver what you promised at the price you quoted and on time. Now everyone wants *more*. More attention. More ingenuity. More surprises. They're never satisfied.'

I asked him, 'When your customers ask for more, do you try to give it to them?'

'Yes,' he said.

'When you give them more,' I asked, 'do you charge extra for it?'

'Of course,' he said.

'When you raise your prices,' I asked, 'do your customers continue paying?'

'So far, yes.'

I found it difficult to sympathize with the man's alleged problem. He had hit the customer jackpot and didn't know it. He had happy customers who were:

- loyal (they stuck with him rather than switch to a competitor),
- price tolerant (they didn't blink when he jacked up his prices); and
- forcing him to grow (they not only increased his business, they improved it).

I can't think of three better qualities in a customer. But I can see how business people turn these pluses into negatives. When a customer is constantly pushing you to do better, it's sometimes easier to focus on the push rather than the fact that the push moves you forward.

Customers wouldn't be customers if they weren't 'pushy'. It's their job to push for a better price, improved service, speedier delivery, and upgraded performance.

Likewise, it's a manager's job to remind people in the organization that their customers are not the source of their stress, frustrations, and failures. They are the source of their profits and growth. Here are three management techniques that jog my memory when I forget what a customer is worth.

1. Manage expectations

When a customer is unhappy, it's usually because of a gap between the customer's expectations and reality. The situation is hardly improved when you realize that customers are in a perpetual state of rising expectations. They always want more.

That's why some energy has to be devoted to managing the customer's expectations.

We see this all the time in our business with the sponsorship of sports events.

I remember the first year we put on the Johnnie Walker World Championship of Golf in Jamaica for United Distillers, the British parent of the Johnnie Walker Black Label brand of Scotch. The concept was an end-of-the-year event that featured the top 26 golfers in the world competing for what was at the time the biggest purse in golf. Although we loaded the field with all of the marquee names in the sport, the event was still a risky proposition. The weather could have been uncooperative and there was no guarantee that the most glamorous names would be at the top of the leader board on Sunday. A comparative no-name from the Australian tour could get hot for four days and run away from the pack, which would have been fine in sheer sporting terms but would probably have disappointed the sponsor.

Fortunately, the stars were in perfect alignment that weekend. Greg Norman and Nick Faldo, then ranked no.1 and no.2 in the world, went head to head on Sunday and finished tied for first after 72 holes. Faldo won in a sudden-death playoff. We could not have dreamed up a better finish if we had scripted it ourselves.

Our problem: what do we do for an encore?

Over the years, we've come to realize that a huge success in the first year of a sponsor's event is a double-edged sword. It's terrific because the event delivered more than we promised. The sponsor got a bonus. The bad news is that the sponsor expects the same result the following year. Unfortunately, you can't deliver that in sports. A golf sponsor doesn't always get a thrilling final-round showdown between two superstars.

In moments like these, managing expectations is as crucial as managing the event itself. We have to be there next to the customer in great years and not-so-great, pointing out the factors beyond our control, reminding the sponsor that 'It won't always be this great,' or if the situation warrants, 'Wait till next year.'

2. Manage your contacts with the customer

It doesn't seem possible that you can have too much contact with a customer. But at some point, overexposure to the customer works against you. The odds of offending the customer – by promising more than you can deliver or not knowing your facts – increase the more you are in the presence of the customer. If you've ever dealt with an overbearing salesperson in a store, you know the feeling. The salesperson seems helpful at first, but after a while, when the salesperson's chatter and charm wear thin, you'd rather be left alone.

After all, there are clear divisions between being out of touch with your customers, staying in touch with them, and touching them the wrong way.

When it comes to managing customer contacts, we can all learn from the great stage performers. They didn't overstay their welcome in front of their customers. They always left the audience begging for more. Salespeople should do the same.

3. Managing your apologies

Effective managers don't enjoy having unhappy customers, but they're smart enough to consider them as opportunities rather than disasters. An unhappy customer usually gives you the chance to correct the situation.

For example, a bad meal at a restaurant may sour me on that establishment forever. If I express my displeasure, some restaurateurs will ignore me or blame me or make excuses. But others are very adept at managing apologies. Some will send over a bottle of wine. Some will tear up the check. Some will invite me back as their guest. Whatever the gesture, it's smart to know how to manage your apologies. If it's true that it costs five times more to find a customer than to keep him, then that free bottle or free meal is the wisest investment a restaurant can make.

It's no different in any other business. If you have a system for keeping customers happy, you should also have a system for dealing with them when they're unhappy.

8

When You're in Charge

LOOK BEYOND THE RÉSUMÉ

The world would be a simpler place if we could hire the best people according to their résumés, references, track record, and the first interview. Unfortunately, none of these traditional criteria are as reliable as we would wish. Résumés are often little more than a chronology of an individual's work life; they conceal as much as they reveal. References are virtually worthless; no job candidate lists a reference who will speak ill of him or her. Track record can deceive too if it doesn't enumerate how much of the credit for a claimed success belongs to the job candidate and how much to others. First interviews, like first dates, display people on their absolute best behaviour; it's the second and third interviews where candidates reveal their true selves.

I speak from experience. I've considered and hired people who had the total package: impeccable résumé, impressive personal connections, a verifiable track record at a rival firm, and suave presentation skills at the job interview. Yet once they're inside our company and their mediocrity is obvious, it baffles me that I overlooked their deficiencies. It could be a simple lack of common sense or an inability to work with colleagues or sheer laziness. Whatever the flaw, I missed it. And there's no way I would have picked it up from résumé, references, track record, or first interview.

Of course, I know these criteria are severely flawed. Like most managers, I rely on gut instinct as much as anything else in my hiring decisions. For example, if a potential hire is overly concerned with salary at the first interview, my gut tells me something's not right. There's nothing wrong with wanting a hefty compensation package, but this grasping behaviour at the start spells trouble to me. No amount of money will ever satisfy this individual. He or she will leave us for the next bigger pay cheque that comes along.

It would be nice if we could formalize this sort of gut instinct. I know one CEO who judges candidates according to body parts. 'I look at a prospect's head, hands, and shoulders,' he says.

He's speaking metaphorically, of course. Head means raw intelligence. Hands refers to people's business skills. Shoulders refers to their ability to lead and accept responsibility.

As hiring metaphors go, these three are not bad. If you added a fourth body part – the heart – here's how it would work for me.

1. What's in their head?

Some bosses and companies – most famously Bill Gates at Microsoft – believe that intelligence is almost everything in a job candidate. Their logic: you can teach smart people anything, but you can't teach dumb people to be smart.

These companies formally test for intelligence with brainteasers such as 'Why are manhole covers round?' and guesstimates such as 'How many barbers are there in Chicago?' How candidates think their way to an answer is apparently important to high-tech firms and big-league consulting groups, where the job is all about problem-solving.

That's not important to me. Intelligence at our company is about making unusual connections between sports and everyday commerce. But it starts with an affinity for sports. Thus, in a job interview, I might camouflage a quiz by casually wondering who won the 1964 PGA Championship. A candidate who wasn't even born in 1964 but somehow knows the answer is Bobby Nichols has sufficient intelligence to impress me.

2. How good are they with their hands?

Good hands means good business skills. But it's not enough to hire people who have the skills for the job at hand. I'm looking for an extra skill or two – because the extra skills allow people and our business to grow.

For example, if I'm hiring an accountant, I don't merely want someone who's good enough to handle our accounting needs. I want an accountant who understands selling or who has strong presentation skills. Those additional skills will come in handy when we need to promote this accountant to another position (if we don't promote him or her, the hire can't be deemed a total success).

The way I see it, I'm not hiring an accountant who happens to be able to sell or get up in front of a crowd. I'm acquiring a future salesperson or executive who happens to be extremely disciplined with money.

3. How broad are their shoulders?

Broad shoulders means people who are not afraid to accept responsibility. This may be the fuzziest area for gauging new hires. After all, how can you assess someone's willingness to tackle everything you will eventually delegate to them.

It's not enough to ask them. People will always claim that they are eager to shoulder more work. But when push comes to shove, a lot of people fall short in this area. They want a clear and steady path of promotions. What they don't appreciate is that they often have to shoulder a lot of responsibilities before they officially get promoted into that position.

In my experience, the best way to assess people on this matter is to examine what they've done in the past. Have they tackled assignments that their colleagues avoided? Have they been working on side projects that don't show up in their job description or their résumé? Do they do more than they're asked to do? If so, their shoulders are broad enough for me.

4. How big is their heart?

Heart means passion for our business. But it has to be more than saying, 'I really want to work for you.' Given our heavy involvement in the sports business, we hear this all the time. Lots of young people really want to work for us.

What I'm talking about is not a passion for getting a foot in our door, but rather a passion to win at all costs once you're in the door. In basketball, coaches and fans always admire the players who are willing to throw their bodies after a loose ball. Those are the players with big heart.

That's the heart I'm looking for in my business.

This is an area where I really have to rely on my gut instinct. But if I'm right, the reward more than outweighs the risk.

DON'T LET COLLEAGUES TAKE EACH OTHER FOR GRANTED

A friend once tried an unusual experiment within the company he had founded. He had a junior executive within the company call a division chief to discuss a promising idea. The purpose of the experiment was to see how long it took the division chief to respond to a colleague.

The junior executive identified himself as a co-worker, but despite this seemingly insider edge, it took four calls to get any kind of a response from the chief – and that response was merely a return call from an assistant asking for something in writing.

Then the same junior executive (on his CEO's orders) called the division chief again with a promising idea. Only this time he identified himself as an employee from a wholly fictitious company. Within seconds the division chief was on the line, eager to hear about the idea.

When I asked my friend if he was surprised by the result, he calmly said, 'Not at all. That's why I did it. I've always thought it's easier for an outsider to make something happen at our company than someone who's already inside.'

I'm not surprised either. I suspect if you tried the same experiment at any other organization you would just as likely get the same result: employees who are more responsive to perfect strangers than to co-workers.

It's not hard to see why, given the nature of most organizations and the competitive forces at play.

The biggest reason why an outsider has a better chance of getting people's attention is that most people take their colleagues for granted. They know that a colleague will not disappear or go somewhere else with the idea. The colleague has no choice but to deal with them. They are the only game in town. And so they are just as likely to take their time getting back to a colleague as to respond instantly. It's a little like the dynamics of a family where siblings know that no matter how much they neglect or abuse each other their brothers or sisters will always be there for them.

A more insidious reason is the eternal issue of who gets credit for a great idea. If that junior executive had ever got through to the division chief to present his idea, I'm sure there would have been at least a split-second of concern on both sides (and probably more) about who would ultimately get credit for the idea. At best, the chief would have to share the glory with a colleague. That issue doesn't come up at all with an outsider. If an outsider calls the division chief, all the glory falls on the chief for bringing the big idea into the company. It sounds silly on paper perhaps, but you can't deny that this vile competitive impulse colours the situation.

The most inexcusable reason, however, is when bosses condone this behaviour. I'm not sure they do so wilfully, but it sometimes happens simply due to benign neglect. If I'm being honest with myself, I'm as guilty as the next CEO. If a junior executive complained to me that a colleague was not responding to his calls, I might be concerned. But I'd also be inclined to make excuses for the offending colleague. Depending on who it was, I might tell the junior executive, 'Well, he has a lot on his plate right now,' and suggest someone else to call. But if that same complaint came from an outsider – someone writing to me about the complete lack of response from someone within my company – my concern would increase by a factor of ten. Frankly, I'd be furious. I would regard such behaviour as corporate irresponsibility of the highest order – as if someone was tossing dollar bills at us and we refused to pick them up. I'd confront the offending colleague immediately and address the problem.

The difference in my response to the two situations worries me. It means I'm tacitly sending a message that I will tolerate internal neglect but not external. Knowingly or not, I've established two tiers of responsiveness at our company, That's not good, and I'm as much to blame for the problem as anyone else – more so in fact because I can do something about it.

As the boss, I can urge colleagues not to take each other for granted. I can remind them that squabbling over turf and credit usually doesn't fool anyone and has the opposite of the intended effect; it makes the combatants look petty and small, rather than clever and creative. I can do all this, of course, but I'm not sure I will ever change human nature to as great an extent as I desire.

The real solution starts with me (and every other manager or boss). It's the boss's duty to set the example of being as responsive to the lowliest insider as to the most important outsider. It's an ideal worth striving for. Without it, your company is missing out on some of its best opportunities – the ones generated from within.

BE WARY OF UNANIMOUS AGREEMENT

I always worry when everyone in our company is in agreement about a new idea or a major decision. If people are unanimously behind a concept, my first instinct is to think there's something wrong with the concept.

In my mind, organizational harmony means people getting along and working together *after* a decision has been made. But in reaching any decision, I don't mind a little friction among the decision-makers. I want our people mixing it up in a meeting, questioning assumptions, challenging their peers and superiors, and tossing out alternative ideas. That feisty sort of debate is how bad ideas are put to sleep and better concepts are allowed to breathe.

If everyone is in perfect agreement about a concept, I get nervous. It means:

1. The concept is too bland

Conventional ideas, by definition, breed convention. They're not meant to inspire debate.

If an idea is bold and unconventional, if it pushes us into new areas, if it involves some risk (and what good idea doesn't?), it's bound to have some opposition. There's always going to be someone in the room who thinks it's too risky, someone who doesn't see how it fits with our current business, or someone who thinks we should tone it down.

That's a good sign. If that opposition helps improve the original idea, that's even better.

2. People don't care

There will always be situations where the people in the room are indifferent to a concept. They don't care enough to argue about it, so they vote along with everyone else. If the vote is yes, that doesn't mean the idea is good. If the vote is no, it doesn't mean the idea is bad or boring. It might simply be that your people are too distracted with their own projects and problems to care either way.

If that's the case, you have to make people care. The easiest way to make your people care is to hit them in their wallets. It's amazing how quickly people snap to attention and treat a concept more seriously once you link the success or failure of the idea to their compensation. If you suspect that people aren't taking a group decision seriously, tell them that their annual bonuses depend on the outcome of their decision. If you weren't getting the full benefit of their brainpower before, you will now.

3. People don't get it

Some ideas simply sail above everyone's head – because they're presented poorly or they're too technical, or they're too complicated. So everyone in the room ignores the concept. Again, that is no reflection on the quality of an idea or its potential to pay off for your company. It only means that you have to make people appreciate the concept in ways that they understand.

I remember sitting in on a major planning meeting at a friend's company. The subject that day was a proposed investment in a new software accounting system. As the company's chief financial officer and his technology consultant explained the technical intricacies of how the system would work, it was easy to see the glaze forming over the other executives' eyes. They had no idea what the two men were talking about. If they approved the multimillion dollar investment, they would be doing so out of ignorance and because they wanted to move on to a more interesting subject. The validity of the idea was immaterial to them because they didn't get it.

To his credit, the CEO sensed this and stopped his presentation. He said, 'Look, I know the rest of you aren't interested in how this works. You want to know what it does. The biggest problem this company has had for the last decade is that we have no control over our expenses and income. This system will tell you for the first time at the push of a button how your divisions are doing. I guarantee it.'

The guarantee was a nice rhetorical touch. But the critical point was telling everyone how the system would make them better informed. That's a concept that anyone can understand.

4. People are intimidated by the group leader

You don't have to be an expert on group dynamics to appreciate that a shrewd and persuasive executive can control a group discussion so that every debate ends with unanimous support of his or her position.

I saw this with my own eyes some years ago when I was on the board of directors of a large industrial company. My fellow directors were not a meek and naive group. Most of them were CEOs or self-made millionaires. They knew how to make smart decisions. And yet we were all like putty in the hands of the chairman and CEO who ran the meeting. He dazzled us with his presentation skills, his mastery of the facts, and his ability to push our hot buttons. Time and time again, we unanimously supported ideas and investments that, in hindsight, look incredibly bone-headed. When people ask me how I could have voted yes on some of our decisions. I tell them, 'You would have voted the same way if you were in that boardroom.'

I keep this in mind whenever I'm running a meeting. As the boss, I know that some people will always agree with me because I am the boss, no matter how preposterous my notions. (Fortunately, we have people who automatically question me for precisely the same reason.) As a result, I often couch my suggestions with phrases that invite disagreement. If I say, 'Maybe this is an idiotic idea, but . . .' it somehow makes it easier for people to point out that it is idiotic.

I'd rather deal with that than unanimous agreement.

CO-OPT YOUR RIVALS, DON'T CRUSH THEM

I was on a sales call not long ago listening to the chief operating officer outline his company's marketing plans for the coming year. One of his strategies for dealing with his main competitor caught me by surprise.

The plan wasn't illegal or unethical, but it was Machiavellian in its ruthlessness. It wouldn't increase the COO's market share. It was only intended to unsettle and irritate this competitor.

Later in a private moment, I asked the COO why he was making such a hostile gesture which could only lead to open warfare.

He said, 'I'll do anything to hack away at those people across town. Doesn't everyone hate their competition?'

Well, actually no.

I've always thought that how you deal with your opponents says a lot about you. You can compete but you don't have to be a bully. You can be a warrior without turning into a barbarian.

Lyndon Johnson fought very hard against John F. Kennedy to win the 1960 Democratic Presidential nomination. Yet losing to Kennedy didn't stop Johnson from becoming his running mate. The same thing happened in 1980 between Ronald Reagan and George Bush. Because Bush derided Reagan mercilessly during the primaries, people were stunned when he agreed to run as Reagan's Vice President. I've always thought the makeup of those two tickets said more about Kennedy and Reagan's savvy than anything else. They competed, they won, and rather than crush their rivals, they co-opted them.

I try to do the same in business, and my reasons are strictly competitive.

In my more arrogant moments, I fantasize that our company has no competition in sports management. When reporters have compared our company to the perceived number two or three firms in our field, I've actually disputed the comparison, contending that lumping us with our nearest rival is like 'comparing General Motors with a neighbourhood garage.'

That doesn't accurately reflect my attitude about competition. The truth is, I'm extremely grateful for my rivals because competition is instructive.

You see this in sports. The best players are willing to rework their game completely if that's what it takes to beat an archrival. They'll analyse their weaknesses from past performance and add specific features – an improved serve in tennis, a quicker shot release in basketball – to give themselves an advantage. It's hard to say if they would make the extra effort if the archrival didn't exist.

Likewise in business. Competition shows you precisely where you have room for improvement. Here are six ways your competitors are good for you.

1. They help you understand market share

If you're Nike versus Adidas, market share is an obvious indicator of how you're performing. In the athletic shoe business, where there's not that much spread between one manufacturer's profit margins and another's, gaining or losing a few extra points of market share can mean the difference between a good year and a bad one. You always want to be adding market share.

It's a little different in our business. If you define your market as, say, the 200 golfers in the world worth representing, adding market share is not necessarily the right move, especially not if the golfers you're adding are closer to the bottom of the heap than the top. I'd rather represent the top 20 golfers in the world than the bottom 180. In that sense, market share is misleading in our business. It's not where the profits are.

2. They give you pricing cues

In golf course design, Jack Nicklaus has historically charged the highest fees. We've always taken our pricing cues from him. An increase in the Nicklaus fee lets us raise our clients' design fees across the board. Of course, we always set the fee fractionally lower than the Nicklaus standard. But the end result is more income for all concerned.

3. They force you to think more than one step ahead

In chess, you can measure the quality of your opponent by how many moves ahead you have to think to stay in the game. A neophyte playing one move at a time will usually lose to someone who has considered his next two or three moves.

Likewise in business, where some clever rivals have forced us to think more deeply about a situation than we were accustomed to. Although we have a dominant position in sports management, there's no end to the new companies entering our field, trying to chip away at our business. Some are small. Some are well-funded and successful in other areas. Because they approach our business from a different angle, they don't quite see things the way we do. As a result, we take them very seriously. They force us to examine our position and rethink our assumptions. As in a chess game, they help us to think farther ahead ('If we do this, and they do that, then we do this. . . .').

Although I would just as soon not face this steady stream of new rivals, a part of me knows they've forced us to be smarter.

4. They improve your profit margins

There's no business that's 100 per cent efficient, that's squeezing all the profit out of its operations. There's always some other operation somewhere that's found a way to do it better. Invariably, it's a competitor. If you can get a dialogue going with these super-efficient rivals (as the Big Three automakers did in the 1980s, visiting Japanese auto plants and learning their methods), it won't cost them a penny but it might open your eyes.

5. They energize your staff

At its most basic level, competition should make your heart beat faster. Perhaps today it's considered unseemly to hate your rivals and use them to stoke your employees. After all, there's a good chance you know your competitors well, you like them, you may even have worked for them in the past or intend to in the future.

But if you can convince your people that their rivals across town are the biggest threat to their pay cheques and promotions, you will teach them a lesson in motivation they'll never forget.

6. They return the favour

When you respect your opponents they usually return the favour. Opponents are less likely to take gratuitous swipes at you when your back is turned if they consider you a friend as well as a rival. I know this is true because of all the opportunities I've had to say less than laudatory things about competitors to prospective customers, and yet I've held back. If the competitor is a friend. I bite my tongue.

But the best reason to respect your opponents is that it prepares you to learn from them. If you truly hate your competition, it's easy to fall into the trap of scoffing at everything they do.

But even the puniest competitors have something to teach you. If they're still in business nipping at your heels, they must be doing something right. And that's worth knowing. Thus, when executives leave an opponent, I am keenly interested in what they have to say. Because I've treated them with respect in the past, these departing employees are more likely to say it to me than to someone else.

DON'T BE AFRAID TO SEND YOUR PEOPLE TO THE PENALTY BOX

One of the best features of sports is that you always know how you're doing. Either the scoreboard or the fans will tell you. And if you've done something wrong, there are rules and officials and referees who will immediately penalize you for it. It's all part of the sport.

That sort of ruthless honesty is often missing in business. Managers don't always tell their subordinates how they think they're doing at their job. They withhold praise when subordinates are doing well. More significantly, they fail to correct a subordinate who has messed up.

I once casually reminded one of our executives of a project that went awry five years earlier and cost us $60,000.

'Wait a minute. Mark,' he said. 'I've always thought that little fiasco was water under the bridge. I can't believe you're still holding that deal as a demerit next to my name.'

Until that moment, I had not realized that I still cared. More important, neither did he.

If I'm being honest with myself as a manager, I have to admit that I'm more to blame for keeping that executive in the dark than he is for not appreciating how I secretly feel. After all, how would he know I've put him in my penalty box if I've never whistled him for a penalty?

I don't usually misfire in this regard. I'm pretty good at letting our executives know of my displeasure when they've messed up. I'm not afraid to blow the whistle and call a penalty on them. And I tend to do it quickly. The quicker I toss them into the penalty box, the sooner I can let them out.

But I know a lot of managers who aren't good at this – and the reasons why vary with each manager.

The biggest reason is that many people, even those in unquestioned positions of authority, don't like confrontation. As bosses, they are mentally hard-wired to be accommodating and nurturing rather than cutting and hyper-critical. The irony is that a boss is actually more nurturing when he is willing to confront an errant subordinate. The method may vary. You can confront with humour or sarcasm or unbridled anger. (I use all of these techniques when I have problems with subordinates and their performances.) But the net result is that, as the boss, you have established a performance standard and informed the subordinate that he has fallen short of that standard, a failure that hopefully will not be repeated. Without the confrontation, neither of you can move forward.

Unfortunately, a lot of bosses can be unhappy with someone but will tell everyone except that individual. I'm not sure what they aim to achieve by this. Are they hoping that someone will pass on their displeasure to the subordinate? That strategy rarely works. For one thing, there's no guarantee that a third party will accurately convey the boss's feelings to the subordinate. Also, the strategy undermines a boss's authority. When employees hear from a third party that the boss is unhappy with them, their first thought is usually, 'Why didn't he tell me so himself?'

Still other bosses keep their displeasure totally to themselves. This rarely corrects the situation or improves the relationship between boss and subordinate. Actually, it's almost guaranteed to make it worse.

A little of this is also the employee's fault, of course. I don't know too many employees who are eager to admit their performance errors or acknowledge that they deserve a demerit. If they've done six positive things during the past year and two negative things, they will naturally focus on the positives and ignore the negatives. That's human nature. It's the rare employee who will toss himself into the penalty box.

A more subtle reason is that many bosses aren't clear about their priorities. The things I expect from an employee are not always obvious. For example, a couple of years ago I was hounding one of our executives to secure an endorsement deal for one of our long-time clients. In the grand scheme of things, this endorsement contract was a minor blip. The client was well past her prime and any deal we got her would involve relatively small numbers. But she could have used the extra income and, in my mind at least, it was a major priority. So, every time I talked to this particular executive, I asked him how he was doing on the contract for this client. And every time he would put me off, saying, 'I'm working on it.'

At year's end, when I reviewed this executive's performance and adjusted his compensation, I told him I was penalizing him a little because of his sorry performance for this client.

He responded by pointing out all the revenue he had generated for the company with several hefty deals – as if those big deals would cancel out the fact that he failed to do what I asked. I guess he thought the priorities he set in his mind were more important than the ones in mine. That review corrected that false impression. But until then, the executive had no idea how one minor lapse (to him) was a major failure (to me).

Of course, that makes it all the more important that bosses become more aggressive, rather than more lenient, about whistling penalties on their employees. If they don't, who will?

UNLEARN ONE ACQUIRED HABIT A YEAR

Ultimately, an executive is the sum total of all the things he or she learns during a business career. But there's something to be said for unlearning facts, insights, and assumptions as well.

After all, none of us is immune to the accumulation of 'bad habits' during an active career. The problem is, they accrue so slowly over the years that we don't notice how strong their influence becomes. It's like gaining weight after college. No one notices if you gain a pound. But if you put on a pound a year, you'll be 30 pounds overweight in your early 50s.

As a result, it's valuable to step back and reconsider some of the tenets we hold so dearly in business. Here are five I'm revisiting.

1. Trust your first impression

You'd think this is one principle that wouldn't be debased or diluted over the years. Not true. As executives get more experienced, they become more cautious. They want more, not less, information before they make a decision. As a result, they rely less and less on their 'gut instinct' or first impression and more on careful, rational, well-researched thinking. Over time, this makes them not only less decisive but less instinctive as well – even though their golden instincts are probably what put them in a decision-making position in the first place.

This isn't a big-problem for me, but I do notice when the tell-tale signs of hesitation creep into my behaviour. That's when it's time to relearn to trust my first impression.

For example, I was interviewing people for an assistant position. The first candidate I saw was perfect. She tested well, had an unimpeachable résumé, and had the right disposition for the job. Yet some cautious part of my brain was whispering to me, 'You can't hire the first person who walks into your office. See more people.' So I did. Yet none of the half-dozen candidates who followed came close to the first candidate. My hesitation not only cost me time but created the risk that the first candidate would take another job while I was treating myself to more impressions.

Extend this simple scenario to every other decision in your life and you'll see the danger here. You'll also see the value of unlearning the bad habit of not trusting your first impression.

2. Be less selective with your facts

A chief executive I know suspected one of his managers of cheating the company. So he conducted an exhaustive audit of the manager's finances. After weeks of poring over documents, the auditor announced the manager was absolutely clean. There was nothing unusual, let alone illegal, with how he handled company monies. Yet despite this complete 'acquittal' the CEO still thinks the manager is 'dirty.'

This is the curse of selective perception. In pursuing our agenda, we exclude certain inconvenient pieces of evidence and focus on those that support our preconceived point of view. As a result, we always find what we are looking for, despite all evidence to the contrary.

This is an easy habit to fall into, but unlearning it is equally easy. It starts with the recognition that your perception is highly selective. It ends when you are willing to admit that you are wrong.

3. Maintain the long-term integrity of the chain of command

What do you do when a junior employee goes around his or her immediate superior to complain to you about something that superior is doing? This is one of the thornier situations for a boss – because it forces the boss to choose between supporting the chain of command and dealing fairly with a possible injustice.

In my early years. I always supported the chain of command, even when it was slightly unfair. But over the years. I've softened slightly. I sometimes dignify the complaint and get directly involved, even at the expense of undermining an executive's authority.

But I now believe this is a policy worth unlearning. Experience has taught me to trifle as little as possible with the delicate mechanics of hierarchy and command. It possible, I always support the chain of command and tell the feuding parties to work it out among themselves.

I've learned that the employees' complaints are rarely serious – in fact, they're usually petty and one-sided. But more importantly, the employee and superior don't need my Solomonic interference. Usually, they just need to talk to each other.

In my experience, the proper solution eventually surfaces. If it doesn't and the problem becomes cancerous, then I step in. But by then the problem is no longer a threat to our hierarchy; it's a threat to our business.

4. Take a close look at the warts

In every business, it's tempting and easy to steer your sights to the rosy picture – the good news that you have a 60 per cent market share, not the bad news that one of your rivals has 30 per cent and is growing much faster than you are.

The best executives, of course, work hard to resist that temptation. They know that complacency and self-satisfaction are the demon scourges of growing enterprises, so they're constantly pointing out the warts in the pretty picture.

But no one is perfectly true to this vision. Maintaining morale and momentum sometimes forces you to focus on the good news; anything less may demoralize the troops. From there, it's easy to see how this rosy view can become habit-forming. That's when it's time to unlearn the habit.

If everything seems like it's coming up roses, enjoy the moment. But at the same time, get real. The thorns are there. You know it. But you have to look for them to avoid being pricked by them.

5. Eliminate a person

For years, I've given each of our senior executives a clear goal of meeting five new people in the coming year. I do it as a reminder that although it's all too easy (and possibly comforting) to get caught up in the affairs of the people you already know, that's no way to grow a business.

I think I should also be checking on them to see what old names they've *stopped calling* – because that's a worthwhile goal too. We all know people who, over time, have simply become more trouble than they are worth. If you've dealt with a person for years, it's often hard to notice or admit that the relationship has survived too long or simply reached a dead end.

I don't wish to sound ruthless or to suggest that we jettison friends the moment we think they are no longer useful to us or don't comport with our sense of personal efficiency. But there's nothing wrong with re-examining your relationships with the goal of making them less draining or pointless.

For several years now people in our golf division have urged me to have dinner once or twice a year with a golfer who is not our client. The desired result is that he will eventually see the error of his ways and hire us to manage his career. I've known this athlete for years and enjoy his company. I also know him well enough to be convinced that he is happy with his current representation and does not want to be represented by us. In other words, the dinners our golf people keep arranging for us are futile.

This year my goal is to act on that conclusion. I've quietly removed that golfer from my personal VIP list. He doesn't know it (and I doubt if he would care). He and I will certainly get together if our paths cross, but seeing him is no longer an annual or semi-annual obligation for me. I'd rather spend my time meeting new people. But I couldn't do that if, at the same time, I didn't also eliminate one or two people who I've been meeting too often and too long.

THE COSTS YOU CAN CONTROL ARE THE COSTS THAT ALWAYS GET OUT OF CONTROL

Like most managers, I run our business based on a very simple model. On the one hand. I'm always trying to increase our *revenues*. On the other, I'm trying to get a grip on our *costs*.

This tug of war between revenues and costs, income and outgoings, is the eternal struggle for a manager. If revenues outpace costs, you have a profitable business. If revenues outpace costs by a large margin, you have a dynamic growing business that can withstand almost any challenge from any competitor. On the other hand, if costs exceed revenues, you have an organization that's in trouble and quite possibly out of your control.

Most managers pay extremely close attention to revenues – because that's where the glory is. It's perfectly understandable. Revenues mean income. Income means sales. Sales mean you did something wonderful to make someone part with his or her money. It's as if you went into battle with nothing but your company's product line and came back with a fistful of cash instead. In that sense, a manager who can keep revenues rising is nothing short of a war hero.

I'm not exaggerating. If you've ever been to a corporate sales meeting and witnessed the accolades showered upon sales managers who exceeded their quotas or broke their division's sales record, you know the kind of awe and gratitude that focusing on revenues attracts.

Contrast that with the attention paid to costs. There's no glory for containing costs, no conferences at lush resorts to honour employees who negotiated a terrific lease or found a vendor who charged 20 per cent less than the previous supplier.

On the surface, I'm as guilty of this bias as anyone else. If you look at my travel schedule, the letters I write, the calls I make, the memos I send to our executives, a large percentage of my time is devoted to developing new prospects and selling to existing customers. I still get a thrill when I hear someone made a great sale.

But if the truth be known, an increasingly large amount of my down time (when I'm just thinking through a problem) and my management time (when I'm executing the solution) is devoted to containing costs.

Again, I like to keep it simple. In my mind, a company has only two kinds of costs: *fixed* costs and *variable* costs.

A fixed cost is something you can't do much about no matter how clever you think you are. The cost of running an office is a fixed cost. For example, it costs close to $15,000 per year per employee to keep the doors open and lights on in our five-storey townhouse office in Manhattan. No matter how much I want to, I can't do much about reducing this cost. Leases, electric bills, and taxes are the sort of expenses that never go down. I guess we could seal off the fifth floor and move a dozen employees to another building to save a few dollars, but that wouldn't be feasible or good for morale. This sort of expense is part of the cost of doing business. I can pay attention, but I can't do much to reduce it.

So instead, I focus on variable costs. These are the costs that I can control if I put my mind to it.

For example, payroll is the largest variable cost at most companies. Unfortunately, it's not the sort of cost that you can reduce without putting the company at some risk. You can contain the cost by limiting raises to, say, three per cent across the board or freezing salaries. But unless the company is in dire trouble and you have to lay off people or make everyone take a pay cut, you can't cut your payroll costs.

It's even worse if the company is thriving. After all, payroll is the one subject that everyone in the company thinks about. The only problem is that they rarely think about it as the aggregate sum – what their salary and everyone else's together is costing the company. They only think about it in terms of themselves – specifically, in how much of a raise they're going to get. If the company is doing well, they expect to do well too. And in truth, they should. Payroll costs should go up if revenues are rising. That's how you keep employees happy and motivated and at your company, not a competitor's.

With all that mental energy devoted to getting raises, it's no wonder that the seemingly easy-to-control expense of meeting a payroll is so often out of control.

That's the paradox. The costs you think you can control are almost always the costs that get out of control. The reason is not too hard to figure out. When people are given the chance to spend money at a company, they rarely choose to reduce that expenditure. On the contrary, they always spend more. What becomes a novel nice-to-have expenditure one year will, if unmonitored, quickly become a necessity in two or three years time.

That's why about seven years ago I formed an Administrative and Operations Committee to keep an eye on costs at our company. This group's mandate is to review every operational expense at our company – from office leases to health benefits to what we spend on phone bills and faxes.

It's amazing what items the committee turns up. Five years ago we were spending $30,000 a year on car services in New York. Five years later we were spending $350,000. Even if we factored in the increased number of employees in New York, that was a huge jump in how many people were using town cars and limousines (as opposed to taxis and public transportation) to get around New York City. It also proved my thesis that a cost ignored is a cost that will soon be out of control.

So we instituted a little more control. Instead of keeping an open account at several car services in the city, we eliminated those accounts and forced people to pay for a hired car themselves and justify it on their expense reports. We're not eliminating car services in New York. We know that there are times when they have a legitimate business purpose. We needed something to make people hesitate, if only slightly, before they automatically reserve a hired car rather than hail a taxi to get to their next appointment.

As I say, there's no glory in rooting out extravagance and waste in an organization. It's a thankless task. But ignoring it is the greatest extravagance of all.

SOME PROBLEMS ARE NOT WORTH KNOWING

The biggest curse of being the boss is that you can't always be sure you're getting the information you need to manage your business.

Sometimes the people reporting to you shade the facts to make themselves appear in the best light.

Other times, particularly if the news is bad, they will withhold critical information from you because they're not sure how you'll take it. They'll do this even though they instinctively know that a) getting the facts to you as soon as possible is the best way for you to deal with the problem, b) the truth will eventually come out, and c) behaving this way is counter to everyone's best interests. They do so because they're afraid you'll shoot the messenger, or that they'll chalk up a career demerit for being straight with you.

It's no different with criticism. You always want your people to be totally candid with you. If you're making a poor decision, you need people who have the guts to tell you you're wrong – and why. You need this sort of candour and openness. But the curse is you can never be sure you're getting it.

Every manager has his or her own methods for dealing with this problem. But the end goal is the same for all of us: we want people to be totally straight and honest with us.

Over the years, because this is such an important issue, I've made a conscious effort to elicit candour from our people. But in recent years, I've noticed a corollary problem arising: sometimes your people tell you too much. Sometimes they raise issues that you need to know but can't do anything about.

This is particularly true whenever I hear internal complaints. For example, I got a chance to catch up with one of our promising executives a few weeks ago. I wanted to see how we was doing and what he thought could be improved in his operation. He was extremely positive in a vague way at first. Everything was fine, according to him. But after a little prodding, I could tell he wasn't completely happy. It turned out he felt neglected by his boss, who was constantly travelling and never available when he needed an answer on a project or approval for some expenditure. It's a real problem, he said. Deals were falling apart and projects were going over budget because little details were falling through the cracks and it took days and weeks rather than hours to get a decision made.

Now, on the one hand, you can say this is precisely the sort of feedback a manager needs. I've been alerted to a problem that, but for the candour of this young executive, would never have reached me.

But in my mind, this situation is even more frustrating than being kept in the dark. When someone grumbles to me about a problem inside the company, as the boss I feel compelled to do something about it.

The problem is, all I've heard is the complaint. I haven't been given any specific evidence. And so, if I bring up the matter with the young executive's boss, he'll deny it. He'll say, 'That's ridiculous. I'm always reachable on the road. Show me one example where my absence has cost us money.'

And, in truth, he has a point. Without any concrete proof, how can I indict or convict him?

So I then have to go back to the complaining executive to give me examples of where the system has broken down. I can do something with examples. I can change our procedures or discipline someone. But I can't do anything without proof.

Of course, the answer to this request is always the same. No one wants to go on record with a complaint because they're afraid – not of losing their jobs (I wouldn't let that happen) but of some subtle reprisal that will stall their career. (This is the familiar cry of the would-be whistleblower.) In the end, telling me the truth without proof is the same paralysis that afflicts the people who won't tell me the truth at all.

Only in this case, it's even more frustrating for me because I know there's a problem but I can't do anything about it. At least in the more distant past, I didn't even know about the problem. Managerial ignorance is bliss compared to managerial impotence.

In moments like these, the challenge for any boss is not managing the problem but rather managing the frustration that you'll never solve the problem.

KNOW WHEN TO LEAVE YOUR WORRIES ALONE

The other day I asked an associate to keep an eye on a pet project while I was out of the country. I knew the executive in charge of the project had a lot of things on his plate and I was worried that he would not follow up in precisely the manner we had planned or, worse, forget it completely.

The associate, who knew the executive well, told me my worry was misplaced. She said, 'You don't have to get excited about this project because he's excited about it. What you have to worry about are all the things that don't excite him.'

I thought that was a perceptive comment. It spawned McCormack's Rule of Worrying, which says, 'You don't need two people worrying about the same thing at the same company. One is enough.'

That's a handy guideline for any manager who isn't sure what he should be paying attention to and what he can leave alone. If someone else is worrying about a situation, you're covered. Worry about the things that everyone else is ignoring. I'd be hard pressed to come up with a simpler system for saving time, delegating shrewdly, and reducing stress.

Of course, it helps if you can size up what worries or excites your colleagues and what doesn't. I suspect this is one area where many of us overestimate how insightful we really are.

Try the following experiment:

Take a few moments to analyse what really excites your closest associate at work. Then write down what you think are his or her five biggest professional priorities. Then ask this associate to write down his or her own priority list. I'd be amazed if the two lists had three items in common. (A more basic, and potentially scarier, version of this experiment: list the five items you think each of your subordinates is working on. Then compare with your subordinates' versions. Again, I doubt if the lists come close to matching.) That's how negligent or unaware most of us are about what's really going on in our colleagues' minds.

I learned this some time ago with my assistant in London. Every executive has certain expectations of a personal assistant in terms of organization, follow-through, handling of correspondence, dealing with appointments, maintaining useful files, etc. This assistant was fully capable in these areas. But it took me years to realize that what really excited her was anything that had to do with travel and entertainment. She loved dealing with hotels and airlines, bargaining for better deals not only for me but for the entire company. She loved arranging my business luncheons and dinners – to the point where she would ask me in June what I wanted served at a luncheon for eight people on October the 8th. She excelled in this area in large part because it excited her.

Her fascination with these areas inevitably cost her a little in other areas of her job. But I learned to deal with it. I never worried or second guessed her about anything having to do with my travel and business entertaining – because I knew she would always have everything under control. (This saved me hours each month.) Instead, I worried about the tasks that didn't excite her as much. As I say, two people shouldn't worry about the same thing. One is enough.

Since then, I've learned to keep a mental checklist of the concepts that excite the 30 or 40 executives at our company who I talk to regularly. It's not a big chore. I know executives who consistently lead off every phone conversation by reporting on the same single project. It doesn't take a genius to figure out that this is the one item on their plate that really excites them. Likewise, I deal with executives who cannot get through any discussion without mentioning a particular client or deal. Again, it's easy to see what turns them on.

Noticing these things is a great timesaver in that it dramatically reduces the number of things I have to worry about. I also suspect it saves a lot of wear and tear on employees. One of the biggest reasons employees lose faith in their bosses is that bosses nag them about things they don't need to be nagged about. If nothing else, at least I'm not hounding people for the wrong reasons.

The only time I worry about people's priorities is when they're in direct conflict with the company's priorities. We've had executives who, with some justification, take pride in a sports marketing concept they created. Unfortunately, that sort of pride is hard to contain sometimes. It compels them to force-feed their pet concept into any and every sales situation. If they're talking to a customer who wants to get involved in sports, the first thing out of their mouth will be the pet concept at the top of their mind, regardless of whether it's appropriate or even if the customer is interested in something else we have to offer.

When an executive's excitement misses the bigger picture, I start to worry – alone.

PAY ATTENTION TO THE 'INTANGIBLES'

It's always fascinating to watch a great coach assess athletic talent. While the rest of us are on the sideline watching a graceful, well-conditioned young man or woman hit a ball or run up and down the court, the coach is seeing a totally different performance. He's breaking it down into discrete and often measurable components. These are the athlete's tools.

In baseball, for example, the essential tools are hitting, running, fielding, throwing, and hitting with power.

In basketball, the tools are running, jumping, shooting, passing, dribbling, rebounding, and defending.

When professional coaches are deciding whether to draft and invest in a star collegiate player, these are the components they study. They haul out their clipboards, tape measures, and stopwatches and put a number to everything. If the college star is going to make the leap successfully into the pros, his numbers will have to measure up to professional standards.

It's not pure science, but it's a lot closer to science than sitting in the stands and enjoying the competition the way the rest of us average untutored fans do.

It's also not just about numbers. You cannot predict an athlete's future success merely by adding up his 41–inch vertical leap to his 4.3 second time in the 40–yard dash. You have to include a few non-physical intangibles in the mix, too.

Baseball scouts call this a ballplayer's 'makeup' – qualities such as his work habits, desire, attitude, and discipline. But talent scouts in every sport are looking for these same personality traits – because they know that the intangibles that can't be measured are the great athlete's real tools. Lots of young people can jump high, run like the wind, and chase down a ball, but the intangibles are what separate the champions from the also-rans.

I bring this up because I sometimes think corporate managers should apply the same talent-assessment procedures to hiring executive and sales talent. They should, but they don't.

I've spent most of my career around supremely talented athletes and I've seen how rigorously a great tennis coach like Nick Bollettieri or a great golf instructor like David Leadbetter assesses athletic talent. The methods that business people use to hire people for responsible jobs – say, a sales manager making a six- or seven-figure salary or a division chief overseeing 3,000 people – don't come close to the rigorousness that sports people employ. More often than not, a company hires someone because they performed well at another company, they came highly recommended by a friend, and there was nothing egregiously alarming in the candidate's résumé. It's not always that simple, but it's close.

I'm guilty of this too. When I hire people, I rely as much on a vague gut instinct about them as any other factor. I wonder what would happen if I applied more rigorous standards.

For example, if I were considering an experienced salesperson, these are the tools I would be analysing:

- *Personality*: do I like them instantly? (If they repulse me, they'll repulse customers, too.)
- *Previous sales*: what's their favourite sale, and why?
- *Communication skills*: can they write a sales letter? Can they speak articulately to large groups? Can they do the same one on one?
- *Time management*: are they punctual, focused, and organized?
- *Creativity*: Can they take concepts A and B, skip C through L, and come up with M?
- *Curiosity*: do they read outside their industry or have interesting hobbies? (This tool has a great deal of impact on the previous item.)
- *Passion*: do they get a visceral thrill out of doing deals?
- *Sympathy*: do they care about customers? Can they put themselves in the other guy's shoes?
- *Listening*: can they do it, period?
- *Contacts*: not absolutely necessary, but nice at the start.
- *Follow-up*: do they do it, period?

If I had the time, I think I could accurately gauge each category, either by quizzing the candidate or asking people who know him or her. But the truth is, like most people, I don't make the time for such intensive scrutiny.

As a result, I put a lot of faith in what I call the salesperson's 'makeup', his desire, competitiveness, attitude, cooperation, resilience, how he deals with rejection. These are the intangibles, the soft skills that people develop growing up via their parents, teachers, and friends. As in sports, they are probably better predictors of sales success than anything else. A candidate with all the tools and none of the intangibles is not a serious candidate in my book.

Of course, you can't gauge these intangibles scientifically. You can't put a number to them. But that doesn't mean you can't trust them. At the least, when you're hiring, you should be seriously considering them.

The wonderful thing about the intangibles when you are shopping for talent is that they are valuable gauges even in areas where you have no expertise.

For example, we have a growing classical music division called IMG Artists, which represents soloists and singers from Itzhak Perlman to James Galway to Thomas Hampson and Dawn Upshaw.

One of our brightest rising stars is the 22-year-old violinist Leila Josefowicz. I'm told the music experts in our Artists group credit me with 'discovering' Ms. Josefowicz because I saw an article about her in *People* magazine when she was ten years old and told our Artists chief to check her out.

I suspect our classical music people get a chuckle out of this because my taste in music begins and ends with the Beatles. It took me years to stop referring to concert intermissions as 'halftime.' But something in the *People* story struck a chord with me. You expect violin prodigies to be able to play the notes and produce a beautiful tone. But the reporter from People raved about the young girl's poise on a local TV show and how supportive but unpushy her family was. The family wanted the young girl to lead a normal, unhurried life. The poise and family situation were the interesting intangibles. I didn't need to know a note of Tchaikovsky to sense that this young girl might be special.

Today, at 22, with a major recording contract and a perfectly shaped concert schedule, Ms. Josefowicz is special.

I guess that's the real secret in assessing talent. You shouldn't fly by the seat of your pants. But if you don't have the time to scrutinize how the candidates measure up in the basic tools department, at least pay attention to the intangibles.

COFFEE SHOULD TASTE LIKE COFFEE

A friend described an interesting scene from his summer vacation. For years, one of the distinct pleasures of spending summer in this particular village was shopping for fresh produce at this one roadside shack. The shack itself was nondescript, but the proprietor had a talent for locating the biggest, juiciest fruits and vegetables and, as a result, attracted an affluent clientele from miles around.

Over the years, as this village attracted increasingly more affluent 'summer people' with increasingly more robust spending habits, my friend watched in fascination as this roadside shack grew with the times. Every year, my friend would return to the village to find that the 'shack' had been physically expanded and that the proprietor had added more dazzling goodies to his product line. One year it was baked goods. Another year it was gourmet cheeses. The next year it was a complete butcher shop with the best meat in the area. The following year it was a full line of hand-crafted beers. (This is a classic entrepreneurial success: you either adapt to your changing customer base or die.)

The year after that the 'shack' began featuring a fully stocked coffee bar, with a dozen coffee urns featuring every flavour imaginable. There were coffees flavoured with everything from almond to raspberry to coconut to Bailey's Irish Cream. With the Starbucks crowd this store attracted, this new feature was probably inevitable. But the proprietor had a puckish streak. Among all the fancy coffees, he had marked one urn 'Coffee-Flavoured Coffee.' And this 'flavour' was far and away the store's best seller.

I suppose this shouldn't be surprising. Once you peel away all the fancy bells and whistles, people still drink coffee because they like the taste of coffee. If they yearned for the flavours of raspberry or almonds, they would buy raspberries and almonds.

But there's a larger business lesson here. The proprietor, in his ironic and calculated way, must have known something about the need to stick to the basics. That's why he gave his customers lots of choices, but he never forgot that, in the end, he was still selling coffee. The fancy flavours were fringe profit centres. The basic beverage was what the majority of people would always want. With his 'coffee-flavoured coffee' urn, he had found a clever way of reminding people of that.

I wish more people in business had this proprietor's instincts. In any type of business, it's so easy to become distracted by the bells and whistles of a concept or the side issues of a transaction that we sometimes forget what the core of our business really is. In other words, we forget that coffee should taste like coffee.

I see this in our business all the time. As our company has grown, we find ourselves dipping our toes into some of the most peculiar projects. We started out managing athletes, which logically led to our involvement in creating sports events (where our athlete clients could perform and earn money) and selling the events to television (to increase the money generated for our clients). Clients, events, television. These are our core businesses in any sport.

And yet our company now has lucrative side businesses. For example, we have a corporate consulting arm that advises companies on how they should be investing their marketing dollars in sport. One of the more unique projects is the work we are doing for Petronas, the Malaysian oil company, which is building a concert hall connecting its twin skyscrapers in Kuala Lumpur. Petronas has hired our classical music division to help create an orchestra for the new hall, hire a music director, book conductors and soloists, and programme the events for the upcoming seasons.

It's an astonishing assignment for our company. If someone had told me 30 years ago, when I was travelling the golf circuit with Arnold Palmer, that my little management company would one day be booking violinists and singers in Malaysia or, for that matter, that we would be involved in classical music at all, I would have shaken my head in disbelief. The connection between golf and music and Malaysia would be impossible to make.

And yet, the connection seems logical and ineluctable if you appreciate that the core of our business is, and always will be, our clients. It was our work with golfers that led us to manage athletes in other sports such as tennis and motor racing and skiing. It was our success in those new sports that convinced us the same skills could be applied to clients in classical music. Likewise, it was our experience in golf which gave us a presence in golf-mad countries such as Malaysia. Thus, the relationship with Petronas.

But it wasn't our presence in Malaysia or our expertise in the classical music field that landed the concert hall assignment.

The fundamental reason is that we have the artists as clients. We have access to them. We talk to them daily. We know their schedules, their repertory, their fees, their short- and long-term goals. And with regular access comes credibility with the artists. If we suggest that they travel halfway around the world to perform in an untried hall with musicians they've never met before, they're more likely to accept it coming from us than from someone else.

As I say, it all starts with the clients. They're the core of our business. Without this core, the fringe opportunities have a way of passing us by.

It's no different in any other operation. If you don't know your core business, everything you do will inevitably become a fringe business.

THINK LIKE A PARENT

I've always thought that one of the toughest transitions to make in a career occurs right at the start, when you are just out of college and ready to conquer the world. The problem isn't youth or inexperience or grandiose ambition. It's authority figures. How to deal with authority figures (i.e., bosses) is another thing you can't learn on the Internet.

It's easy to see why bright young people (and many more like them) have problems with their new bosses. It's the way they were trained. For the first two decades of their lives, every authority figure they've dealt with has been someone who has their best interests at heart.

A wag I know calls this the 'This Hurts Me More Than It Hurts You' syndrome. That's the line parents use when they are punishing their child for some unpardonable act of negligence or disobedience. They're punishing the child for his or her own good, so the child won't repeat the error. It's a learning experience.

Young people face the same instructional dynamic with virtually every authority figure in their lives from nursery to graduate school.

A teacher who knows they are not living up to their potential tells them,

'It kills me to give you a bad grade, but that's the only way to teach you not to hand in shoddy work.'

A coach suspends a star player for missing practice. The suspension hurts the coach and the team, but the overriding objective is to teach the player a lesson about discipline.

Each of these authority figures is looking out for the young person's best interests.

All that changes when they enter the workplace. Suddenly they're working for a boss who doesn't necessarily have their best interests at heart. This new authority figure in their life is looking out primarily for himself.

That's a dramatic transition for a lot of young people, especially if they don't recognize the change they're going through. The sting of being berated or punished by a boss is no longer softened by the implicit understanding that 'this hurts me more than it hurts you.' The truth is, it doesn't hurt the boss at all!

Fresh-faced youngsters straight out of college aren't the only ones who experience this rude awakening. It can happen when people switch jobs. If you leave a paternalistic company where everyone treats you like 'family' to work for a hard-boiled, every-man-for-himself organization, you might have problems with your new superiors, especially if you don't appreciate the different styles.

There's a managerial irony here, too. I realize the current 'lean and mean' management gospel promotes a corporate culture where bosses have to look out for their own best interests. When the daily themes being pounded into managers' heads are 'cut the fat,' 'produce or perish,' and 'what have you done for me lately?' it's not hard to see why bosses are less empathetic and nurturing than our parents, teachers, and coaches.

But here's the rub: despite all the economic pressures that currently favour the cold, heartless boss who never loses sight of the bottom line, I still think managers are better off if they model themselves on parents, teachers, and coaches. In the long run, a company where the authority figures have the employees' best interests at heart (and the employees know that) will outlive a company where they don't.

It's easy to pay lip service to this noble sentiment. It's tougher to practise it. Let's say I promote someone because he has a big account in his pocket. I give him a hefty salary increase and an important title commensurate with the huge revenue he is adding to our coffers. Let's also say that a year after the promotion, he loses the account.

As a manager, I have two options here.

I can look out for my interests and that of the company. He's failed. So I punish him by cutting his salary, giving someone else his fancy title, and if he loses another account, getting rid of him. In strict economic terms, that's the right thing to do. It's cold but it makes sense. No one can fault me for it.

Or I can put his interests ahead of mine. I can see that he's hurting and going through some bad times. If I care about him as a human being and support him when he's down, and if everyone in the company sees me doing that, then I've created more of a warm family feeling in the company. It makes people feel more secure. I'm behaving more like a parent than a boss. Carrying this employee until he gets his bearings again might cost the company some money in the short term, but you'll never convince me that this isn't the right approach.

EVERY ORGANIZATION CAN IMPROVE ITS INTERNAL COMMUNICATIONS

An advertising executive was describing the challenge of creating a global campaign for a bank. The biggest obstacle was what he called 'the silo mentality' of the bank's divisions. Each division operated as a self-contained unit, hunkered deep in its own silo, with no regard for anything beyond the silo walls. The investment bankers didn't talk to people in the retail division who, in turn, didn't talk to the credit-card division, and so on.

Said the ad executive, 'It's tough to come up with a unifying global theme for an organization whose component parts are not unified and don't act as if they are global'.

I can certainly sympathize with this advertising executive's dilemma (and I have even more empathy for the bank's CEO). My biggest managerial challenge as the head of a company with 80 offices around the world is getting our far-flung executives to communicate with each other.

Let me be clear what I'm talking about here. I'm not talking about executives cooperating with each other, or getting along, or operating in a synergistic manner that meshes the company's various resources.

My concern is much more elementary. I worry that the people in our Stockholm office don't talk to the people in our Sydney office. I worry that they don't know our people in Sydney. Worse yet, I worry that they don't even know we have a Sydney office!

(It's not a far-fetched problem. It's very real. Think about your organization. How many people in other offices – or other departments – do you know or talk to?)

Before you can attack this problem, you have to say goodbye to some false assumptions.

You can't assume that geography is the easy solution. You can't presume that people who work in close proximity at the same facility are actually communicating with each other, or that putting them in close quarters will somehow improve communications.

For example, I have been under a lot of pressure during the past few years to consolidate our London operations – where we have four different office buildings – under one roof so everyone can have coffee together and run into each other at the water cooler.

That is a worthy sentiment. Yet I can't help recalling two of our executives in Cleveland, one in our golf division, the other in tennis, who on paper were virtually identical twins. They were both in their early 30s, married with children, living in neighbouring suburbs, and personally outgoing and interested in sports. One worked on the 14th floor, the other on the 11th floor. In my mind it seemed fair to assume that at some point over the years they would have run into each other in the elevator or gotten together to trade ideas or commiserate about business or simply because they had so much in common. In reality, they had never met. They were so busy working away in their particular 'silo' that they never had the opportunity or inclination to get together.

You also can't assume that the new technologies for communication – the cell phones, e-mails, and pocket communicators – can eliminate the problem.

For example, in late 1999 the head of our women's tennis division, Stephanie Tolleson, signed up as clients the dynamic tennis playing sisters, Venus and Serena Williams. It was a coup for our tennis division and, quite appropriately, we announced it via e-mail to everyone in the company. Stephanie deservedly received dozens of e-mails congratulating her. But every message was from *someone who already knew her.* That's the problem with the new technology. Cell phones and e-mail ease the *process* of reaching other people, but you still have to know who those people are. You still need a pre-existing relationship with them.

Nor can you assume that mutual professional interests will somehow get people talking. I know one media magnate who oversees a stable of magazines as well as a book publishing house. The two operations are housed in separate buildings in midtown Manhattan. This magnate employs some of the smartest, most aggressive editors in the business. Whether they're publishing books or monthly magazines, these editors have the same agendas. They're always chasing the next big story, pursuing the best writers, and scouting for the next major trend:

'You'd think that the book editors would occasionally talk to the magazine editors about ideas or up-and-coming writers – and vice versa,' he said to me. 'But with few exceptions, they don't.'

I guess internal communication is his biggest challenge, too.

Once you appreciate that people are not talking to each other, you realize that you have to force the issue.

In our London office, for example, we organize regular lunches where we invite people from different divisions to break bread around the table and, if nothing else, put a face to a name they may have heard along the way.

In our North American operations, we now require all our line executives to summarize their deals on behalf of clients during the past three months. We then publish these items as pithy news bulletins in a Quarterly Report. Because of the nature of our business, some of these items are familiar to our employees from the daily sports pages. But it's amazing how many people use this report to learn that so-and-so is a client or that we have a lucrative relationship with XYZ Corp. Without this Quarterly Report, they'd never know. Who would have told them?

Personally, I do my bit, too. If I have forty conversations a day with people who work for us, I'd bet that at some point in at least thirty of them I urge the other person to communicate with someone else in our company. 'Will you please tell that to (fill in the blank) . . .' is probably my favourite phrase in business.

Perhaps it should be every manager's as well.

THE BEAN COUNTERS HAVE MORE POWER THAN YOU IMAGINE (AND THAT'S ALL RIGHT)

It's fashionable to automatically deride a company's 'bean counters.' They're the calculator jockeys whose devotion to budgets and fiscal sanity allegedly stifles the creative entrepreneurial impulses of the salespeople and line executives who are doing the 'real work' at the company. All they know is numbers. They don't understand how the real world works.

It's safe to say this view is more myth than reality now. It's certainly the case at our company, where we give our 'bean counters' a lot of power and discretion now.

It wasn't always that way. In the early days of our company, I wasn't very sophisticated about accounting or auditing. No one in our company had ever heard the word 'internal audit.' In those days, we would simply send the auditor out to an office and say, 'Find out where they screwed up.'

It took me a while to realize that this approach is fine when you're a small organization of 30 or 40 people. When you're that small you have a good idea of what's going on in every part of the company. Everyone knows each other and gets along. You need an accountant, not a police-man or spy who makes people nervous.

But when your company gets to a certain size – about the time when the CEO no longer knows the name of everyone who works for him – and new people are getting hired and travelling around the world and doing deals, you have a totally different need. You need maximum oversight and total cooperation from the people being overseen.

We gradually learned that for our internal auditing to be effective, we had to present it to our people in a way that convinced them they were being helped by the process. We had to reassure executives that we were looking for efficiencies, not wrongdoing – and we had to do it in terms our people could appreciate. For example, an auditor who recovers a $50,000 double payment of an invoice delivers an economic benefit equal to a salesperson who sold a $250,000 client endorsement with a 20 per cent commission to our company. When we started positioning auditing in terms that our executives understood, they became more supportive.

Over the years, I've become very aggressive about injecting auditors into situations where our executives at first did not welcome them. But over time I've seen our people appreciate how much value an auditor can add to some of the most mundane or innocent transactions.

For example, we always have an auditor involved from day one in any acquisition. That may seem obvious now, but it didn't to us for a long time. When we were negotiating to acquire another company or sports property, we usually let the executive who initiated the acquisition work out the deal points. Eventually we realized that the dealmakers in our company weren't necessarily the best people to establish the true value of the acquisition. They didn't know how to inventory assets or place a fair and fully depreciated value on the equipment. In a lot of cases, the dealmakers also weren't as objective as they should be. After all, they were acquiring the assets of a friend, someone who they would be working with after the deal was done. We learned that injecting an auditor into the negotiation – and letting him or her be the bad cop – almost always delivered a better deal for us.

We've also found auditors to be valuable in our joint ventures. We partnered up with another company to create 'The Skins Game'. When you do business with a partner who is a friend, you tend to trust each other implicitly. When you have a hit, no one on either side tends to challenge the system or speculate whether you should be making even more money. Both sides are happy. Why rock the boat? An auditor is good for rocking the boat. In the case of The Skins Game, our auditors determined that both we and our partner could be doing better on some of our contracts. We recovered money, which not only made our side of the ledger look better, but made our partner happy too.

We also rely on auditors to make sure that our clients receive the proper royalties from their endorsement and licensing deals. This isn't extraordinary. Royalty audits should be conducted by auditors. But our auditors have uncovered things in their reviews that have totally reshaped how we negotiate licensing agreements.

A few years ago, for example, I felt that one of our major licensing clients was getting shortchanged on a licensing agreement. The merchandise bearing the client's name was flying out of stores, but we were seeing only a fraction of the money we expected. An audit of the books revealed that our Japanese partner wasn't cheating us. The flaw was in the contract our executives had negotiated, specifically two words that paid our client a royalty based on the cost of goods in Japan rather than on the greater 'landed cost' of goods when they arrived in the US. It was a costly lesson. But since that audit, we have revamped the way we negotiate offshore licensing agreements.

I could continue with examples of how much influence the 'bean counters' have assumed at our company. But the point should be self-evident. If you think the financial types at your company don't have both feet firmly in the real world and, as a result, don't include in any important transaction, you're costing your company money.

NOT EVERY BUDGET DESERVES YOUR RESPECT

A great restaurateur I know was overseeing the opening of a new restaurant in New York City. He had committed several millions dollars to the design and construction of the dining room, which he hoped would become one of the city's most distinctive salons. Every few days he would visit the site to check in with his contractor and make sure that the construction was going smoothly.

On one particular morning, as the job was nearing completion, the restaurateur was disturbed by what he found. The finish work on the mouldings in the ceiling was sloppy. The door fixtures the contractor had ordered were not of the highest quality. The curtain rods should have been a higher gauge of steel.

The restaurateur, a courtly but street-savvy man who knew every trick a contractor could use to shave costs from a budget (and increase his profit on the job), was not happy and let the contractor know it on the spot.

The contractor protested. 'Hey, I'm doing the job on schedule and, better yet, I'm exactly on budget.'

The restaurateur exploded 'I don't care if you are on budget. Budgets are for mediocrities. I'm trying to build the best restaurant in the world. I expect you to be *over* budget!'

I'm not sure this logic works for every kind of business. But the restaurateur instinctively knew that showmanship – the grand gestures and the occasional display of excess – makes up a big part of elegant dining. He also knew that showmanship carries a high price tag, and he was willing to pay whatever it cost.

In his line of work and at his level of ambition, a robust contempt for budgets is not only healthy but probably the only way to do business.

I suspect the same sort of contempt for budgets might be useful in other organizations as well. After all, given the choice of being a) over budget with the job done, b) on budget with the job not done, or c) under budget with the job not done, I would always choose (a). I may have overspent, but at least I have something to show for it. I can't say that with the other options. If sticking to the budget means I didn't get the job done, I've wasted all the money.

It doesn't take a genius to see this. But like the contractor above, some people have an almost religious obeisance to budgets. They tremble at the thought of exceeding their spending authority. What they fail to see, of course, is that budgets are elastic and ever-changing estimates, and they should be treated with enlightened scepticism (if not with outright contempt).

Even when we were a young company, I was sceptical of budgets. I could see how, in a vague way, they let us control spending during a fiscal year. But I always had a problem with the self-fulfilling nature of budgets. If you give some people $10,000 a year to spend on travel and entertainment, they'll spend their limit even if some expenses are unnecessary.

I also think budgets can be self-limiting. Adhere to them too strictly, and you are risking eternal mediocrity. How, in a dynamic industry, can you presume to forecast accurately your budget needs 12 months down the road? And what do you do if you're wrong?

Say we have a tennis division consisting of a dozen executives and client managers, a dozen assistants, and three financial people to handle income and outgoings. Managerial common sense will tell you that, with 27 employees in a division, you must have a budget. The division head has to be in control of his people's salaries and travel and entertainment expenses. But I wonder: what good does that do? What if by December the division head has spent his travel budget, but for $5000 he could fly to Australia and sign up some 17-year-old who is going to be the next Pete Sampras. Am I going to say, 'You can't go?'

I don't think so. If the difference between having a great tennis division and a mediocre one is the difference between being on budget or $5000 over, I will always break the budget.

If consistency is the hobgoblin of small minds, then too much respect for budgets is the curse of the eternally mediocre.

Relying on budgets inevitably creates a profit-centre mentality in an organization. Suddenly, every expense and income stream has to be allocated to a specific part of the company. But that can be a two-edged sword. On the one hand, divvying up income and outgoings this way certainly tells a manager how a particular group is doing and what each group is contributing to the whole.

On the other hand, it creates internal rivalries and jealousies. Group heads bicker about how much of 'their' money is being charged to overhead or the legal department. They want to know why they should have to pay for a computer they didn't ask for. When a big deal is in the works, rather than having two senior executives in agreement saying 'Let's get this contract for the company,' I find them more likely to say, 'I want it for my profit centre.' Ultimately, they will start feuding over this, and the company always loses from this fight. I spend so much time in that sort of dialogue that I wonder if profit centres, as a management tool, are worth it.

But perhaps the worst problem with budgets, is that they don't always provide an accurate picture of what's happening. People can never be strictly defined or judged by numbers.

For example, in our client management business, we basically represent athletes, classical musicians, models, and writers. Every once in a while we take on a client who doesn't quite fit in any of these categories, which was the case recently when we began working with Senator Bob Dole after his 1996 run for President. A few months into the relationship, one of our New York executives used her contacts with an ad agency to get the Senator a lucrative contract for a television commercial. It was a nifty sale for her and she logically assumed that she and her group would be credited with the income. Our accounting people thought otherwise. The commercial was a one-time non-recurring event. To book the income into her group would distort the group's true performance in its core business. So, as a matter of bookkeeping convenience, we allocated the income into the catchall area of 'special projects.'

I'm told this upset the woman. She was worried that, at her year-end review, we would look at her group's numbers and overlook the wonderful sale she had made for Dole. I doubt if that would happen. But I can see why she was upset. If you have too much respect for budgets, you begin to think that everyone else does, too. I can't help thinking that a healthy contempt for budgets would have eased her mind and let her enjoy her triumph regardless of where the income landed in our budget system.

9 Etiquette for the New Millennium

THINK TWICE BEFORE YOU SPLASH SOMEONE, OR WHY EVERY BUSINESS IS LIKE A SMALL TOWN

A friend of mine has a theory that people behave differently in small towns than they do in big towns. If you're driving on Main Street in a small town and accidentally run through a puddle and splash a pedestrian, you would stop the car and get out to apologize to the person you soaked. That's quintessential small-town behaviour – because everyone knows one another in a small town. And you behave differently when people know who you are and you, in turn, know them and expect to see them again in the near future.

It's different in a big town. If you drove down Fifth Avenue in Manhattan and splashed a pedestrian, you'd probably keep on driving. That's quintessential big-town behaviour. It's very unlikely that you know the pedestrian or that the pedestrian recognizes you, and even less likely that you will run into each other again. The different circumstances – particularly the fact that most people are strangers in a big city and remain that way – dictate different behaviour.

My friend was making a larger point though. There will be times when you find yourself in a big town, surrounded by strangers with big-town ways. On those occasions you shouldn't forget your small-town roots. Even in a big town, small-town behaviour is the right approach.

I can't think of too many situations in business when big-town ways are preferable to small-town ways. In my experience, every business is like a small town. The people you deal with – from the regular customers and clients to the prospects who never return your phone calls – may seem like strangers but they are really your neighbours. And you should behave accordingly. Think twice before you splash them. And if you do splash them, apologize – because they'll remember if you don't, will tell their neighbours' who'll remember it as well, and eventually it will come back to haunt you.

You could build a whole world view around this small town/big town dichotomy where every action that people take is explained by whether they know the other parties involved and expect to have dealings with them again.

Once you're aware of it, you can see this dichotomy rearing its pernicious head all the time in business.

In our business of athlete representation, for example, almost anyone can call themselves an agent. All you need is an athlete willing to turn over his or her affairs to you. As a result, given this low cost of entry, our business attracts a lot of dilettantes. Many of these people have one or two clients and conduct themselves 'professionally' as if they are just passing through.

I recall some years ago when one particular agent decided to get out of the golf management business. As he was severing his industry ties, a problem arose with his one major client. Because he was leaving the business for good, this manager ended up in a nasty lawsuit with his golf client. He did things that he never would have done if he had remained in the business. But he was passing through and didn't care about the repercussions of his behaviour.

At our company we have a vested interest in the long-term health and integrity of our industry. I doubt if we would stay in business very long if we resolved all our problems by suing our clients. We can't behave as if we're passing through town, because this is where we live and everyone knows us and we know them.

The most resounding argument for small-town behaviour occurs in thorny contractual situations when the reality of a situation clashes with the terms of a contract.

In theory, contractual problems call for classic big-town behaviour. You hammer out the terms of a contract as aggressively as your personality allows and stick to the terms through the life of the deal, regardless of how onerous or unfair they may turn out to be to one side or the other. A deal's a deal. If you don't intend to honour it or enforce it, why bother having a contract?

The reality is a little different. Changed circumstances can transform a perfectly fair contract into a miserably lopsided one. That's great for you if you're the one benefiting from this unexpected tilt. But what if the other party, the one on the short end of the deal, is unhappy and expects some relief from you?

If you never expect to do business with them again, you might stick to the original terms. That's big-town behaviour.

If you hope to continue doing business with them, you should yield in some way that's fair to both of you and makes them happy. That's not just appropriate for small-town scenarios. It's the right thing to do in any business situation.

I remember a problem that arose with Arnold Palmer's savings account many years ago.

When we first started handling Arnold's business affairs, he and I had a very simple client-manager agreement, sealed with a handshake. It was simple and elegant. For managing all of Arnold's business affairs, we received a 10 per cent commission on all his income. I emphasize the all. There were no codicils or amendments excluding certain types of income.

One of the first things we did with Arnold's money was set up an interest-bearing savings account. As I recall, in the first year. Arnold earned $140 interest on his savings. Our commission came to $14.

In the ensuing years, as Arnold's success on and off the golf course grew, so did his savings account – to the point where our commission on his interest income alone came to a healthy five-figure sum.

Arnold took me aside one day and pointed out that he didn't think commissioning savings account interest was fair. It may have been our agreement but it didn't reflect the spirit of our relationship. He also added that commissioning interest was a double dip. After all, we had already taken our commission on the income before he deposited it in the bank. Why were we commissioning the money again?

It took me about two seconds to see Arnold's point and agree to the change.

In these sorts of binds I always remember Lew Wasserman's advice that the only value of a contract is that 'it is a document which provides the basis for negotiation.' Sometimes you have right on your side, sometimes the other side has the upper hand. In either case, if one side is unhappy, it doesn't pay to stick to your guns. Even if you never expect to do business with the other side again, it's much more admirable (and profitable in the long run) to behave as if you will.

SHRINK YOUR WORLD INTO A SMALL TOWN

Let's stay with this small town idea for a little while longer – because there are worthwhile lessons here.

Whenever I visit Los Angeles and stay at the Peninsula Hotel, I have to remind myself that I'm in the sports business and that I'm a stranger in a town that is the capital of the entertainment industry. But the Peninsula makes it tough for a guest not to feel like a Hollywood mogul.

It starts with the newspapers you find at your door in the morning. Where most hotels give you the local daily, *USA Today*, and maybe *The Wall Street Journal*, the Peninsula provides all of these plus exotic material such as *Daily Variety* and *The Hollywood Reporter*. Naturally, I read them. But these 'industry trades' are dangerous. After a week of immersing myself in their tales of Hollywood gossip, box-office grosses, and who's suing who at the film studios, I sometimes harbour fantasies that I, too, should be putting together movie deals and TV series.

Fortunately, I only visit Los Angeles for a week at a time and this feeling passes the moment I leave town.

But the effect of these publications is interesting. Los Angeles is a sprawling, complicated city with a rich mix of business. It's not just an 'entertainment industry town.' It only seems that way if you read *Daily Variety* and *The Hollywood Reporter*. These publications somehow manage to reduce a huge city into a small town where everyone knows everyone else's business and no one is more than a phone call or two removed from anyone else.

That's not necessarily bad. No matter how expansive your territory, there's a lot to be said for operating in it as if it were a 'small town.'

For one thing, it's easier to get things done in a tight, insular community with shared interests and goals. It's easier to reach people and explain yourself. You have a shared history. You speak the same language and can almost communicate in shorthand.

More importantly people behave differently in a small town. When people know they will have to see their neighbours again in the near future, they tend to be nicer. They're more polite, more accommodating, more willing to yield on the tough issues – precisely because they might need their neighbours to yield on a tough point tomorrow.

For those reasons alone, it would seem wise for us to construct scenarios that tighten up our universe of clients, customers, and contacts and make it feel like a small town. But most of us don't. We're constantly striving to enlarge our sphere of influence and expand our circle of contacts. Ironically, the opposite tack is better.

I noticed this a few years ago at a business conference. Of the three thousand conference attendees. I suspect I could have had a productive private meeting with a third of the people there. Yet over the course of the four-day event, I found myself gravitating to the same two-dozen people, nearly all of whom I had known well or in passing before the conference. If the purpose of going to conferences and trade shows is to learn, to network, and to advertise yourself – to hand out your business card to the maximum number of new faces – then I failed miserably.

On the last day of the conference, I hosted a dinner for these two dozen friends. It was a beautiful and rewarding evening, during the course of which it occurred to me that if I never left that room again, I could still run a thriving business simply by staying in touch with the people in that room. These were my friends. We thought alike. We had common interests. They knew our company's capabilities. And I had a pretty good idea of what we should be doing for them. More important, they had friends outside the room, and if I did my job well for them, they would tell their friends.

Virtually all of the business we've done as a result of that conference has derived from the two dozen people at that dinner, and virtually none has derived from the dozens of strangers with whom I exchanged pleasantries and business cards during the rest of that week.

In hindsight, I realize I had turned a large conference into a small meeting of friends – a big city of strangers into a small town of neighbours. And the results were hard to ignore.

Remember this the next time you feel overwhelmed by all the people you have to see, all the phone calls you haven't returned, all the prospects that seem to be falling through the cracks because you're just too busy. If your universe is getting too big to handle, perhaps it's time to size it down, to turn it into a small town where everyone you meet treats you like a friend and neighbour. I can't see how this would be bad for business.

BE NICER TO THE PEOPLE BELOW YOU, TOUGHER ON THE PEOPLE ABOVE

A few of my associates and I were in a large meeting at another company. The company's CEO was running 20 minutes late, we were told by the senior vice president who had arranged the meeting, but it was all right to start without him. I generally hate starting off meetings without the top decision-maker present, but this meeting has stuck in my mind because of the remarkable behaviour of this senior vice president.

He was a crisply tailored man in his early 40s. Even if he hadn't been sporting monogrammed cuff links and flashy yellow suspenders adorned with golfing bears, I could tell this man was clearly vain and a little too pleased with himself. The giveaway: his imperious and uncivil treatment of his associates. In the course of those first 20 minutes, this man managed to interrupt, contradict, or insult each of the five associates present at least once. (That's quite a feat. Most corporate boors would need one or two hours.)

Then the CEO walked in.

The alteration in the man's behaviour was impossible to miss. With the CEO sitting next to him, he became as warm and cuddly as the golfing bears on his suspenders. He was polite and willing to listen. Towards his boss, he was deferential to the point of sycophancy. In front of our eyes, he had transformed himself from a jerk to a classic 'yes man' (although to many people these are one and the same thing).

It's striking how often people get sycophancy wrong.

They think the best way to impress their superiors and get ahead is to obey their superiors. For the most part, that's a wise strategy. It's certainly better than being habitually contrary and disobedient. But people take it too far. They think obeying the boss is the same as never challenging the boss. Worse yet, they are willing to obey the boss at any cost – even if it comes at the expense of their peers and subordinates. They think that if they are extremely careful with the people above them in the hierarchy, that gives them a licence to be careless with the feelings and welfare of the people below.

Not true. The reverse strategy is much wiser: you should be nicer to the people below you and tougher on the people above.

Consider, for example, this common business scenario. A man arrives at an airport ticket counter to learn that his flight has been cancelled. He will do anything to get on a plane. Unfortunately, doing anything to him means turning into a bully. Instead of pulling back and calmly assessing the situation, he reacts emotionally and aims his emotions at the easiest target – namely, the ticket agent. He berates the agent (who is blameless), curses the airline, demands to see the supervisor, and generally makes a fool of himself. The venting makes him feel good for a moment. But it has hardly endeared him to the ticket agent. The agent, who has surely seen this behaviour before, is standing there thinking, 'Keep screaming, fellow. But there's no way you're talking to my supervisor or getting on a plane today!'

The man's mistake is simple: he was rough to the wrong person.

The correct response would have been to be extremely nice to the agent and say, 'Look, I know this isn't your fault and you're really busy. But I really need to get on a flight. Can you direct me to your supervisor or someone in customer services who can help me?' That, at least, would get the man to the next step in solving his dilemma. Then, if necessary, he can take a tougher (though not rude) position with the supervisor. That's a big reason supervisors exist – to catch flak from angry customers and solve their problems.

It's not much different in any other work place environment. If you're rough and unmannered to your subordinates, you're hardly making a positive impression on them. They'll put up with it for a while. But eventually they'll find an escape route that leads to more civil pastures.

You're also not impressing a boss like me.

Over the years, I've heard reports of executives in our company who have been less than polite to underlings. A part of me thinks, 'Gee, that's odd. I've never seen them behave that way around me.'

A bigger part of me, however, is not surprised. After all, I'm the boss. They're on their best behaviour around me.

But a much bigger part of me is disturbed by this duplicity. As the boss, I want people to be completely candid with me. I need that candour. It's the only way I can be sure I'm getting solid information on which to base my decisions. But as a boss, I also realize that candour, especially when it contradicts me or comes in the form of unexpected bad news, is precisely what many subordinates are most afraid to give me.

That's why it's disturbing when I hear about people behaving one way around me and the opposite around their subordinates. It's not only rude and abhorrent behaviour. It makes me wonder which is their true personality. If they're talking differently to me than to everyone else, it makes me suspect the truth and value of everything they tell me. As advisors, they are almost useless to me.

That's why it's infinitely more impressive to be nice to your subordinates and tough with your superiors. Try it sometime. Everyone will notice. You will not only gain your subordinates' loyalty and commitment, you will gain your bosses' respect and trust.

FRIENDS DON'T ASK THE IMPOSSIBLE OF THEIR FRIENDS

The playwright Henrik Ibsen said, 'The trouble with friends is not what you have to do for them but what you can't do because of them.' I was reminded of this when I called a meeting of several executives to deal with an emergency we were having with a sports federation. After reviewing the problem, the best solution we could come up with involved asking one of the federation's major corporate sponsors to intercede on our behalf. (This wasn't a particularly elegant solution. Ordinarily, I'd prefer going directly to the federation rather than the indirect route of an intermediary. But it was a touchy situation that seemed to demand a third party to press our case.)

At that point in the meeting all eyes turned to one of our senior executives – because it was well known that he had a close personal relationship with the president of one of the federation's biggest corporate sponsors.

The two executives had done a lot of business together over the years. They vacationed together with their families. They talked to each other nearly every day. In short, they were buddies. And now we were asking this executive to get his buddy to lean on the federation to help us out.

To my initial chagrin, the executive refused. I was dumbfounded. All that time and effort cultivating the friendship, I thought, and the friendship doesn't do us any good when we need it!

But our executive had his reasons.

He said it would put the president in a tough spot, forcing him to advocate a position that benefited us more than him or the federation. Furthermore, the repercussions of such interference were hard to measure. In a worst-case scenario, we could end up with three sides mad at each other rather than the current stalemate of two sides mildly annoyed. The request also had the potential of fracturing his friendship with the man, which meant more to our executive than any single business deal.

Put that way, it was hard to argue with his position. Our executive understood instinctively that there were certain lines in business you shouldn't cross with friends and that doing so can ruin a friendship, It's a point that, sadly, escapes a lot of people. They automatically turn to a friend in a pinch, blithely unaware that such a request has consequences. It's not that these people are cavalier about their friendships. On the contrary, that's what friends are for – to turn to in a pinch. Rather, they are blind to the aftershocks of asking a favour. They don't appreciate that there are rules in business about what you should and shouldn't ask of a friend.

The most common mistake, I suspect, is when you ask your friends to solve a problem for *you* that creates a problem for *them.*

It's not hard to find a business lesson for any occasion in *The Godfather*. But people often forget that the plot line of *The Godfather* pivots on a test of friendship. The ambitious thug Solozzo wants to team up with the Godfather, Don Corleone, in selling drugs and narcotics, an heretofore forbidden avenue of crime. To do so successfully, Solozzo needs the protection of all the judges and politicians that Don Corleone has in his hip pocket. The Don refuses, explaining that it's true, he has many friends in politics, but they would not be so friendly if his business were narcotics instead of a harmless vice such as gambling. No matter how attractive the profit margins would be in drugs, it would be a disaster in the long term if it cost the Corleone family its political muscle. Thus, he declines Solozzo's offer, which leads to the attempt on his life that jump-starts the entire narrative.

There's a nugget of wisdom about friendship buried in this scene. The

Don played out the scenario in his mind a few steps beyond what he stood to gain in terms of money. He saw what no one else was looking at: when you ask your friends to solve a problem for you that ends up creating a problem for them, nobody wins.

The other mistake I've noticed is when people ask their friends to promise to try to help out. They're not expecting miracles. All they want to know is that their friends 'tried.'

This is almost worse than asking friends to do something that might run against their best interests. In effect, you're asking for the impossible. You are asking your friends to do something that you don't think they can do. The end result of this scenario is rarely pretty. Your friends fail to help. You are disappointed (and further behind than when you started), and your friends feel foolish for not being able to rise to the occasion. They feel they have let you down even though they sense you have sent them on a fool's errand.

Most friendships are solid enough to endure this sort of messiness. But a smart business person would be wise enough to play out the scene in his or her mind to its logical conclusion. A smart business person would never ask a friend to promise to try.

DEVELOP A GENIUS FOR FRIENDSHIP

Some years ago I attended a memorial service in New York for a friend, a successful lawyer who had died suddenly and too soon. The people who spoke at the service provided a memorable tribute to the man. But even more memorable were the people in the pews who didn't get the chance to speak. Among the man's family and mourners were some of the wealthiest people in America, a former Vice President, several Cabinet members, movie stars, celebrated broadcasters, distinguished authors, college presidents, the owners of two local sports teams, and superstar athletes. Until that moment, I had no idea this man had such a wide and impressive circle of friends – friends who, like myself, felt close enough to him to attend his memorial service. He was someone we would all miss dearly.

Later on, as I talked to the other guests about their connection to the man, it became singularly clear that he had a talent for meeting and bonding with people. He had, as one speaker put it, a 'genius for friendship'.

That phrase made a big impression on me. It struck me that where other people in life devote their time to all sorts of pursuits – some to making money or raising a family, others to charitable causes or public service, still others to lowering their golf handicap or perfecting any of a thousand avocational skills – this man had, with an almost scary discipline, devoted his life to making friends.

The life he led is not for all of us. But the goal he set for himself is a worthy one – and worthy of emulating in some part by all of us.

Fred Adams, who is my oldest friend in the world, likes to tell a story about the first time we met. We were on the first tee at the Chikaming Country Club in Lakeside, Michigan, playing in a schoolboy golf tournament. I was 14, Fred was 16. As Fred remembers it (quite accurately. I might add), he shot a 78 that day while I shot a 67. That's the moment, he says, he decided he wanted me as his friend rather than his adversary.

My point is this: if you want to improve the cast of friends in your life, you have to approach the acquisition of friends proactively rather than reactively. You can't wait for friends to seek you out because a) there's no guarantee it will happen with the ease and pace that you expect and b) you have ceded control over who your friends will be. They are choosing you. You are not choosing them.

To get to this stage in life, you have to make a conscious decision about the importance of friendship in your life. Most people never think about it. They believe, perhaps correctly, that they already have enough friends. They don't have the time for more friends. They can barely handle the ones they've got.

This is one of the great delusions about personal relationships. There's no law that says you can only accommodate three or four truly close friends, professionally or personally, at any one time. But first you have to believe that having more friends in your life is a blessing, not a curse. Believe me, it's a lot easier when you dictate who is or isn't your friend.

Another lesson about developing friendships comes from Benjamin Franklin who said. 'To make a friend out of thine enemy, ask him for a favour'. His point was that when someone does a favour for someone else, a bond is formed, not as you would expect because the person on the receiving end feels a need to reciprocate but rather because the giver somehow feels connected to the person receiving the favour. The act of doing a favour for someone makes you feel protective of them. You have an investment in their welfare, in whether the favour helps them or not.

Think about it. When was the last time someone allowed you to help them out. The act of doing something nice for another person surely made you feel as good as the other person felt. (That's a truism: if you want to feel good about yourself, make someone else feel good.)

But let's take it to the next level. What if the favour doesn't get the job done. This person still needs help. How do you feel now? Chances are you'll continue to help until the problem is solved. Without realizing it, you are interested in the outcome. You have an emotional investment in seeing that it turns out well. In short, you've acquired a new friend.

It's a simple turn-the-tables strategy. If you want to make new friends, stop doing favours for strangers. Let them do favours for you.

A final point about friendship: I have always contended that, all things being equal, people will do business with a friend. In fact, all things not being equal, people will still do business with a friend.

But there's an important caveat to this: if you're doing business with a friend, don't forget to be friendly.

Incidental slights and tiny errors tend to be magnified out of proportion when friends are involved. This isn't necessarily fair, but it's the way of the world. And it goes a long way to explaining why clients abandon seemingly solid relationships for the flimsiest excuses.

I could be doing mind-blowing work on contracts, investments, and taxes for a golf champion. But if I neglect the personal touches, such as congratulating him on a victory or asking him about his stroke, I shouldn't be too surprised when he turns to someone more thoughtful. At that point, the damage is done; no amount of backtracking or fence-mending will get us back in his good graces.

When it comes to friends in business, I genuinely believe you can do 50 per cent less professionally if you give 25 per cent more personally.

(This is by no means a licence to substitute phoniness or fake charm for quality work. But it does point up that quality in a service or product is not what you put into it. It is what the client or customer gets out of it.)

This is certainly true in our business, and probably applies to law firms and brokerage houses and advertising agencies as well. I even think people will stick with a doctor who doesn't heal them as quickly but who has a reassuring and confident 'bedside' manner.

READING PEOPLE REQUIRES MORE THAN ONE READING

I'm a big believer in the notion that you can pick up important insights about people by aggressively observing their behaviour on the golf course, the tennis court, what they order in restaurants, etc. Of course, this begs the question, 'Why can't you do the same thing reading people in straight business situations?'

The reason I think insights from the golf course or tennis court are important is precisely because they take place outside of the normal business routine, on weekends or in relaxed venues, where people let their guard down and, consciously or not, let the more interesting elements of their true character come out. That's less likely to occur in 'straight business situations' when everyone is wearing their 'game face' and studiously working to make the best impression.

The larger point: people clues can be found anywhere anytime, but the social and recreational fringes of business are a particularly rich (and underappreciated) source of insights.

The biggest problem I have with trying to gauge people in strictly business situations is that many clues are misleading or impossible to interpret. I know one extremely successful European conglomerateur who, five minutes into every meeting, pulls out an elaborate chain of silver worry beads and plays with them. If I didn't know him better, I might conclude that he was nervous or superstitious. If I wanted to overthink the situation, I might take special note of the subject we are discussing the moment he pulls out the beads – as if that were a valid indicator of the subject's importance to him. I eventually learned that the beads indicate nothing – except they have helped him quit smoking. They are certainly not a sign of weakness or vulnerability.

The best way to pick up clues is to have a clear idea of what you're looking for. Before most meetings, I make a mental checklist of reasonable expectations. For example, if I'm calling on someone at their office, I can reasonably expect them to be cordial, to be punctual, and to hold all phone calls during our meeting. If they fail to meet one or more of these minimum requirements, that tells me something about them or, at least, about their attitude toward me.

Not long ago two associates and I drove from New York to Pennsylvania for a noon meeting with a computer software company interested in developing a software product around one of our clients. Since we had been on the road for three hours and arrived at 12 o'clock sharp, it was not unreasonable for us to expect our hosts to serve us lunch. As we entered the building, I turned to my associates and said, 'Let's see how clued-up these people are. Do you think they've thought about lunch for us?' It turned out they hadn't. They gave us a tour of the facility and hauled us straight into their conference room, never asking if we were hungry. I remember thinking then that this oversight was a bad omen. No matter how good the company's products were, the people would overlook some of the 'real world' details in marketing them. In hindsight, that's what happened. They made a great product with our client, but had no idea how to sell it.

Of course, it's dangerous to pigeon-hole people on first meeting. The clues they send out take time to appreciate.

A few years ago I had back to back meetings in a midwestern city with two nationally prominent entrepreneurs. Each of these men were powerful forces in their sports-crazy community and I thought it would be worth-while to meet them and tell them about our company.

The first meeting was with a banking tycoon who could not have been more hospitable. He knew all about me and our company. He said he had been eager to meet me for years. He literally bathed me in the warm glow of his respect and admiration. I left his ornate wood-panelled chambers thinking, 'That was a great meeting'.

I then went across town to meet Tycoon No. 2 who could not have been less hospitable. He knew nothing about me or our company, he hadn't bothered to read the material I had sent, and took at least five calls from his stockbroker during our discussion. It seemed all he wanted from me was some free marketing ideas for one of his under-achieving divisions. He had no interest in charming or impressing me or making me feel comfortable. As I left his office, his subordinate who had brought us together actually apologized for his boss's rudeness.

I mention this as a caveat about reading people too quickly. Over the years we've done a lot of business with 'rude' Tycoon No. 2 and absolutely nothing with the 'friendly' banker. And yet the day of our first meetings, I would have bet the opposite would be true. In hindsight, I think the banking tycoon was so nice because he knew no business would transpire between us; he treated my visit as a social call. On the other hand, I can see now that Tycoon No. 2's no-nonsense style was a positive signal. That's the way he does business with everyone. In that sense, his rudeness was merely the opening move in his negotiating strategy.

That's the tricky part about insights. You can't rely on one clue. You have to accumulate clues constantly. You have to analyse them and play them against each other. And be sufficiently open-minded to adjust their meaning. Only then can you pick up insights that will give you an edge.

A 'HEADS UP' HAS CONSEQUENCES TOO

Have you noticed how many times your friends in business call you to give you some small but vital titbit of information on the off-chance that you can put it to good use in your career? I call this sort of exchange a 'heads up' – as in, 'I heard that your client was interviewing other agencies about taking on some of your business. I thought you could use this heads up.'

It's not quite gossip. It's not secret information. It doesn't involve betrayal of a confidence or a fiduciary trust. It's more like a warning to you from a second party about a third party who can affect your livelihood.

It's also not new. People have been trading casual information about their neighbours and acquaintances ever since there was information to be traded. But with the emergence of modems, e-mail, intranets, the internet, cell phones, and other personal communications systems, it seems to me that we are in the middle of a heads up epidemic. I don't have statistics to back up this claim. It's merely an observation that with all the emerging tools and formats for creating and obtaining information, its inevitable that more people will be sharing this information with each other.

In truth, there's nothing wrong with giving and receiving a heads up. In some ways, how you deal with this sort of casual information says a lot about how connected and effective you are. The greater your network of sources who feed you this information the better informed you are. In an age built on information, it's more true than ever that knowledge is power.

But this sort of knowledge comes with caveats. Consider the following my personal heads up to you about the art of the heads up.

1. Information is a two-way street

To receive heads up information, you have to be willing to do the same for your friends. In effect, you are constructing a personal network of reporters who have your best interests at heart – and vice versa. Remember this the next time someone calls you with a heads up. If you like the information and want to keep it coming, you probably will have to return the favour. That requires a savvy awareness of what is and is not a heads up.

2. A heads up is not gossip

Gossip is idle, or speculative, or malicious. It is also usually false or only half true. Worst of all, gossip damns its messenger as much as it damages its subject.

A heads up is not gossip. For one thing, it should be based on solid evidence. It also doesn't aim to hurt its subject. Rather, the purpose of a heads up is to warn a friend to look up and pay close attention to a situation that he or she has been ignoring. In other words, it is based on good intentions.

3. A heads up doesn't betray a confidence

There's a difference between telling a friend something that he or she might need to know and revealing something that he or she has no right to know. The former is a heads up. The latter is betrayal of a confidence.

In your eagerness to help a friend, it's easy to cross over the line and reveal confidential information. Unfortunately, while you may be helping a friend, you are probably not helping yourself. You're not only exposing yourself to the professional consequences of breaking a confidence, but you're probably also raising doubts among your friends. They would be well within their rights to wonder what else you are telling other people about them.

I can see how anyone can get confused by this. Some years ago a former associate who was a little down on his luck visited me in my office to discuss his next venture. I happened to be privy to some confidential information about a planned merger between two larger groups that would have competed with and quickly wiped out this man's venture.

It was not a pleasant quandary. On the one extreme, I could keep my secret information to myself and let the man sink all his money into what I knew would be a sure loser. On the other extreme, I could tell him everything I knew, which would earn his eternal gratitude but would not be ethical.

In the end, I found a way to steer him to one of the principals in the newly merged venture. He figured out their plans, quickly cancelled his own venture, and eventually talked his way into a job in the newly merged company.

A heads up shouldn't hurt other people's reputations. Don't let it hurt yours.

4. A heads up has consequences

If you give someone a heads up, don't be surprised if it has serious consequences. You can't predict or control the fallout once you put your information out there in the marketplace.

A few years back we offered one of our clients to a major sports sponsor. Our concept was good, but unfortunately we presented it to a slightly dim executive who hated the idea. So we took the concept to one of his competitors, who immediately liked it and made a very fair offer that was acceptable to our client. A deal was struck, contracts to follow.

One of our executives happened to be meeting with a senior executive at the original company that had rejected our proposal and mentioned that we had found an interested party. It was a true heads up, a courtesy rather than a negotiating tactic. The senior executive was taken aback. He was unaware of our original proposal but he insisted that we shouldn't sign anything with his competitor until he could come back with an offer.

Ordinarily we consider two hungry competitors bidding for our client's services to be the ideal negotiating position. It can only drive the price higher.

But in this case it put us in an awkward position. We had already accepted the first offer. To let the company that had originally turned us down back in the game meant going back on our word. But it also meant that we weren't getting the best deal for our client.

Fortunately, the client made it very easy for us. There was no question in his mind about keeping his promise. His word was more important than a few (or even a lot of) extra dollars.

But the situation would never have arisen if someone in our company had thought about the consequences of a seemingly harmless heads up.

THE BOSS CAN ASK A STUPID QUESTION (AND NOT SOUND STUPID)

Not long ago I was distressed to learn that a company with whom I had assumed we had a healthy working relationship had signed a major contract with one of our Pacific Rim competitors to produce a sports event. Now, I don't usually get upset when we lose out on deals, even when they involve our 'friends' and our rivals. I've come to accept that no one can have 100 per cent share of market. But in this case, I thought we had an inside track at the company. One of our executives – at least, according to his memos and expense reports – was spending a lot of time and money with the company, suggesting that we would be the first to know if something good developed.

It didn't work out that way. So I pointedly asked the executive what went wrong. I told him that if I had been spending as much time with the company as he appeared to be doing, I would have known their plans inside and out. I would have been peppering them with questions every chance I got and building a complete dossier on their sports needs.

'That's right, Mark,' he said. 'You would have. But there are some questions I can't ask of people at another company – and you can.'

I thought it was a lame excuse for poor intelligence gathering. But as I thought about it, he had a point. As a CEO, I assume I can say or ask almost anything inside our company. But CEOs of successful companies also have an edge in how they communicate outside their organization, particularly in the kinds of questions they can ask.

I know in my case there are at least four provocative questions I can get away with that other people can't. For example:

I can ask a stupid question – and not look stupid

As the head of a successful company, I carry some positive baggage into a situations. People give me the benefit of the doubt because I run a sharp company. I have smart people working for me. Therefore, I must be smart. Thus, if I'm in a meeting about the sport of curling and someone mentions the greatest curler of all time, the 'Babe Ruth' of curling who is known to everyone with even the remotest interest in curling, I can raise my hand and ask. 'Who's that?' – and not elicit the eternal derision of everyone in the room. A junior executive couldn't get away with that (and probably wouldn't raise his hand).

I can pry about salaries – and not look nosey

In an era where virtually no topic is taboo, people's salaries are still off limits. People will tell you how much they paid for their home, how much, it costs to send their daughter to college, perhaps even how much they have tucked away in their savings account. But they clam up when the subject turns to how much money they make or, for that matter, how much other people make. There's nothing wrong with that. Privacy is still a virtue and most of us have the good sense not to pry.

And yet . . . I could easily get into a salary discussion with the CEO or senior-level executive at another company. If I asked the CEO, 'What does a chief financial officer of a big company like yours make these days?' I'm sure I would get a straight answer – and I wouldn't be perceived as prying. It would be a form of shared intelligence among equals. An executive of lower rank couldn't get away with that.

I can ask about a company's profit margins – and not sound as if I'm going to misuse the information

A company's profit margin is amongst its most precious data. If you know the other side's profitability on a project, you know how much or how little room they have to negotiate. It's not the sort of information that people freely hand out to anyone in a negotiation..

And yet . . . if I'm at the negotiating table and ask the CEO, 'Look, I want to make this deal work. How much profit do you need to make on it?' it doesn't sound intrusive. It sounds as if I'm being constructively curious. The CEO knows that, depending on his answer, I have the authority to adjust my end of the deal to make it work for both of us. A junior person asking the same questions might not be able to do anything even if he did get a straight answer.

An even bigger problem with asking this sort of question at a lower level, of course, is that lower-level people are not in a position to know. The CEO knows. So I ask.

I can ask personal questions – without being intrusive

If someone outside the company whom I didn't know well referred to one of our executives and asked me, 'Does he still have a drinking problem?' I would think the question was inappropriate and impertinent. If I responded at all, it would be no more revealing than, 'What makes you say that?'

And yet, a fellow CEO asking the same question would probably not be out of line. With another CEO, I would assume it wasn't just idle curiosity. The CEO had a good reason for asking. Perhaps he's observed something that I should know about. Perhaps he wants to help. Either way, if a CEO opens this sort of door, I won't automatically shut it. I'd expect the same response if I was asking the personal questions.

In my experience, when a CEO asks a personal question, it sounds as if he's concerned and wants to help. When someone at a lower rank asks the same questions, it rarely sounds like altruism.

The point of all this is not to brag about my superior ability to gather intelligence, but to point out how anyone at any level can get the same edge.

Take the simple act of asking a seemingly stupid question. We've all been taught since we were little children that there's no such thing as a stupid question, and that if you don't know, ask. But we forget these truisms when we get into a room full of people, many of whom are in a position to judge us and may not be as charitable as our parents and teachers were in our youth. Unlike the highest-ranking people in the room, who are usually presumed to be intelligent by virtue of the status they have earned, the rest of us demonstrate our brilliance by speaking up when we know what we're talking about and remaining silent when we don't. It's not that we think we're so smart. It's that we're not sure when we aren't.

It's easy to diffuse this, of course. All you have to do is confess your ignorance by prefacing your question with the phrase, 'Maybe this is a stupid question but . . .' No one can fault you for ignorance if you already admit to it. The real truth, though, is that there are probably other people in the room who are glad that you asked. In my experience, if you don't know, chances are at least one other person in the room doesn't know either.

The smartest people are not afraid of asking so called stupid questions. They don't pretend to know it all.

The same goes for any other kind of intrusive or impertinent question. No matter what your position or status, if you can erase the suspicious motives behind your questions, you can ask almost anything with the same freedom and authority as the most powerful CEO.

Learn the art of picking up the check

A good friend went out to dinner with clients and business associates. At meal's end, when the check came, his tablemates started kidding each other about how short their arms become when the bill arrives. They all seemed to take a slightly perverse pride in their skill at avoiding picking up the check.

'I didn't see what the fuss was about,' said my friend, 'since I always pick up the check (as I did on this occasion). But these fellows had turned the simple act of paying the bill into a contest of wills, as if picking up the check meant you blinked first and you were a chump,'

My friend's tale alarmed me slightly – because it never occurred to me that people in business need instruction in the protocol of paying the bill.

For my part, the protocol is simple: I always pick up the check. I'm at a point in my career where I can afford to. But even in my early years, when I couldn't always afford it, I still had very 'long arms' when it came to reaching for the bills. I guess it was, in part, because I preferred having the other party feel indebted to me (in whatever small way someone feels indebted to you because you were their host at a meal) rather than the other way around. But the bigger reason was surely that I was almost always in selling mode during these meals. I invited the other party to lunch. I had a sales agenda. Ultimately, I wanted something from them. Picking up the check was one way – out of many – for me to make a positive impression.

As a general rule, you should pick up the check if a) you suggested the meal; b) you are most obviously the senior person at the table in terms of status and/or compensation (it's expected of you, so don't disappoint your guests'); c) you are hosting people from out of town (they should return the favour when you visit them); d) you are obviously trying to extract something from the other party (money, information, contacts, etc.); or e) you sense any hesitation or doubt about the bill coming from the other people at the table.

That last item is the tricky one – because a lot of people do indeed have short arms when the check arrives. They're noticeably uncomfortable, or they excuse themselves from the table, or they look around the table waiting (and hoping) for someone else to make the first move. That awkwardness has always appalled me. If nothing else, being quick to grab the check avoids the awkwardness.

The best news about picking up the check, though, is that over time you will acquire a reputation for being a generous and possibly magnanimous host. The payoff may not be apparent immediately. But believe me, eventually it will mark you – extremely positively – in people's minds. No one will ever turn down your offer to meet over lunch or dinner. People will always agree to meet with you if there's no doubt about who's footing the bill. That's a nice edge on the rest of the short-armed world.

A final point: the value of picking up the check depends a lot on how you do it. You shouldn't be theatrical about it or draw attention to yourself. The simpler the effort the better. (The best gesture of all, of course, is the check that never comes – because you have an account at the restaurant.)

About 20 years ago I happened to be at a festive dinner with half a dozen people that cost nearly $1000 (which would be something like $5000 in today's economy). When the bill came, a world famous athlete at the table – who had been a great amateur but had recently struck it big as a professional – reached across the table to pick up the check before anyone else could touch it. He paid in cash, and I remember thinking, 'What a great guy!' Later on, someone at the table pointed out to him that at least four business people at the table could have put the bill on their expense accounts. This visibly upset him, as if his momentary act of generosity had been silly or slightly unworldly. Actually, we were originally charmed by it. But as he continued to fret about it as we parted, I couldn't help thinking that some of the magnanimity of his gesture had evaporated. Upon hearing that the evening could have been paid for out of someone else's pocket, he should have said, 'In that case, it was even more of my pleasure to be your host.'

As I say, sometimes the value of picking up the check is all in the execution.

But this great athlete had the right impulse. And he shouldn't have worried about it. The people who don't grab the check have more to worry about than those who do.

YOU DON'T NEED TO TELL THE WORLD YOU'RE NETWORKING

Among the peculiar customs of career-minded executives, surely none has been more abused or cynically regarded than networking. The time-honoured concept of developing relationships and nurturing contacts in business seemed to reach rock-bottom in the late 1980s with the advent of the 'networking party,' a torturous ritual where young people would pay a fee to gather together in a noisy public room with dozens of like-minded strangers to exchange business cards and fatten their Rolodexes. In the current version of the 'networking party,' everyone in the room has their eyes on Internet riches; the business cards are simply e-mail addresses jotted down on everyone's Palm Pilot. I'm not sure how well I could nurture a relationship in a room seething with so much naked ambition and artificial goodwill. But people starting out constantly need to expand their base of contacts. The networking party fitted the bill for a few dull moments.

I guess my big problem with any form of aggressive networking is the essential artificiality of it. The care and feeding of contacts – whether you do it with phone calls or by gathering friends at a monthly lunch or by going to industry conferences or by thumbing through your college's alumni directory or by joining a club – should be a natural extension of your business life.

1. Don't be obvious

In other words, don't tell the world your networking. People may help you, but they tend to be suspicious of anyone who is so obviously 'on the make,' who so obviously wants something from them.

When I was starting out as a lawyer in Cleveland, I was encouraged by my firm to join the Junior Chamber of Commerce. It was a good place to get a feel for the local business community and, not incidentally, meet potential clients. At meetings you could tell the people who were using the group for their own ends. They would be taking down names, handing out cards, or talking up the wonders of life insurance. I always thought it was more personally attractive to contribute something to the Jaycees before you tried to extract something from the group. I got my chance when I offered to organize a golf exhibition and fund-raiser featuring Arnold Palmer for them. The event was a success and very quickly I was perceived as a giver rather than a taker. Had I chosen to, I think I could have made the Jaycees a core group in my personal network after that.

The first rule of networking is simple: help someone else before you help yourself.

2. Know why you're networking

Networking has three basic purposes: to get information, to get business, or to get a job.

When networking, you should make it absolutely clear which of these goals you are pursuing. Like most people, I've received phone calls from casual acquaintances who claim they are 'just touching base.' It's possible there's a blunt purpose for these calls, but how would I know if the caller doesn't come out and say it? I often end these conversations wondering, 'What was that all about?' That's not effective networking.

I would find it refreshing if the other party admitted, 'I need you to help me reach Joe Smith,' or 'I need this deal.' That's something I can understand and act on.

A few years ago an executive at another company took me to lunch where he very forthrightly began the meal by announcing, 'I've asked you here because I need your help in finding a new job.' He had a specific company in mind and a specific position and knew I had strong contacts there. We spent a big part of lunch developing a campaign to land the new job. Now, in most cases, that would have been the end of it. I would have gone back to my office, made a few phone calls on his behalf to test the waters, and let him take over. But I recall making some extraordinary efforts for him. I even hosted a dinner where he could mingle with his future employers. I went out of my way for two reasons. First, I owed him. Over the years he had been extremely helpful to me and our company. He had never asked me for anything. Second, he knew exactly what he wanted and told me. In the face of such honesty, I had to respond with an honest effort.

3. Know your network

A lot of people have no idea who is actually in their network. If you've ever been disappointed by a colleague or customer or friend when you needed help, you know how it easy it is to misjudge the cast of characters in your personal network.

The solution is simple: make a list. Ask yourself this question: 'If you lost your job today, who's the first person you would call?' I don't care if it's your spouse, lawyer, college roommate, or plumber, but that's the point person in your network. Now, who are the second, third, and fourth people you'd call?

If you're devoting most of your 'career development' time to names not on this list, you need to rethink your approach.

Don't forget your old friends

A lot of people make the mistake of networking with people they want to do business with. That's not networking; that's selling.

The best people to keep in touch with are the ones with whom you are already doing business – namely, your customers, clients, and suppliers. Over the years, some of the best advice, the best introductions, and the most lucrative connections we've made at our company have come from our customers and clients. Athletes have literally taken us by the hand into companies they thought we should know better. This isn't standard operating procedure, nor do we expect it. But if you make a point to stay in touch with customers and clients about matters that concern them, it's almost inevitable over time that they will be curious about matters that concern you. They'll volunteer to help you.

That is the essence of effective networking: people helping you out whether or not there's anything in it for them.

Index